Celtic Christianity

Celtic Christianity
Making Myths and Chasing Dreams

Ian Bradley

Edinburgh University Press

© Ian Bradley, 1999

Edinburgh University Press
22 George Square, Edinburgh

Reprinted 2001

Typeset in Monotype Ehrhardt
by Norman Tilley Graphics, Northampton
and printed and bound in Great Britain
by The Cromwell Press, Trowbridge, Wilts

A CIP record for this book is available
from the British Library

ISBN 0 7486 1048 0 (hardback)
ISBN 0 7486 1047 2 (paperback)

Contents

Illustrations

Introduction

Interest in and admiration for 'Celtic' Christianity is booming. Books pour off the presses retelling the stories of fifth- and sixth-century British and Irish saints, providing anthologies of prayers in the Celtic tradition and offering a Celtic model of mission and church organisation. Tapes and compact discs of Celtic chant, miniature reproductions of Irish high standing crosses and prayer cards decorated with the motifs found on ancient illuminated manuscripts fill the shelves of visitor centres and tourist outlets as well as religious bookshops. An ever-increasing number of people take part in pilgrimages to Celtic holy sites and attend workshops, quiet days and conferences on the theme of Celtic spirituality. The appeal seems to extend across the theological and denominational spectrum, and well beyond the company of Christian believers. New Agers, post-modernists, liberals, feminists, environmentalists, evangelicals and charismatics identify with Celtic Christianity and call for a recovery of its key principles today.

In the context of the current revival, it is tempting to suggest that Celtic Christianity is less an actual phenomenon defined in historical and geographical terms than an artificial construct created out of wishful thinking, romantic nostalgia and the projection of all kinds of dreams about what should and might be. When I asked a group of students half-way through an MA course on Celtic Christianity what they understood by the phrase, their definitions included 'an intense sense of presence and place', 'an intimate liaison between humanity and the totality of creation', 'a poetic rather than rational approach to faith', 'an indigenous Trinitarian form of Christianity designed for free spirits', 'wholeness and mystery', 'a loving God revealed through his creation' and 'a church specially rooted in place and culture'. I suspect that if I had asked what they found most lacking in the contemporary church and modern forms of religious expression, I would have received remarkably similar answers.

Ours is not the first generation to cast longing glances back at the beliefs and practices of the native Christian communities of the British Isles in the period between the fifth and seventh centuries. They have had a recurrent appeal over the last 1,300 years. In the pages that follow, I attempt to chart the course and describe the main characteristics of six distinct movements of Celtic Christian revivalism, including the present one. The first took place as long ago as the eighth and ninth centuries when hagiographers first created idealised portraits of the Celtic saints and Bede compared the purity of the golden age of Aidan and Cuthbert with the corruption of his own day. The second significant revival took place in the twelfth and thirteenth centuries, stimulated partly by the new Anglo-Norman rulers of the British Isles and partly by the outburst of romantic imagination that produced the Arthurian legends and the Quest for the Holy Grail. The Reformation brought a new interest in and appropriation of the Celtic Church as a prototype of sturdy independent British Protestantism. During the eighteenth and nineteenth centuries antiquarianism, growing national consciousness, denominational rivalries and the influence of the romantic movement combined to give further shape and appeal to the entity that was now coming to be known as Celtic Christianity. The early part of the twentieth century saw a fifth distinct period of revival, in part growing out of the Celtic Twilight movement and focusing on Iona as a place of exceptional spiritual power, ecumenical potential and renewal of the church. The closing decades of the twentieth century have witnessed a sixth revival which so far shows no sign of waning.

Certain themes recur again and again in these successive movements of what I have chosen to call Celtic Christian revivalism. Their leading protagonists have generally, although not exclusively, been non-Celts. From the Anglo-Saxon Bede and the Anglo-Norman chroniclers of the thirteenth century to the predominantly English enthusiasts in the van of the current revival, it has largely been outsiders who have identified a distinctive 'Celtic' strain of Christianity and found it particularly attractive. Part of the reason for Celtic Christianity's recurrent appeal is undoubtedly its apparently exotic and peripheral quality. Much has been made of its different and 'alternative' nature. An important aspect of this has been its perceived closeness to native pre-Christian and pagan religions. In virtually every revival, this in turn has led it to be seen as being more syncretistic and more friendly to the natural world than other forms of

Christianity. Its simplicity and deep spirituality have also been recurrent themes. A persistent vein of nostalgia has allowed those Christians who lived in the sixth and seventh centuries, about whose faith and work we know next to nothing first hand, to become paragons of a pure and primitive faith. Most of the revivals have also been at least partly inspired and driven by denominational and national rivalries, ecclesiastical and secular power politics and an anti-Roman Catholic agenda.

This book attempts to chronicle the long love affair that the British, and others, have had with their 'Celtic' Christian origins. In this affair, myth-making, legend-building, inventing and reinventing history for propagandist purposes have all played a significant role. Much of the story told in the following pages is unedifying and I must confess that of all my books, this one has given me most pain and least pleasure to write. It has, I fear, a deconstructionist tone and will strike those who have read my earlier works on this subject as an example of the reductionist academic approach that I have myself attacked. To them I would say, first, that I think this story has to be told, and, second, that I do not believe that in the telling of it the essential integrity and preciousness that lies at the root of what, for better or worse, has been called Celtic Christianity is lost or destroyed. I still believe that the distinctive voice of the early indigenous Christian communities of the British Isles speaks to us through all the layers of distortion and fabrication with which it has been overlaid. This book is not about that voice or those people. It is concerned not with the actual faith and achievements of Patrick, Columba, David, Cuthbert and their contemporaries, but rather with how they came to be perceived in the centuries after their deaths. In many ways, the historical figures emerge as more rather than less saintly, in the true sense of that word, when the layers of hagiography and idolisation are stripped away.

One theme is especially marked in all the revivals discussed here. Celtic Christianity has been a vehicle through which people have chased their dreams. In medieval times these were often dreams of fantastic voyages and epic quests. In more recent times they have been dreams of deeper spirituality, a gentler and 'greener' Christianity and simpler and more open church structures. There have also been dreams of avarice, ecclesiastical and political one-upmanship and national and denominational point-scoring.

I dedicated my book *The Celtic Way*, which has played a small part in promoting the present revival, to 'all doodlers and dreamers, poets and pilgrims'. In the years since its publication, I have had cause to modify some of the more romantic and fanciful statements that I made there. Yet I remain happy to dedicate this more sober and, I trust, scholarly volume to those who dream dreams and see visions. Patrick was a dreamer and a visionary. So, I believe, was Columba. If Celtic Christianity, however reconstructed and reshaped, can help us not just to dream but to put our dreams into reality by changing ourselves and our world and moving forward in imitation of Christ and towards the Kingdom of God, then that for me is its ultimate justification. I also happen to think that such a role is in keeping with its original spirit, in so far as we can discern it through the mists of time, the clouds of romanticism and the fog of legend that have enveloped and obscured it over the centuries.

Acknowledgements

I have been greatly helped by comments and suggestions from Donald Allchin, Oliver Davies, Ursula Hall, Donald Meek, Tony Nolan, Hilary Richardson, Robert Runcie, David Selwyn, Ray Simpson, Henry Stapleton and Jonathan Wooding. My researches have been greatly eased by the hospitality and friendship of Oliver Davies and Fiona Bowie in mid-Wales, Alastair Graham and Des Gilmore in Dublin and Michael and Joyce Classon in Donegal.

I am grateful to the following copyright holders for permission to reproduce illustrations: Historic Scotland (Plate 1), the Master and Fellows of University College, Oxford (Plate 2), the National Museums of Scotland (Plate 3), the Syndics of Cambridge University Library (Plate 4), the National Galleries of Scotland (Plate 10), the estate of John Duncan (Plate 11) and the Department of National Mission, Church of Scotland (Plate 12).

For all the saints who from their labours rest

The first wave of interest in Celtic Christianity, *c*.664–800

The concept of Celtic Christianity is almost invariably associated with the notion of a golden age between the mid-fifth and mid-seventh centuries. This period saw the flourishing of the best-known Irish and British saints –Patrick, whose arrival in Ireland in or after 432 could be said to mark its start Brigit, Ninian, David, Columba, Columbanus and Aidan, whose death in 651 perhaps marks its end. It also saw the founding of the great monasteries at Clonmacnoise, Derry, Durrow, Glendalough, Iona, Llantwit Major and Lindisfarne. Often described as the age of saints, it seems to have combined missionary zeal, spiritual energy and simple faith in exceptional measures.[1]

It is almost entirely thanks to the work of writers and artists living long after this period that we think in these terms. From the centuries concerned we have virtually no direct evidence, either literary or archaeological. The early Christians were probably too much involved in missionary work and setting up churches and too preoccupied with thoughts of imminent judgement to reflect on their times or leave records for posterity. Such literary production as did take place, in a society in which literacy was probably very limited, was largely confined to the basic biblical and liturgical texts needed to carry on an itinerant preaching and sacramental ministry. Early churches and monastic buildings were constructed of wood or wattle and daub and have left less obvious traces than the stone buildings of later centuries. It is very doubtful if British and Irish Christians in the sixth and seventh centuries saw themselves as living in a golden age or regarded some of their contemporaries as saints. Indeed, one of the very few contemporary accounts of the state of the church that has survived from this period, Gildas' *De Excidio Britanniae*, written in the mid- to late sixth century, paints a picture of almost universal gloom and looks back longingly to the days of Roman occupation. For this British monk, at least, the Celticity of the early British church was a matter for lamentation rather than celebration.[2]

It is, of course, the misty and vague aura surrounding this age that accounts for much of its appeal. The absence of hard facts has allowed hagiographers, romantics and propagandists for various causes to weave myths and spin legends. This process began in the mid-seventh century, in circumstances and for reasons that will be explored in this chapter, and has continued ever since with particular bursts of enthusiasm occurring in the eleventh and twelfth centuries, around the time of the Reformation, during the latter part of the nineteenth century and in our own day.

The first and perhaps most influential of these successive waves of rediscovery and reinvention involved the writing-up of certain individuals from the fifth and sixth centuries as saints. This process of hagiography, which was inspired to a large degree by ecclesiastical power politics and the scramble by certain churches to prove their supremacy over others, has profoundly coloured our perception of Celtic Christianity. It has focused attention on a handful of figures like Patrick, Columba and David. That these particular individuals led holy lives seems highly likely, but their status as spiritual supermen almost certainly owes more to propaganda battles being waged long after their deaths than to their actual achievements. One of the most distorting aspects of the cult of the Celtic saints has been to create a small group of 'star performers' and neglect the life and work of many other pioneer evangelists. Recent research has revealed, for example, the number of British and Irish missionaries active in Ireland before Patrick.[3] It has also shown that neither Columba nor Ninian deserves the accolade of apostle of Scotland and that the Picts were almost certainly converted by monks whose names have largely been forgotten.[4] The personality cult is only one unfortunate aspect of this concentration on saints. It has also almost certainly given us a highly misleading picture of spiritual Power Rangers charging around performing spectacular miracles and founding hundreds of churches.

If these men were the spiritual supermen that their later hagiographers made them out to be, then it seems strange that nothing was written about them in their own lifetimes, nor, indeed, in most cases, for 100 or more years after their deaths. It is just conceivable that contemporary accounts of their lives were produced and subsequently lost. The Viking raids, which first hit Ireland in 795 and inflicted huge damage on monasteries around the British Isles over the next 100 years, undoubtedly destroyed many early manuscripts. In his seminal work on the sources for the early ecclesiastical history of Ireland, James Kenney points to the almost complete dearth of hagiographical material existing in Ireland in the pre-Viking period.[5] Several of the earliest surviving manuscripts of saints' lives are, in fact, to be found in Continental libraries, notably in northern Italy and Germany where Irish monks first penetrated during the sixth and seventh centuries and increasingly settled in the aftermath of the Viking incursions. The earliest known lives of both Welsh and Irish saints were actually written on the Continent. The seventh-century life of Samson, which may be the earliest extant biography of a Celtic saint, was written in Brittany, as were all subsequent lives of Welsh saints produced until the time of the Norman conquest. The mid-seventh-century life of Columbanus, unusual in being written very soon after its subject's death, was the work of Jonas, an Italian monk who had entered the monastery of Bobbio in northern Italy in 618. Another early Irish life, that of Fursa, who died around 649, was produced by a member of the community that he had founded in Gaul.

It is surely not coincidental that those Welsh and Irish monks who left their native shores were the first to be eulogised and crowned with the hagiographical haloes of Celtic sainthood. Again and again it has been outsiders and exiles rather than native Celts who have been most attracted to Celtic Christianity and most assiduous in identifying and celebrating its distinct ethos and character. Distance lends enchantment to the view culturally and geographically as well as chronologically. The appeal of what was later to become known and recognised as Celtic Christianity was perhaps first felt in mainland Europe. There are many testimonies to the high regard with which wandering Irish monks on the Continent were held because of their scholarship and spirituality. This is not simply a case of prophets being more honoured outside their own homelands. The experience of exile has also been an important element in promoting the appeal of Celtic Christianity, as it has in spreading Celtic romanticism more generally. The Welsh monks who went to Brittany and the Irish monks who settled in mainland Europe, especially those who had been forced to emigrate by Anglo-Saxon and Viking harassment, could be excused for harbouring an idealised view of the land and the church they had left behind. They helped to reinforce two of the most potent themes that were to become associated with the idea of Celtic Christianity, a wistful sense of longing for a lost homeland and a perpetual sense of exile and pilgrimage.

In comparison with this activity on the Continent, the lack of local interest in the lives and achievements of the pioneer Christian missionaries of the British Isles in the century or so following their deaths seems all the more striking. This neglect was relatively short-lived, however. The late seventh century saw the beginnings of what was to become a significant monastic industry, the systematic production of Latin *Vitae Sancti*, celebrating the lives and achievements of the Celtic Saints. The total corpus of these works is not huge – just over 100 Latin *Vitae* covering sixty saints have been identified, ranging in date from the late seventh to the fourteenth century but with the great majority being written in the earlier period. They form a distinct and highly influential genre. Perhaps their most striking characteristic is that their subjects were all dead, and in most cases long dead. Virtually all those whose lives were written up belonged to the fifth and sixth centuries. It is entirely a retrospective exercise. As Richard Sharpe has pointed out, 'all the positive signs suggest a complete lack of interest in the heroes of the contemporary church'.[6] There are no *Vitae* for such key figures as Maelruain of Tallaght (d. 792), who seems to have been instrumental in the eighth-century monastic reform movement associated with the Céli Dé, or Blathmac, a monk of Iona put to death by the Vikings in 825 when he refused to reveal the location of Columba's shrine, thus making him one of the few Celtic Christian martyrs. There was no attempt to write about these figures in later *Vitae* and bring them into the company of Celtic saints. Even thirteenth- and fourteenth-century lives continued to regard the mid-seventh century as a cut-off point after which there were no more saints.

There is, indeed, a strong sense in the early hagiography that the more distant the past, the more saintly were its inhabitants. A 'Catalogue of the Saints of Ireland', thought to date from the first half of the eighth century, divided the religious history of Ireland, which was regarded as coming to an end in 665 rather than at the time the manuscript was written, into three epochs, each with its own order of saints in a descending degree of sanctity. For the period from 432 to 544 an *Ordo sanctissmus* of 350 holy bishops and founders of churches was listed. The 300 bishops and priests recorded as living between 544 and 598 constituted an *Ordo sanctior*, while the 100 bishops, priests and hermits listed for the period from 598 to 665 were accorded the lesser status of an *Ordo sanctus*.[7]

What accounts for this apparently sudden desire to recapture, and rewrite, early indigenous Christian history and why were the mid-660s taken as its stopping point? In Ireland, 665 was the year of a great plague which seems to have caused numerous deaths, not least in the monasteries. Possibly its devastating effects provoked a realisation of the urgent need to put down in manuscript form what had hitherto been transmitted orally, as well as stimulating thoughts on the coming day of judgement. Recognition of the need to record the past more systematically may well have coincided with a stage in monastic development where the initial missionary push had slackened and there was more time to devote to history and reflection. There is also some evidence that following the plague there was a slippage of standards in Irish monasticism and a slide into worldliness. It is from this period, for example, that the practice arose of having lay abbots appointed through hereditary succession. Reaction against these trends, which showed itself in the Céli Dé reform movement, may also have inspired a nostalgic looking back to a lost golden age of asceticism.

In the ecclesiastical history of mainland Britain, 664 is a key date as the year of the Synod of Whitby, that great set-piece debate between representatives of the 'Celtic' and 'Roman' churches. It is, in fact, highly questionable whether this was as important or decisive an event as it has often been portrayed. What is undeniable, however, is that there were tensions between British/Irish and Anglo-Saxon/Roman usages and attitudes and that Whitby did mark a significant victory for the latter. It may well have left those on the 'Celtic' side feeling the need to assert its roots and traditions. One of the immediate consequences of Whitby was the retreat by Colman, the defeated Bishop of Lindisfarne, and his followers back to Ireland to set up their own monastery there. It would hardly be surprising if this and other similar communities in exile became centres of self-conscious 'Celticism'. The outcome of the Whitby debate may also have promoted a new interest in the early Celtic experience on the other side. As we shall see, there are reasons for believing that the late seventh-century lives of Patrick and Columba were written by enthusiastic 'Romanisers'. Perhaps we encounter here for the first time a phenomenon that has played a significant role in the successive revivals of Celtic Christianity over the last 1,300 years. Just as outsiders and exiles tend to give more honour to prophets than their own kinsfolk do, so victors are apt to romanticise what they once sought to destroy. There are plenty of examples in history to show how a despised and marginalised culture suddenly becomes attractive and quaint to those who have succeeded in subduing it. One only needs to think of the transformation in the perception of Highland Scotland by the English and Lowland Scots that took place after the suppression of the Jacobite rebellions. Something similar may have happened to the perception of 'Celtic' Christians after Whitby. No longer a serious threat, they became, in the eyes of those who had defeated them, heroic, almost tragic remnants of a pure and primitive Christianity.

The identification and idolisation of certain individuals as saints in this period was not an isolated insular phenomenon. Peter Brown has charted how saints' cults developed throughout Latin Christendom, beginning with the veneration of martyrs in the fourth and fifth centuries and spreading so that by the end of the sixth century 'the graves of the saints ... had become centres of the ecclesiastical life of their region'.[8] Across Europe, growing concern about sin and judgement, possibly stimulated by the rise of the ascetic movement, brought a new emphasis on the need for patrons and friends within the company of heaven. Saints filled this role. With miracle stories demonstrating that their powers extended beyond death, they came to be seen as invisible companions, role models and intimate protectors. Where the British Isles, and Ireland in particular, seem to have differed from the Continent is in the extent to which cults of purely local saints arose. Whereas in other parts of early medieval Christendom these were not much in evidence before the ninth century, Ireland already had a good many well-developed local saints' cults by the end of the eighth century. There is no Continental parallel to the *Martyrology of Tallaght*, which dates from around 800 and commemorates a very large number of native saints. It is almost certainly because of the proliferation of these local cults that Ireland has such an exceptionally large number of saints. It has been said that more saints seem to have lived on that one island in two centuries than in the rest of the world in the entire period since. In fact, as Professor Padraig Ó Riain has demonstrated, a relatively small number of actual early saints was almost certainly expanded into a multitude because of the tendency of Irish cults to fragment and localise. Many of those whom we think of as different saints are probably simply variations on the name of a single original.[9]

The development of monasticism in Ireland and Wales (and so by extension into what we would now think of as Scotland and northern England) from the seventh century onwards played a key role in shaping the cults of Celtic saints. Almost without exception, the saints whose lives and miraculous achievements were celebrated in the *Vitae* were monks. In some cases, indeed, of which Patrick is perhaps the leading example, they were almost certainly made more 'monkish' than they actually were in real life. Their lives were written by other monks, generally from monasteries with which they were associated. The overall effect may well be to give an over-monastic bias to the picture that we have of Celtic Christianity. Wendy Davies has argued that this distortion certainly applies in the case of Wales.[10] The prime requirement for sainthood in this first wave of hagiography and Celtic Christian revival was the foundation of a monastery or, better still, a family of monasteries. From the mid-seventh century onwards there seems to have been a great scrabble among churches and groups of churches to attribute their foundation to a saint from the golden age of *c*.450–650. From the eighth century onwards virtually every church in Ireland traced its origins to the church-planting activities of one of the early saints. Almost 3,000 ecclesiastical sites across the country have the name *cill* (church) coupled with the name of a saint from this early period.

Claims to foundation by a particularly holy and venerable figure were not, of course, peculiar to churches in the British Isles. Continental Christianity also looked to saintly patrons, following the example of the church in Rome which claimed establishment by Peter and Paul. Lacking martyrs, and anxious not to boost the territorial claims of bishops, the rising monastic communities of Ireland (those in mainland Britain would follow somewhat later) looked to their own in the search for founding fathers. This explains two of the most striking and distinctive features of those who were 'canonised' in the great wave of hagiography that characterised the first period of Celtic Christian revival. They were local figures and were almost without exception founders of monastic churches, or at least cast in that role by their hagiographers. It is also undeniably true that, in the words of Kenney, 'the importance of each is commonly in proportion to the subsequent fame of his chief foundation'.[11] The fact that we regard the likes of Patrick, Columba, Brigit and David as the greatest Celtic saints perhaps has less to do with the actual holiness of their lives than with the success of the monastic establishments which they actually or supposedly founded.

We are brought face to face here with the rather unedifying agenda that lay behind the deliberate creation of the idea of an 'age of saints' in what must rank as one of the most successful and enduring pieces of brand-labelling in the history of marketing. Perhaps we should not be too cynical about what was happening. It seems reasonable to believe that the particular individuals chosen to carry the role of monastic founders and patrons were already known and popular for the sanctity of their lives. The dynamic between actual reputation and popular devotion on one hand and formal hagiography on the other is sadly all but impossible to explore because of the almost total absence of sources in the former areas. While oral tradition must surely have fed into the written lives produced by the hagiographers, we cannot be sure how far this led both real-life memories and popular folk beliefs to find their way into the *Vitae* which are so often our only source for the lives of their subjects and one of very few sources for the nature of Celtic Christianity in its golden age.

What, for example, are we to make of the miracle stories that so dominate the *Vitae* and which have proved so disconcerting for post-Enlightenment rationalists but so attractive to post-modern charismatics, mystics and New Agers? Are they there because they actually happened or did the hagiographers fill their pages with accounts of wonder-working to echo the miracle stories in the Gospels or to cast their subjects in the mould of the great heroes of pre-Christian Celtic mythology? Was this, indeed, what public opinion demanded? Kenney has argued that

> Saintship itself was, to the popular mind, a concept of the magical order. Its essential characteristic was not moral goodness but the possession of that mysterious power which works miracles. The 'sanctifying grace' of the legendary saint neither arose from habitual virtue nor resulted primarily in holiness: it was the Christianised counterpart of the magic potency of the druid.[12]

The extent to which pre-Christian material was woven into early Celtic Christian literature is fiercely disputed among modern scholars and lies at the heart of the debate between nativists and anti-nativists in the field of Celtic studies. What is in no doubt, however, is that the prominence and prevalence of miracle stories in the *Vitae Sancti* has played a significant role in forming one of the most powerful and enduring impressions about Celtic Christianity, namely its fusion of pagan and Christian themes.

In fact, there was quite possibly a more prosaic, political reason for the prominence of miracle stories in the *Vitae Sancti*. They fulfilled a vital function in the hagiographer's prime task of promoting the claims of a particular monastery. Whatever they may have been like in life, and it is well nigh impossible for us to know, the Celtic saints had one overriding role in death and that was as key players in the game of ecclesiastical power politics. It was, indeed, in order to play that role that they were turned into saints. The main purpose of a *Vita* was often not, as tends to be assumed, to encourage the faithful but rather to demonstrate its subject's sanctity and superiority over other saints, in the interest of promoting the authority, prestige and financial interests of the monastery which claimed him or her as founder or patron. For this purpose sanctity meant power, defined in the ability to work miracles, preferably more spectacular than those practised by the patrons of other rival communities. The emergence of the *Vitae* in the late seventh and eighth centuries coincided with the development of the cult of relics which further enhanced the miraculous powers of saints. Often, indeed, a *Vita* was written specifically to accompany and explain a set of relics in the possession of the monastery whose claims it was promoting.

There is a formulaic character to most *Vitae* which is partly explained by the hagiographers' tendency to draw inspiration from the Old and New Testaments and from earlier saints' lives. Certain themes and categories of story occur again and again throughout the genre. We first encounter them in the earliest known Life of a Celtic saint, the early seventh-century *Vita Samsonis*. The saint comes of noble parentage, his birth is foretold in angelic visions and signs from God highly reminiscent of the Annunciation, his miracles echo those performed by Jesus (in Samson's case, healing the sick, banishing devils and raising a dead boy to life) and are particularly aimed at proving Christianity's superiority over pagan magic and at impressing kings. There is also a strong emphasis on personal holiness and asceticism – Samson is depicted as progressively withdrawing from the world, retreating from his monastery at Llantwit Major first to Caldy Island and then to a cave in a forest – and on the saint's personal foundation of numerous monasteries.[13] These themes, and variations on them, recur again and again in the saints' Lives which appeared over the next seven centuries or so. Their repetitive character has bred a weary cynicism in some historians:

> There is no development in the genre; seventh-century texts are practically indistinguishable from twelfth-century ones, and the same tedious formulae recur time after time, often borrowed shamelessly from one life to another. With few exceptions, the Saints' lives are a dismal swamp of superstition and perverted Christianity, dreary litanies of misplaced reverence and devotion.[14]

It is on the distinctly shaky foundations of this 'swamp of superstition' that much of our understanding of Celtic Christianity is founded. This can be seen by a brief examination of the way in which hagiography established the posthumous reputations of the three figures who remain the biggest names in the Celtic Christian pantheon: Brigit, Patrick and Columba.

We know next to nothing about the real historical Brigit. The Annals of Ulster give the year of her birth as 452 and report her death, at the age of 70, in 524, 526 and 528. She is generally thought to have founded a major church at Kildare around 500 although there is no direct contemporary evidence for this. There is evidence of popular devotion to her in the late sixth century. A poem thought to date from around 600 describes her as 'another Mary', providing an early taste of the Marian identification which was to be an important feature in her cult. Two Lives of

Brigit, one by Cogitosus and the other the so-called *Vita Prima*, appeared around 680, about 150 years after her death, making them the earliest known *Vitae* of an Irish saint. Both seem to have been written for propaganda purposes and reflect the secular and ecclesiastical politics of their day. The *Vita Prima* closely identifies Brigit with the cause of the kings of Leinster, the province in which Kildare was situated. It describes one king having a vision of the saint going before him into battle with her staff in her right hand and a column of fire blazing from her head. The Leinstermen were victorious in the battle and Brigit remained their patron and 'Sovereign Queen' until the eleventh century. Cogitosus' Life seems to have been written primarily to forward the claim of the church at Kildare to supremacy in the Irish church. For him, Kildare is as much the hero as Brigit: 'It is the head of virtually all the Irish churches and occupies the first place, excelling all the monasteries of the Irish'.[15]

Cogitosus' *Vita Brigiti* contains virtually no details of Brigit's life but is rather a string of miracle stories intended to illustrate her sanctity, her great faith and her charitable disposition. More than most saints' Lives, it appears to have been written to edify and set an example as well as to press the claims of a particular monastic foundation. Several of its stories convey the message that God helps those who help others. When Brigit gives away to the poor all the butter and milk that she is supposed to have given to the dairy where she works, for example, God miraculously answers her prayer and supplies her with her quota and more. Similarly when she gives some pork to a begging dog, the amount left in the trough is not diminished when she comes to take it out.

The miracles recounted in Cogitosus' Life present a curious amalgam of pagan and Christian themes. Some seem to have come straight out of the realm of pre-Christian fairy lore, like the story of how Brigit hung her cloak on a sunbeam. Others have clear Scriptural precedents. Her action in turning water into beer for a group of thirsty lepers is directly linked in the *Vita* to Jesus' miracle at the wedding feast at Cana. She is shown curing blindness, moving a river and terminating the pregnancy of a woman who had taken a vow of chastity and then been involved in a casual affair. Other stories may echo elements in Irish pre-Christian worship of the triple goddess Brigit. According to a ninth-century glossary, one of the three sisters who made up this pagan deity was the patroness of smithwork and there is a strange story in the *Vita Brigiti* which portrays the saint smashing a silver dish against a stone to divide into three exactly equal pieces for lepers. The repeated emphasis in the Life on the production of food may also pick up the theme of fertility associated with the pagan triple goddess.

The *Vita Prima* makes more explicit and overt links with pre-Christian themes. Brigit's birth is foretold by a druid and she is born out of wedlock on a threshold. *Ultan's Hymn*, a seventh-century poem which may conceivably pre-date the two *Vitae*, describes the saint as 'a golden, radiant flame' leading the faithful to the 'brilliant, dazzling sun'.[16] The sacred fire at Kildare supposedly established by Brigit and tended by her nuns may link with worship of a goddess of sun and fire. Later Lives took up more pagan motifs. *Bethu Brigte*, which dates from the late eighth or early ninth century and is the earliest surviving saint's life written largely in Irish, has Brigit being raised in the house of a druid and provides further examples of her fertility in turning water into milk and curing a woman of infertility by treating her with water enriched with her own menstrual blood.[17] It also describes the female saint being consecrated a bishop. The date established for her feast day, 1 February, was the day of the Celtic festival of *Imbolc* which seems to have had links with milking and fertility.

It is difficult to assess how consciously the hagiographers from Kildare and elsewhere who created the cult of St Brigit were seeking to graft pre-Christian elements into her story as a way of increasing her appeal and impact in what was still a partly pagan society. Dorothy Bray, the modern historian who has made probably the most detailed study of the Brigit cult, sees an element of synthesis at work in the making of the saint: 'She derives her image from the most powerful female representative in Irish tradition, the great goddess; however, she owes her existence as a saint to the traditions and beliefs of Christianity'.[18] Dr Bray has also pointed out that the feature of the pagan goddess figure which is most conspicuously missing from the portrayal of the saint in poems and *Vitae* is her overwhelming sexuality. Brigit the saint is presented as being distinguished above all for her virginity and spiritual purity. Are we here witnessing the chasing of a dream of pure womanhood, idolised in terms of chastity and charity? If so, then it is not the only dream that went into the making of the Brigit cult. Elva Johnston has pointed out that 'its manipulators successfully drew on the Marian cult, pre-Christian traditions and royal patronage'.[19] Some 300 years after her death, Brigit had acquired the status of superhero (the gender is significant – her portrayal by hagiographers was much more akin to that of her male counterparts than to other female saints), military protector, archetype of moral purity, Christianised goddess and bringer of fertility. She had doubtless also become the object of much fantasy and wish-fulfilment.

The cult of Patrick, which also arose in Ireland in the mid-seventh century, shows many similarities with that of Brigit. It also has one unique feature. Unlike any other 'Celtic' saint, Patrick wrote an account of his life that has survived. This enables us to compare the actual life as it is recorded for us by the man himself with the myths and legends that grew up around him several centuries after his death. The details and dates of Patrick's life are not without their own problems but, considering the academic controversy that they have provoked, there is remarkable scholarly agreement about the authenticity of the document known as the *Confessio*. It is generally thought to have been written in the 470s when Patrick was probably aged around 60. The opening words set a tone which could not be further away from the superhuman wonder-worker of later legend: 'I, Patrick, a sinner, am a most uncultivated man, and the least of all the faithful, and I am greatly despised by many'.[20]

It is true that Patrick recounts one miracle wrought by God through him when a herd of pigs suddenly appears in front of him and his starving comrades on their twenty-eight-day sojourn through the wilderness after escaping from slavery in Ireland. It is true also that he comes across as a visionary and dreamer – indeed the *Confessio* is the self-portrait of a man who through following his dreams is led to escape from slavery, to his life's work of missionary activity and to intense spiritual experiences of both the devil and the Holy Spirit. The overall tone of the *Confessio*, however, is of its author's unworthiness, the testing of his faith by the devil and his trials and tribulations at the hands of his enemies, who notably are more often fellow Christians than pagans. The abiding impression created is of a life of danger and persistent unpopularity. It is also a life of compromises and somewhat shady deals – having to give presents to chiefs for safe passage and stipends to those who travel with him. The *Confessio* presents the picture of a figure who may have a deep spirituality and a burning missionary zeal but who is also defensive and lacking in self-esteem.

Patrick is generally supposed to have died soon after writing the *Confessio* (i.e. in the 470s or 480s). Kenney writes that he 'was not entirely forgotten, but such evidence as we have regarding the 200 years following his death seems to show that his memory had slipped into the background of old and far-off things'.[21] There is, in fact, one isolated piece of evidence for the development of a cult of Patrick in the early years of the seventh century. It is a hymn, *Audite Omnes*, which was probably the work of Bishop Colman Elo (d. 611), who came originally from Antrim, where Patrick's own missionary activities seem largely to have taken place, but founded a church near Durrow in County Offaly. Colman may well have been among the first to spread the story and fame of Patrick outside Ulster and into the Irish Midlands. Significantly, perhaps, it was two clergymen from that region who wrote the first known Lives of the saint in the latter part of that century. Together with another hymn in his honour, *Ymnum sancti patrici magister scotorum*, which appeared in the Antiphonary of Bangor (680–91), these two *Vitae* seem to have played a significant role in propagating the cult of Patrick. Each has a slightly different focus – Muirchú, who was attached to the church at Sléibte in Leinster, portrays Patrick as the heroic figure who almost single-handedly defeats paganism in Ireland, while Tírechán, a bishop in Meath, concentrates on his role as the founder of churches. Both portray Patrick as a hugely successful national apostle and miracle worker, in marked contrast to the picture of humility, difficulty and disappointment contained in the *Confessio*.

The most dramatic story which both Muirchú and Tírechán put into their lives of Patrick is completely absent from the *Confessio*. The saint's Easter-eve encounter with Leagaire, the high king of Ireland, and his druids on the hill of Tara has become a key element in the Patrician legend and is intimately linked in popular piety with what is perhaps the best-known literary relic from the golden age of Celtic Christianity, the hymn entitled 'St Patrick's Breastplate'. Most historians are agreed as seeing this story as a piece of pure fabrication, on the part either of one of the two late seventh-century hagiographers or of one of their predecessors. It has anachronistic elements – there was no high king of Ireland in Patrick's day – and there are conflicts between the story as it is related in the two *Vitae*. Muirchú describes Leagaire being converted to Christianity after a contest of magic which culminates in a house being set on fire. While Patrick escapes unscathed from the half of the building constructed out of dry wood, the druid ensconced in the half made of green wood is burned to death. Tírechán makes no mention of this contest, nor of the conversion of the king. Ludwig Bieler has suggested that Muirchú's story may be modelled on the victory achieved by Peter over Simon the magician in the apocryphal *Actus Petri cum Simone*, while Charles Doherty argues that it was modelled on the drama at the court of Nebuchadnezer in the book of Daniel.[22] Others point to the strong elements of magic and pagan symbolism in the accounts of this confrontation between the forces of the new religion and the old which is portrayed as taking place within sight of the most sacred place in pre-Christian Ireland, the hill of Tara. When Leagaire orders his men to kill Patrick and his followers for their effrontery in kindling the paschal fire in defiance of the pagan ceremonies being enacted on the hill, the Christians miraculously metamorphose into a herd of deer and escape. There seem to be echoes here of Celtic shape-changing as well as of other primal and pre-Christian themes.

The clearest message of the story of Patrick's encounter with Leagaire as recounted by Muirchú and Tírechán is the superiority and triumph of Christianity over paganism. This is a recurrent theme in subsequent literature promoting the cult of Patrick. The prologue to the *Martyrology of Oengus*, written around 800 in the monastery of Tallaght, for example, consists of a series of verses chronicling the overthrow of paganism and the triumph of Christianity, one of which proclaims: 'The pride of Leagaire has been stifled; Patrick's splendid revered name is spreading'.[23] Subsequent hagiographers made more and more of Patrick's supernatural powers. The ninth-century *Vita Tripartita* cast him in the mould of a druidic wonder-worker and depicted him casting magic spells with malevolent as well as beneficial intent, cursing people who crossed him and making rivers barren when fishermen refused him a share of their catch. As with Brigit, the tales got taller and the pagan elements more predominant as the cult progressed.

Patrick's reputation was taken up and embellished to provide a host of churches with a foundation legend and to bolster the claims of one particular church to primacy over all others in Ireland. This was almost certainly the principal engine driving the development of his cult and the main motive for Muirchú's and Tírechán's *Vitae*. Both men made a strong claim for the primacy of Armagh and linked it to Patrick's growing role as the national apostle of Ireland. The development of *paruchiae* or federations of churches was a marked feature of late seventh-century Ireland. Several churches in the midlands put themselves under the protection of Armagh, which was emerging as one of the strongest and most stable ecclesiastical centres. We know that Muirchú's church in Leinster had been placed under the jurisdiction of Armagh, and so incorporated into the *paruchia Patricii*, by Aed, the bishop of Sléibte, and it was apparently at his behest that Muirchú's *Vita* was written around 690. Tírechán's *Acta Patricii*, which dates from the same period, was addressed to the clergy of Meath and set out to show that all their churches and those of the neighbouring Connacht region were founded by Patrick and so belonged by right in his *paruchia* and under the protection of Armagh.

The use of Patrick's name and fame to forward the claims of Armagh to supremacy over all other churches in Ireland was already well advanced by the time Muirchú and Tírechán produced their supportive *Vitae*. It is not clear exactly when the abbot-bishops of Armagh first styled themselves coarbs, or heirs, of Patrick. Their assertion of supremacy over ecclesiastical establishments with a more direct Patrician connection, notably Saul and Downpatrick which both claimed to be the saint's burial place, as well as over rival centres like Brigit's Kildare, involved a good deal of skilful invention of history. Perhaps their most successful piece of propaganda was the *Liber Angli*, which possibly dates from the 630s or 640s. It has been described as 'a sort of contract between God and St Patrick, giving St Patrick authority over the entire ecclesiastical establishment of Ireland, and establishing the dignity of Armagh and its bishop'.[24] In keeping with the visionary character of the author of the *Confessio*, Patrick is portrayed as falling asleep by a spring and being visited by an angel who tells him: 'The Lord God has given all the tribes of the Irish as a *paruchia* to you and to this city which in Irish is named *Ardd Machae*'. The implications of this encounter are spelt out in the clearest possible terms:

> This city has been specially dedicated by the angel of God and by the apostolic man, the holy bishop Patrick. It therefore has precedence, by a certain privilege and by the heavenly authority of the supreme bishop, its founder, over all churches and monasteries of all the Irish.[25]

The *Liber Angli* records a subsequent encounter between Patrick and Brigit at which she is informed in friendly but businesslike terms that her *paruchia* will be under his protection.

Other factors in the ecclesiastical and secular politics of late seventh- and early eighth-century Ireland may also have helped the cult of Patrick. It may not be coincidental that the earliest lives of the saint were written in the region that seems most readily to have conformed to the Roman method of dating Easter. Heinrich Zimmer argued that the Patrick legend was an invention of those 'Romanisers' who wanted a closer union between Irish and Continental Christianity.[26] There was considerable tension between churches in the north of Ireland (Patrick's own heartland), who tended to keep to the old 'Celtic' ways, and those in the midlands and south who had adopted Roman usage. What better way of unifying them than by claiming the northern Patrick as national apostle and proving his impeccable Roman credentials? Ludwig Bieler has suggested that there may be a link between the flowering of the cult of Patrick in the late seventh century and the 697 Synod of Birr which reconciled northern and southern Irish churches, apparently on the basis of an acceptance of the Roman dating of Easter and tonsure in the north and recognition of Patrick as national apostle in the south.[27] Others have suggested that the Irish were keen to find a patron saint to take the role that Columba was fulfilling for the *Scoti* of Dal Riata and Aidan for the Northumbrians.

It may be that these theories are too clever and suggest a degree of political sophistication that was not present in seventh-century Ireland. Nonetheless it is clear that political and dynastic factors played a major part in the development of Patrick's cult. It was, for example, vigorously promoted by the powerful northern Uí Néill clan who claimed sovereignty of Tara, and thus the high kingship of Ireland. Muirchú and Tírechán seem to have been propagandists for both the ecclesiastical primacy of Armagh and the supremacy of the king of Tara. The story of Patrick's encounter with Leagaire may possibly have been developed to serve both claims. In 737 Aed Allán, Uí Néill overlord and self-styled king of Tara, promulgated the 'Law of Patrick' which put all clerics in Ireland under Armagh's protection.

It seems highly doubtful that Patrick, apparently largely forgotten in the two centuries after his death, would have become the central figure that he has in the pantheon of Celtic saints had it not been for his posthumous enlistment to promote Armagh's claim for ecclesiastical supremacy in Ireland. The success of that campaign, and the backing that it received from the Uí Néills and others, established him as the national apostle. As Armagh's power and pretensions grew, so its chosen patron and protector became an increasingly idealised and larger-than-life figure, portrayed in one foundation legend as another Moses who was shown the pattern of the great monastic city in a vision from God as he stood on a hilltop. Having been built up, his reputation was exploited for financial gain. In 734, certain of his relics said to have been donated by him to the church of Armagh were carried into other districts to encourage the payment of tribute. Thereafter the coarbs of Armagh regularly went on circuit, carrying the saint's relics around the country and demanding what came to be known as 'Patrick's pence'. A late tenth-century poem attributed the conversion of the Norsemen of Dublin to Patrick and declared that his successors at Armagh were therefore entitled to tribute in gold from them.

Patrick's posthumous fame was achieved at the cost of grossly distorting his actual character and achievements in life. The self-doubting wandering missionary of the *Confessio* became the confident miracle-worker and power-evangelist of the *Vitae*. He was claimed as the founder of hundreds of monasteries and churches in places where he had almost certainly never set foot. The extent to which the character of the historical Patrick was deliberately distorted to serve the interests of the cultic saint is demonstrated in the *Liber Ardmachanus* (Book of Armagh), a dossier of documents assembled around 800 to support Armagh's claims to primacy. Alongside Muirchú's and Tírechán's *Vitae*, it included a truncated version of the *Confessio*, deliberately edited in the opinion of one leading modern scholar to remove the passages that spoke of Patrick's humiliation and weakness. Even in its emasculated form, with twenty-seven of its original sixty-two paragraphs cut, the language and style of the *Confessio* must still have jarred with the rest of the book's contents. In the words of Daniel Binchy:

> The contrast between the real Patrick and the 'conquering hero' of his late seventh century biographers, Muirchú and Tírechán, in the same manuscript, who marches from one territory to another at the head of a band of lay and clerical retainers and pulverizes his opponents, often by a display of 'bigger and better' magic than the local druids can produce, would have been all too obvious.[28]

There is particular irony in the fact that Patrick the Romano-Briton should have become patron saint of Ireland. The *Confessio* is the heartfelt account of one who regards himself as a victim of Irish aggression and who equates Ireland with paganism and barbarous practices like slave-owning. His emergence three centuries after his death as the supreme symbol of Irish national identity is just one instance of how profound the difference is between Patrick the man and Patrick the saint. In that latter incarnation he came to play many roles and to serve many interests and causes. With every new Life, the legends and miracle stories concerning him became ever more elaborate and fantastic. It is hard not to share Daniel Binchy's verdict that

> the effect of these and similar fables is the exact opposite of what the writers intended: far from glorifying Patrick they diminish him, and had his own writings perished, his biographers would have effectively obscured the true greatness of the man, his humility, his fortitude, his courage and his charity.[29]

Columba was the object of a similar posthumous cult in the seventh and eighth centuries, characterised by ever more extravagant claims as to his miraculous powers in life and death. Unlike Patrick, however, he did not have to wait long for his 'canonisation' (if one can use that phrase about a process that was wholly unofficial and not yet a complex ecclesiastical process). It began soon after his death and was a much more domestic affair than Patrick's, being largely the work of his successors and kinsmen as abbots of Iona.

Although there are no contemporary accounts of Columba's life and work, eulogies written shortly after his death have survived. The earliest of these, the *Amra Choluimb Chille*, was almost certainly written very soon after his death in 597. It is attributed to Dallán Forgaill, an Irish poet who clearly had access to material from Iona. The emphasis in the *Amra* is not on Columba's miraculous powers but rather on his earthly asceticism and particularly on his learning. It celebrates the life of a scholar whose interests stretched well beyond Biblical exegesis and theology into the realms of mathematics and astronomy. Even in this early work, however, there is acknowledgement of the saint's posthumous powers as patron and protector. The last verse confidently proclaims: 'He will protect us in Zion'.[30] Dallán also seems to have drawn on the language used for pre-Christian heroes to locate Columba in the tradition of the Celtic warrior aristocracy.

There is evidence of the conscious development of a Columba cult on Iona in the century following his death. Ségéne, the fifth abbot of Iona (623–52), appears to have organised a systematic trawl to collect hagiographical material. One of its results was the production by his nephew, Cumméne, of a *Book of the Miracles of Columba*. Although only a tiny fragment survives, it shows a shift in focus from Columba's actual life and achievements towards his supernatural encounters and posthumous miracles. Two poems written around 650 by Beccán mac Luigdech, a hermit associated with the Iona monastic *familia* and possibly living on the island of Rum, emphasise the themes of exile and asceticism that were to become a potent element in the romance of Columba and the appeal of Celtic Christianity more generally. His verses portray the saint leaving his beloved Ireland and tossing about on the waves in an act of penance. They also depict a heroic ascetic who forswears the comforts of bed and sleep to 'embrace stone slabs' and 'crucify his body'.[31]

The classic *Vita* written by Adomnan, abbot of Iona from 679 to 704, marked a decisive final stage in Columba's 'canonisation'. Its stress was almost entirely on the saint's supernatural and miraculous powers, as attested by the themes of its three sections – prophetic revelations, miracles of power and visions of angels. Adomnan's self-proclaimed aim was to provide proofs of his venerable subject's sanctity. Unlike previous hagiographers, he included posthumous miracles, some of which he claimed to have witnessed himself, and demonstrated how the saint's protective powers were available not just to those who had contact with his relics but to all who mentioned his name in the context of prayer and praise.

Adomnan had several reasons for wanting to idealise Columba. Like nearly all the abbots who ruled Iona in the seventh century, including Ségéne, he was a close blood relation of the founder and his *Vita* can be read as a work of familial piety and respect. It was also undoubtedly written to assert Iona's primacy over the far-flung Columban monastic *paruchia* and promote its close links with the ruling house of Dál Riata, the Irish colony in Argyllshire which was making substantial inroads into the land of the Picts. It is significant that Adomnan cast Columba in the role of a king-maker who, under divine inspiration, chose the kings of Dál Riata and presided over what appears to have been the first recorded Christian coronation in Europe. A recent monograph has suggested that this last episode may have been invented by Adomnan to give authority and tradition to an arrangement which had only developed in his own time whereby the abbots of Iona consecrated the rulers of Dál Riata. The vexed Easter question may also have played a role in promoting Columba's cult. Adomnan was apparently converted in 688 to the new Roman system of dating but had difficulty in persuading the monks of Iona over whom he ruled to abandon the old method. It has been suggested that he wrote his *Vita Columbae* to prove his Columban credentials and attachment to the founder in the hope that this might persuade the monks that it would not be a matter of disloyalty to change their ways in this instance.[32]

More, perhaps, than any other Celtic saint's Life, Adomnan's *Vita Columbae* shows the strong influence of the wider early medieval hagiographical tradition established in the fourth century by Athanasius' *Life of Antony of Egypt*. It shows a particular reliance on the model provided by Sulpicius Severus' *Life of St Martin of Tours* which is, indeed, quoted verbatim at several points. As with Brigit and Patrick, the miracle stories seem to involve drawing on both Biblical precedents and pre-Christian Celtic mythology. Several of Columba's superhuman feats, such as turning water into wine, stilling a storm, raising a dead boy to life and driving out demons, directly parallel miracles recorded in the Gospels. Others, like the drawing of water from the side of a hard rock, recall episodes in the Old Testament.[33] There are also clear Biblical echoes in the 'Annunciation' stories which describe the saint's birth being foretold by a series of signs and wonders. Adomnan's frequent references to Columba's sightings of both demons and angels probably owe more to Biblical influences than a conscious or unconscious assimilation of Celtic fairy lore. When he writes of the saint confronting 'a line of foul black devils armed with iron spikes and drawn up ready for battle' and seeing 'holy angels fighting in the air against the power of the Adversary', for example, he is simply echoing the language of Revelation.[34]

Other miracle stories in the *Vita Columbae* involve interaction with pagan religion and do not have such close Biblical precedents. Several describe the saint baptising and 'converting' a pagan shrine, such as a well or spring, usually by blessing it. On a number of occasions Columba is portrayed taking on wizards and sorcerers and out-performing them with the power of his magic. In one passage that is reminiscent of the story of Patrick's encounter with King Leagaire, Adomnan recounts a trial of strength taking place between Columba and the pagan wizards at the court of Brude, king of the Picts. The saint wins the day by causing a stone to float, healing the king's chief wizard and opening the locked gates of the royal fortress by signing the cross over them. The clear message conveyed is that Columba was engaged in tit-for-tat contests with representatives of the old pagan religion. As Donald Meek has observed, their theme seems to be 'Power Evangelism in the Dark Ages'.[35]

While the enduring image that these stories have created is of Columba as a spectacular miracle-worker, they may originally have had a more political message. Commenting on the striking story of Columba quelling the Loch Ness monster, Owen Dudley Edwards has noted that 'the essence of being an Irish missionary was in general to take a stage stance in which any sign of concession to the home-grown opponent is a self-destructive indication of weakness'.[36] It is noticeable that most of Columba's miracles, and all of those which involve confrontation and bettering an opponent, are set in Pictland. Gilbert Markus has suggested that the stories of the subduing of the Loch Ness monster and the slaying of a wild boar on Skye by the power of the saint's terrible word were inserted by Adomnan into his *Vita* to present the Picts as a hostile people and to show the Gaels' superiority over them.[37] By contrast, animals encountered by the saint in the Irish colony of Dál Riata, and especially on Iona itself, are portrayed as universally friendly and evoke a very different response from Columba. The prime example of this is, of course, the crane which he prophesies will fly in from Ireland and commends to the special care of his monks. Several commentators have argued that this bird symbolises the land of Ireland. The difference between its treatment and that of the hapless boar which has the misfortune to live on the Pictish island of Skye is certainly striking.

By Adomnan's time, monks from Iona, along with other Gaelic-speaking *Scoti*, were penetrating the Pictish strongholds of northern and eastern Scotland. Together with other later saints, notably Moluag and Maelrubha, Columba was adopted as the patron of this movement of Gaelic colonisation. In particular, he was taken up by the rulers of Dál Riata as they extended their influence northwards and eastwards across the Scottish mainland. There is no doubt that Columba's fame and status were greatly boosted by the close links between Iona and the royal house which was eventually to provide the rulers of the new united kingdom of

Scotland. Support in high places also played a key role in promoting his cult in Ireland. The *Amra Choluimb Chille* seems to have been commissioned by Aed mac Ainmirech, king of the Cenél Conaill sept of the all-powerful Uí Néill clan. In 753 Domnall Mide, king of the southern Uí Néill, having wrested the high-kingship of Ireland from his northern cousins, promulgated a 'Law of Colum Cille' in a vain attempt to halt the onward march of Patrick and Armagh and make all Irish churches acknowledge the primacy of Iona.

Royal patronage also brought the cult of Columba into England. When his father was ousted from the Northumbrian throne in 617, Prince Oswald escaped to the sanctuary of Iona where he was baptised and drank deeply of the Columban legend. After seventeen years, the Anglian prince, by now thoroughly Celticised, felt emboldened to claim his father's throne and sallied south to challenge Cadwollan, the Welsh king who had seized it. According to Adomnan, during the night before the battle, Oswald had a vision of Columba who promised his protection and prophesied that Cadwollan and his forces would be routed. Events went as the saint had predicted, and one of Oswald's first actions on becoming king of Northumbria in 634 was to ask Ségéne to send down a missionary bishop from Iona to establish a church in his extensive kingdom which stretched from the banks of the Forth to Yorkshire. This request led to the mission of Aidan, the founding of Lindisfarne and so to northern England gaining its own set of Celtic saints and its abiding attachment to Celtic Christianity.

While the cult of Columba spread far and wide, Iona remained its heart and focus. Its relationship to the saint was very different from that of Armagh with Patrick. Columba had founded the island monastery, lived there for the last thirty-three years of his life and died there in circumstances described by Adomnan in one of the most moving passages in all Christian literature. Although Columba's hagiographers were concerned to champion Iona's supremacy over the growing family of monasteries spread across Scotland and Ireland, they never made the wild and excessive claims for it that were made for Armagh. Their poems and stories rather encouraged a romantic view of the island as a remote rocky haven of spirituality and asceticism. Early in the eighth century Columba's body seems to have been taken from its simple underground burial place and moved to a portable shrine inside the monastic church. George Henderson has argued that this enshrinement may well have been the occasion for the production of the magnificent illuminated gospel book known as the *Book of Kells* which, he suggests, both in its ecstatic visionary quality and its specific iconography, strikingly echoes themes in

Adomnan's *Vita*. If he is right in his assertion that 'the Book of Kells was specially fashioned for St Columba who was for the monks of his own community their own particular mediator' then this most splendid and venerated of all the surviving artefacts of Celtic Christianity turns out itself to be an early tribute to the golden age of the saints.[38]

If Columba's cult seems to have had a more spiritual dimension than Patrick's, it was not without its political and propagandist side. Throughout the ninth century it was harnessed with considerable effect to the gradual Gaelicisation of Pictland and the emergence of the new Dál Riatan-dominated kingdom of Alba. Kenneth Mac Ailpín, who is usually hailed as the ruler who united the Picts and Scots although he was by no means the first king of Dál Riata to rule over the Picts, was a fervent devotee of Columba, and in 849 he moved several of the saint's most precious relics to Dunkeld in Perthshire at the heart of the new Scottish-Pictish kingdom. His ostensible reason for bringing the relics to the Scottish mainland was to save them from the thieving hands of the Vikings who had first raided Iona in 806 and were only prevented from seizing the shrine containing his body during another raid in 825 through the heroism of Blathmac who faced death rather than reveal the secret location where it had been hidden. Other relics, including the gospel book that now bears its name, were removed to a new Columban monastery at Kells in the middle of Ireland. There is some suggestion that the relics originally taken to Dunkeld were also moved to Ireland in 878, possibly to avoid the Viking raids which were penetrating ever deeper into the Scottish mainland.[39] Although Kells assumed supremacy within the Columban *paruchia*, its abbots styled themselves abbots of Iona, a testimony to the enduring hold of the little island which in its isolation became the subject of numerous poems (many of them attributed to Columba himself) on the themes of exile and yearning.

The Scots' gradual ascendancy over the Picts in the ninth century brought a significant revival of Irish influences in the church throughout the new kingdom of Alba and considerably boosted the cult of Columba. Kenneth Mac Ailpín's successors gradually extended their control over the more northerly Pictish territories, helped, in the words of Sally Foster, by 'the aggression of a revitalized Gaelic Church, promoting the language of St Columba'.[40] There may be a depiction of the saint on Sueno's Stone, a twenty-foot-tall carved cross-slab near Forres dating from the late ninth or early tenth century, which seems to commemorate a significant victory of the Christian Scots over the pagan men of Moray, perhaps one of the last outposts of Pictland. One side of the stone depicts a bloody battle while the other has a large carved cross under which two

Plate 1. Panel on the west face of Sueno's Stone, Moray, possibly showing Columba and Andrew 'present' at the coronation of a Scottish king.

elongated figures appear to be bending over a smaller figure in the middle. Anthony Jackson has suggested that this scene may represent the coronation of Kenneth or one of his successors and that the figures on either side of him are those of Columba and Andrew, representing 'the joint blessing of the defender of the old Scottish Christianity and the new defender of the Catholic Church'[41] (Plate 1).

If this is indeed the case, then this monument provides an interesting early portrayal of the two men who would posthumously vie for the honour of becoming Scotland's patron saint. Columba was, not surprisingly, the favoured candidate of the Gaels. The Picts backed Andrew, the apostle, whose cult seems first to have been championed in Northumbria, notably by those on the 'Roman' side in the Synod of Whitby, and was probably introduced into Fife in the early eighth century by the Pictish King Nechtan who had close links with the Northumbrian church. Ultimately, of course, the apostle was to win out against the Celt, largely thanks to some shrewd public-relations work by the inhabitants of northeast Fife and the sheer weight of the ecclesiastical establishment in late medieval Scotland. There was a considerable period, however, when Columba rather than Andrew was looked to as the nation's patron saint. His crosier, which was kept at Dunkeld, was carried as a protective device by Scottish armies facing the invading Viking armies at Corbridge in 918 and became known as the *Cathbhuaidh*, or battle talisman. The *Brecbennoch*, or blessed shrine, associated with the casket known as the Monymusk Reliquary, which may have been built to house a relic of the saint in the eighth century, was also regularly paraded before Scottish armies. Columba's psalter, which had been removed from Iona to Kells along with other relics in the mid-ninth century, was encased in the late eleventh century in a silver casket known as the *Cathach*, or battler, and jealously guarded by its hereditary keepers, the O'Donnells of Donegal, who carried it three times round the battlefield before any military encounter in the confident belief that it would bring them victory.

It is ironic that the relics of the gentle monk who was known as 'the dove of the church' should have become battle standards and tribal totems. Military power and royal patronage did much to spread and enhance Columba's fame and ensure Iona a continuing role long after it had ceased to be the centre of the monastic *familia*. Altogether forty-eight Scottish monarchs are said to have been interred on the island in the tenth and eleventh centuries, together with four from Ireland and eight from Norway. The half-pagan Norsemen venerated Columba, believing that he had many of the qualities of the Viking war-god, Odin.

Although Patrick and Columba were undoubtedly appropriated for political and propagandist purposes, there was also a less calculated side to the appeal of 'Celtic Christianity' in the early medieval period. Even as early as the seventh century it was bound up with a sense of nostalgia and a yearning for a world that was no more. This is particularly evident in some of the speeches made at that great set-piece confrontation between 'Celtic' and 'Roman' Christianity, the depiction of which by historians has done so much to shape a romantic view of Celtic Christianity as a gentle, anarchic, deeply spiritual movement crushed by the authoritarian weight of Roman bureaucracy and imperialism. The significance of the Synod of Whitby has undoubtedly been over-exaggerated and the position of the losing side over-romanticised. Studying the accounts of the debates that took place in 664, however, it is impossible not to be struck by the veneration felt by the 'Celtic' protagonists for Columba and the good old days and ways that he represented. While the appeal of Wilfrid, chief spokesman on the Catholic 'Roman' side (and leading champion of the cult of Andrew) to Petrine authority and universal practice has an undeniable logic and tidiness, there is something deeply moving about Colman's counter-appeal to 'our most reverend father Columba and his successors whose life, customs and discipline I will never cease to follow'. Even Wilfrid has to concede that however misguided and ignorant they were, these were men 'who in their rude simplicity loved God with pious intent'.[42] In that remark, patronising though it is, we find an acknowledgement of that quality of primitive purity that has been one of Celtic Christianity's most attractive points in the eyes of its many admirers over the centuries.

Perhaps no one did more to foster this impression of a vanished golden age than the historian through whose eyes all subsequent generations have viewed the Whitby debate. The Venerable Bede is often portrayed as an apologist for Roman Christianity and as one of the chief architects of the notion of Englishness.[43] I firmly believe that he was also largely responsible for initiating the British, and more especially the English, love affair with 'Celtic' Christianity. His monumental *Ecclesiastical History of the English People* idealised the spirituality and purity of church life in sixth- and seventh-century Ireland and north Britain. Completed in 731, it appeared at a critical time in both the political and religious history of the British Isles, when the identity of its constituent nations was being forged and the era of itinerant missionary activity was giving way to one of more settled ecclesiastical structures. As a historian, Bede's natural inclination was to look back, and he presented the pure and primitive 'Celtic' Church as a model against which the church of his own day was judged and found wanting. In so doing, he established an approach to reforming perceived abuses in the church that was to be very influential for many centuries to come. In the words of one recent commentator, 'From now on the case for reform would be presented as restoration of pristine conditions, distilled from the collective memories in the hagiographies of Bede and others'.[44] The fact that these pristine conditions came to be associated especially with the Celtic Christian communities of the fifth to seventh centuries was largely a consequence of the prominence that Bede chose to give to this particular element in the early ecclesiastical history of the British Isles.

The geographical location of Bede's work was as significant as its timing. Of all the ecclesiastical communities in the emerging English nation, the Northumbrian church was the most steeped in Irish influences. It was both Celtic and Anglo-Saxon, drawing inspiration from Iona as much as Rome. While the monasteries in which Bede had been brought up, Wearmouth and Jarrow, were both unequivocally Roman and Anglo-Saxon in foundation and outlook, 'Celtic' Lindisfarne, the offshoot of Iona, was nearby and, perhaps because he was not part of it, he looked on this Irish neighbour with the wistful eye of one who feels the grass is greener on the other side of the hill. Bede's treatment of Lindisfarne and its traditions, like his language about Columba, Fursa, Colman, Aidan and other Irish monks, is noticeably warmer and more enthusiastic than his remarks about his fellow Anglo-Saxon clergy and their monastic foundations. Bede's Northumbrian background had another important consequence. It gave his history a northern bias. Portraying the lands north of the Humber as being at the heart of the formation of English Christianity, he largely ignored the significant early Christian communities existing in the south of Britain, among both Britons and Saxons.[45] This perspective almost certainly led him to over-exaggerate the importance of the Irish influence on early English Christianity. His statement that the English were instructed 'by their Scottish masters ... in the rules and observance of regular discipline' was certainly true of his native Northumbria, but in the south there were other important missionary teachers, like the the Franks who supplied Canterbury with a bishop before Augustine.[46]

Several enduring myths about Celtic Christianity can be traced back to the pages of Bede's *Ecclesiastical History*. His much-quoted passage about the evangelisation of the Picts (Book 3, Chapter 4) greatly over-estimated the contribution of Columba and Ninian and led to these two saints vying posthumously for the accolade of apostle of Scotland while the work of other missionaries active among the Picts was largely ignored. Patrick Wormald has pointed out how it was Bede rather than Adomnan who had Columba 'convert the Picts to Christ by his words and example', a claim for which there is virtually no evidence.[47] Bede's mention of Ninian had even more dramatic and distorting consequences. Without it, the Galloway saint would almost certainly not have come to occupy his high position in the pantheon of Celtic saints. Once again, the Northumbrian bias played a key role here. In Bede's time, Galloway was under Northumbrian rule and Whithorn, its ecclesiastical centre, was being developed as a large monastic city. Ninian was taken up as a figure who could give legitimacy to Northumbrian aspirations to rule Scotland and as a focus of devotional feeling who would attract significant numbers of pilgrims to Whithorn. Pecthelm, appointed to the newly created Anglian bishopric of Whithorn in 729, seems to have been instrumental in promoting the cult of Ninian, building on Bede's description of him, which is unsupported by any other early references, as the evangelist of the southern Picts.

Bede almost certainly over-exaggerated both the peculiar missionary zeal and the monastic character of the Irish church. It is to him, as much as to the authors of the early *Vitae*, that we owe our image of the Celtic saints as super-charged evangelists rushing round and single-handedly converting whole regions and kingdoms to Christianity. His distortion of source material to produce this impression can be clearly seen in the case of his treatment of the Irish monk, Fursa. A modest reference in a Merovingian *Vita* to Fursa softening the barbarous heart of an East Anglian king is turned by Bede into a description of the full-scale evangelisation of East Anglia by the Irish monk who 'followed his usual task of preaching the Gospel, and converted many unbelievers by the example of his virtue and the encouragement of his preaching'.[48] Wormald points to the distorting effect of Bede's emphasis on 'the monastic note' in Irish Christianity, most notably his remarks on the primacy of abbots over bishops which 'led almost all historians until recently to see abbatial rule rather than episcopacy as characteristic of the "Celtic Church" '.[49]

There is no doubt that Bede viewed Celtic Christians through rose-tinted glasses. He portrayed Columba's successors as abbots of Iona as being 'distinguished for their great abstinence, their love of God, and observance of the Rule' and even excused their erroneous method of calculating the date of Easter on the grounds that they had no one to bring them the synodical decrees on the subject 'since they were so far away at the ends of the earth'.[50] In that statement we find one of the first expressions of what were to become among the most enduring and attractive features of 'Celtic' Christianity, its remote, marginal, slightly anarchic quality in which deep and simple piety mingled with a slightly stubborn determination to be out of kilter with Rome. Wormald is surely right to conclude that 'Bede has done more than anyone, more even than Adomnan and picturesque scenes of beehive huts, to make these 'Celtic' saints lovable'.[51] One might add that it is he who is also largely responsible for giving the other 'Roman' side to early British Christianity its negative image. His description of the meeting that took place around 600 on the borders of the West Saxon kingdom of Hwicce between Augustine and the British bishops to discuss differences over dating Easter and other variances between Celtic and Roman usage (Book 2, Chapter 2) left an impression of Roman arrogance that was to remain deeply embedded in the British psyche for many centuries. Augustine's failure to stand to greet the British bishops became a touchstone of Roman imperialism and reinforced the image of Celtic Christians as a gentle people crushed by the might of their haughty big brothers. As we shall see, this episode was frequently cited by post-Reformation historians seeking to establish the independent, proto-Protestant credentials of the early British church.

Bede also played a significant role in promoting the idea of Ireland as a particularly holy place. Although he never explicitly used the phrase 'the land of saints', this is the clear impression that he leaves in the minds of his readers. He refers several times in his history to English priests seeking life-long exile in Ireland 'to obtain hereafter a residence in heaven' and speaks particularly warmly of those who followed Finan and Colman back to Ireland in the aftermath of the Synod of Whitby 'either for the sake of Divine studies, or of a more continent life'.[52] Here, as in his other panegyrics to the Celtic tradition, he may well have been pointing up a contrast with the state of spirituality and learning in the English church. Peter Hunter Blair comments:

> Bede's almost idyllic picture of *Hibernia* was perhaps coloured by his knowledge that Ireland had been at once the source of so much Christian teaching among the English, and the inspiration of so many English who had gone there to be taught by Irish scholars at a time when no such teaching was to be had in England.[53]

In this case at least, Bede's favourable portrayal of Celtic Christianity over his own Anglian Church was almost certainly justified. He was not alone in pointing to the particularly high standards of Irish scholarship and spirituality. These were widely recognised on the Continent, not least at Charlemagne's court in Aachen from where around 800 the English monk Alcuin noted that Willibrod, the Northumbrian-born and -educated missionary to the Frisians, had gone to Ireland 'because he heard that scholarship flourished there and also because he was attracted by the reputation of certain holy men'.[54]

Bede's greatest praise is reserved for the Celtic founders of his own Northumbrian Church. It is here that his use of an idealised picture of a vanished golden age of Celtic Christianity to draw attention to the faults of the church of his own day is most explicit. Having shown, for example,

how Aidan practised what he preached, by spending his time in reading
the Scriptures and learning the psalms, distributing to the poor what
he was given by the rich and traversing the country on foot rather than
horseback, Bede comments 'his course of life was so different from the
slothfulness of our times'.[55] Similarly, he contrasts the simple austerity of
the monastic life at Lindisfarne under its first three Scottish-trained
abbots, Aidan, Finan and Colman, who eschewed stone buildings and
constructed their churches out of hewn oak covered with reeds, with the
more extravagant and ostentatious ways introduced by the Anglo-Saxon
abbot, Eadfrith, who took the thatch off the monastic church and covered
the roof and walls with plates of lead (Book 3, Chapter 5). There is evidence that Bede was uneasy with the opulence of Wearmouth and Jarrow
with their stone buildings, vestments, altars, stained glass windows and
pictures. He was sad to see these features being introduced at Lindisfarne
and its daughter houses at Lastingham and Coldingham. He was unhappy about other aspects of Northumbrian church life in his own
time, notably the lack of missionary zeal among clergy and monks, the
tendency for monasteries to become family possessions, passed down
from father to son, the increasing wealth of the church and the spread of
bogus monasteries which were set up by those wishing to avoid taxation
and military duties. It is not difficult to read between the lines of Bede's
idyllic picture of the devotion of the early monks at Lindisfarne and
detect a criticism of the increasing wealth and worldliness of contemporary churchmen:

> The whole care of those teachers was to serve God, not the world
> – to feed the soul, and not the belly ... The priests and clergymen
> went into the village on no other account than to preach, baptize,
> visit the sick, and, in a few words, to take care of souls; and they
> were so free of worldly avarice that none of them received lands or
> possessions for building monasteries.[56]

Ironically, Bede himself played a significant role in increasing the
wealth of Lindisfarne by enthusiastically promoting the cult of Cuthbert
as its patron saint. Cuthbert, who died in 687, stands as the last great
representative of the heroic age of Celtic saints. Bede's *Vita*, penned
around 721, followed the usual pattern and was made up largely of
miracle stories, many of which were posthumous and involved both
corporeal relics like bones and incorporeal or representative relics like
clothes and shoes. It presented its subject in highly idealised terms as an
exemplary monk, ascetic and bishop. Alan Thacker has shown the extent
to which Bede's portraits of both Cuthbert and Aidan drew on the

qualities of the ideal pastor as defined by Gregory the Great. In his *Dialogues*, Gregory had listed these as ascetic discipline, regular withdrawal and retreat from the world, episcopal humility and above all leading by example and practising what you preach. He had especially commended the work and life of Benedict. In Thacker's words:

> Cuthbert is presented as an exemplary, monk, ascetic and bishop
> ... He is seen as the Northumbrian equivalent of the great holy
> men of the Christian past, and as the ideal Gregorian, who acts in
> the spirit of the Benedictine Rule and closely resembles Benedict
> himself.[57]

It is ironic that Bede's *Vita*, which like his *Ecclesiastical History* was to play an important part in establishing the Celtic origins of the English Church and its independence of Rome, should have been inspired by a Papal model and a desire to present Cuthbert as a true European.

Bede's *Life of Cuthbert* undoubtedly played a part in promoting another widespread conception about the distinctive nature of Celtic Christianity. His delightful picture of the saint being befriended by otters, who rub against his legs to dry them after his long prayer vigils in the North Sea, was taken up by medieval illustrators and undoubtedly helped to foster the notion of an especially strong bond between the Celtic saints and animals (Plate 2). More immediately, the *Vita* gave a boost to an already flourishing pilgrim trade to Lindisfarne of which Cuthbert himself would surely not have approved. He seems to have deliberately retreated to his hermitage on the remote island of Farne to die and expressed the wish that his body should be buried quietly there. However, shortly before his death he apparently reluctantly acceded to the monks' request that his body should be taken back to Lindisfarne for burial. His corpse was robed in vestments and placed in a stone sarcophagus. Eleven years later his body was raised and put in an elaborately carved wooden chest on the floor of the monastic church where it could be visible to pilgrims. The enshrinement may have been celebrated by the production of the sumptuous illuminated manuscript known as the Lindisfarne Gospels.[58]

Cuthbert was by no means the only Celtic saint to have his remains re-housed in the late seventh century so that they might be venerated by pilgrims. The bodies of Aidan, Cedd and Chadd underwent similar treatment and King Oswald's hand was enshrined in a metal casket. An account of posthumous miracles performed by Ninian produced at Whithorn at the end of the eighth century was probably associated with the enshrinement of the saint in the monastic church there. *De Abbatibus*,

Plate 2. Twelfth-century drawing of otters drying Cuthbert's feet in a manuscript of Bede's *Life of Cuthbert*. (Source: University College Oxford MS 165.)

a poetic tract written around 803 in one of the daughter houses of Lindisfarne, described the enshrinement of an Irish monk, Ultan, and reported how a sick monk had been cured after the dead saint's hand was laid on his forehead.[59] This new development, which affected the cults of Anglo-Saxon and Continental as well as Celtic saints, brought new wealth to monasteries like Lindisfarne and Whithorn as pilgrims flocked to view the relics enshrined in their bejewelled caskets. It also brought a new danger to those remote outposts of Celtic Christianity that had survived the assaults of the Romanisers. It is doubtful if the Vikings would have been very interested in attacking the monasteries around the coasts of Britain and Ireland in the ninth century if they had not been crammed full of glittering treasures.

The Viking raids played their part in increasing the romantic appeal of Celtic Christianity. When news of the first Viking attack on Lindisfarne in 793 reached Alcuin in Aachen, he was devastated even though he had never been there: 'Behold the church of the holy Cuthbert bespattered with the blood of God's priests, robbed of all its ornaments, the most venerable place in all Britain given over as a prey to the pagans'.[60] Laid waste and deserted, their monks martyred or fled, the ruined monastic

sites around the coasts acquired a new melancholy romance and spoke
even more eloquently of a vanished golden age. Many Irish monks emi-
grated to the Continent, taking with them their manuscripts and their
nostalgic memories, soon to be compounded by the yearning of the exile.
Another significant wave of emigration in the ninth century, probably
prompted by Anglo-Saxon rather than Norse incursions, took monks
from South Wales to Brittany from where the first substantial collection
of Welsh saints' lives was written.

The displacement caused by Anglo-Saxon and Viking incursions may
have increased 'Celtic' consciousness among the native peoples of the
British Isles. It was in the ninth century, perhaps under the pressure of
invasion and the threat to their identity, that the Gaels seem to have
developed an origin legend which portrayed them as one of the lost tribes
of Israel which had wandered the world until they landed up in Ireland.
Perhaps the most potent element in this legend, and certainly the one that
was to have most influence in the developing conception of 'Celtic'
Christianity, was its emphasis on the Celts as a wandering people. The
theme of wandering monks constantly engaged in *peregrinatio pro Christe*
was to become an important element in the image and appeal of Celtic
Christianity. As with other elements, it had a strong basis in fact. Partly
as a result of invasions from the Continent, many Irish and British monks
did find themselves in exile on the Continent. Doubtless, too, the strain
of *wanderlust* in the Celtic temperament played a part. The German
scholar Walafrid Strabo wrote in the early ninth century of the Irish
peregrini 'to whom the custom of travelling into foreign lands had become
second nature'.[61] More fanciful and idealised notions of journeying and
fantastic voyages would also play their part in developing the romance of
Celtic Christianity as we shall see when we examine the stories of St
Brendan's Voyage and the Quest for the Holy Grail.

There is one further aspect of the first wave of interest in Celtic
Christianity which remains to be considered in this chapter. During the
ninth century, poems and hymns began to appear which were attributed
to saints and monks who had lived three or more centuries earlier. We can
be fairly certain about dating this material because there are features in
both the language and the script which are not found in earlier manuscripts. It is, of course, just possible that poems which did date back
several centuries and had previously been transmitted orally were being
written down for the first time, perhaps in the wake of the disruption
caused by the Norse attacks. It seems more likely, however, that this trend
represents a further development of hagiography. As the cult of a saint
grew, poems, prayers and hymns were written that could be put into his

mouth. Perhaps the most common genre that falls into this category are the *lorica* or breastplate prayers which invoke divine protection with language reminiscent of that in St Paul's Epistle to the Romans. Poems of this kind dating from the ninth century are ascribed to Fursa, Colman, Columba and most famously to Patrick. Significantly, 'St Patrick's Breastplate' (best known to us in Cecil Frances Alexander's translation which begins 'I bind unto myself this day') is not mentioned in either Muirchú's or Tírechán's elaborate accounts of the saint's encounter with Leagaire at Tara which is supposed to have been the occasion for its composition. Nor is it mentioned in the late ninth-century text of the *Vita Tripartita*. Kenney, who states that the language forms cannot be older than the eighth century, points out that it is not, in fact, until the eleventh century that it was first linked to that story and given its nickname 'The Deer's Cry'.[62] Other much-quoted verses attributed to Columba also appear to have been written in this period, including 'The path I walk, Christ walks it', 'That I might bless the Lord who orders all' and several poems looking fondly back to Erin.[63]

Among the ninth- and tenth-century poems which were put into the mouth of a sixth- or seventh-century monk is a distinct group which enthuses about the pleasures of life in the open. These 'hermit' poems, which number fourteen in total, have been much quoted to illustrate the 'green' credentials and closeness to nature of the early Celtic monks. The image that they present is of hermits siting their huts close to woods and pools and deriving considerable pleasure from their close proximity to animals and birds. One of the most striking consists of a dialogue between Guaire, king of Connaught, who lived in the first half of the seventh century, and his half-brother Marbán the hermit. It contrasts the spiritual poverty of the king's materialistic urban existence with the riches enjoyed by the hermit who lyrically lists the many different animals and birds who visit his hut. In fact, the verses, which were written at least 200 years after Guaire's death in 663, are most unlikely to have been the work of a real hermit. Donnchadh Ó Corráin, who has recently submitted the fourteen poems which make up the main body of this collection to a penetrating and devastating literary analysis, has commented on the 'disconcertingly unrealistic' nature of the poem with its complete absence of references to the discomforts of hermit life:

I doubt very much if hermits wrote poems like this. Rather, it seems to me to be a conscious work of art and in no sense a record of a life lived. It belongs to a genre of literature in which the goods of the hermit life, far from stress and bustle and from the strains of communal living, are idealized and extolled by literary men whose own lives were lived out, as teachers and administrators, in the great monastic towns and the schools attached to them.[64]

Ó Corráin finds similar tell-tale clues of romantic idealisation in other verses which are so often taken to indicate the particular appeal among Celtic monks of the simple eremitic life and their closeness to nature. A poem attributed to Abbot Manchin Leith who died in 665, which begins: 'I wish, O Son of the living God, for a hidden little hut in the wilderness', he finds to be not about the eremitic or anchoritic life but rather about 'the idealized new foundation – a common topos in Christian literature and life of all ages. It has a strong utopian streak about the founding of a monastic settlement.'[65] He also detects a strong note of nostalgia in the poem which is 'calling for a return to what was imagined to be the simpler monastic life of earlier days'. He delivers a similar verdict on another much-quoted poem in this genre, 'All alone in my little cell'. Overall, in Ó Corráin's view, the hermit poems are not 'the ingenuous product of the primary emotions and experiences of the hermit life' but 'sophisticated works of art ... here religious life is seen through the conceits and tropes of cultivated and scholarly men writing to meet the needs and taste of a cultural élite'.[66]

Similar strictures have been applied to much of the material that has come out of subsequent revivals of Celtic Christianity. As we shall see in a later chapter, Alexander Carmichael has come in for much the same criticism for re-working and prettifying the crude and earthy Gaelic poems and prayers that he collected in the Outer Hebrides in the latter years of the nineteenth century for his *Carmina Gadelica*. On the whole, those who have been drawn to the purity of Celtic Christianity have been cultured and educated and it is perhaps inevitable that they should have turned it into something more sophisticated and learned than it was, even as they rejoice in its spontaneity and simplicity. In the case of the 'hermit' poems of the ninth century, Ó Corráin's verdict does seem somewhat over-harsh. Even if their authors were not themselves hermits, and had no intention of becoming so, they do seem to have had a genuine love of nature and a feel for its spiritual qualities. They may not have mentioned the hardships of life in the outdoors but they cannot have been totally unaware of them. Even a large monastic city like Glendalough, with a population of several thousand monks, was far from being an urban centre in the modern sense. Surrounded by lakes, mountains, trees and fields, its inhabitants would have been well aware of the sights, sounds and fickleness of the natural world. It is nonetheless true that these poems are not what they purport to be and that they were written by monks living in rather different circumstances from those described in their verses. Several of the hermit poems are first found in old Irish glosses written on Latin manuscripts which have been preserved in Continental monasteries, a fact which rather surprisingly Ó Corráin does not mention. May we not be dealing here again with the idealised nostalgia of the exile? It is not hard to imagine an Irish monk sitting in the stuffy scriptorium of a large monastery on the flat plains of eastern Europe and dreaming of the hills and woods of home.

All our modern instincts are to dismiss these productions as fraudulent fabrications. Yet we cannot apply the same judgements to them as we would, say, to hymns written today and passed off as long-lost works of the Wesleys. The fact is that for those living in the early Middle Ages the communion of saints was a living reality rather than a mere hollow doctrine. Saints were as real and close a presence in death as in life. The divide between past and present was blurred, just as the thinnest of veils separated this world from the next. We need to remember this when we read the *Vitae Sancti*. To modern eyes, they appear to consist of pure invention and fantasy. This is certainly how they have been viewed by most scholars. Ludwig Bieler described the average medieval saint's life as 'a kind of religious romance' in which the subject's temporal activities were mentioned only incidentally and 'accuracy or completeness were not essential'.[67] D. P. Kirby regarded the whole genre as 'essentially destructive to some extent of historical truth'.[68] There was even some contemporary criticism of the hagiographers' predilection for tall stories. A ninth-century Irish scribe bewailed 'the Irish habit of prefering fiction to true history'.[69]

It is undeniable that the *Vitae Sancti* which started appearing in the later seventh century and the cults which they promoted have greatly distorted and idealised our perception of such figures as Brigit, Patrick, Columba and Aidan. They exemplify an approach to the lives and character of the famous which is the exact opposite of that adopted by both popular journalists and serious biographers in our own age. In a culture such as ours where no opportunity is missed to denigrate and bring down the reputations of the dead as well as the living and the search is relentless to expose feet of clay and find skeletons in every cupboard, it is hard to comprehend an attitude of hero-worship and devotion which sought to build up reputations rather than destroy them. The factors which lay behind the production of the *Vitae* of the Celtic saints, and the wider idealisation of the period in which they had flourished, were many and various. Lives were written to point a moral and provide an example as well as to support the claims of a particular church and to promote a lucrative pilgrim trade. Romantic wishful thinking, idealistic dreaming and self-projection also played their part in creating the myth of a golden age of pure and primitive Christian witness.

It would be wrong to give the impression that all of this was simply contrived and manufactured by medieval monastic spin-doctors. There is also evidence from an early stage of genuine popular affection for the Celtic saints as well as of widespread devotion to their cults. Historians are cynical creatures who are always looking for hidden agendas and dubious motives. Some at least of the early medieval love affair with Celtic Christianity we should simply take at face value. As one of the leading modern authorities on medieval saints' cults has written:

> The saints were not fictions created by monastic hagiographers to serve a useful end, but lively presences who owned property, appeared in visions, cured the sick, and dispensed justice. Hagiography provided the prism through which relics were viewed and interpreted, but a literary genre could not invent the presence of saintly patrons.[70]

NOTES

1. For a recent use of the term 'golden age' for this period by an academic, see the title of Chapter 8 of D. Ó Cróinín, *Early Medieval Ireland*. For the 'Celtic Age of Saints', see G. Williams, *Religion*, p. 111. See also T. Joyce, *Celtic Christianity* (Orbis Books, Maryknoll, New York, 1998), p. 56.
2. M. Richards, 'Places and Persons in the Early Welsh Church', *Welsh History Review*, Vol. 5, 1970, p. 347.
3. See, for example, R. Sharpe, '*Quatuor sanctissimi episcopi*: Irish saints before St Patrick' in Ó Corráin, *Sages*, pp. 376–99, and De Paor, *St Patrick's World*, Ch. 5.
4. This is discussed in Bradley, *Columba*, pp. 35–42.
5. Kenney, *Sources*, pp. 294–5.
6. Sharpe, *Medieval Irish Saints*, p. 10.
7. A useful summary of this document can be found in Kenney, *Sources*, pp. 478–9.
8. Brown, *The Cult*, p. 3.
9. P. Ó Riain, 'Towards a Methodology in Early Irish Hagiography', *Peritia*, Vol. 1 (1982), pp. 146–59.
10. Davies, *Wales*, pp. 141, 148.
11. Kenney, *Sources*, p. 298.
12. Ibid., p. 303.
13. The most accessible edition of the *Vitae Samsonis* is the reprint of Thomas Taylor's 1925 edition (Llanerch, Felinfach, 1991).
14. Ó Cróinín, *Early Medieval Ireland*, p. 211.
15. De Paor, *St Patrick's World*, p. 207. This provides the most accessible English

text of Cogitosus' Life. The *Vita Prima* can be found in the *Journal of the Royal Society of Antiquaries in Ireland*, Vol. 119, 1989, pp. 14–49.

16. Ultan's hymn can be found in W. Stokes and J. Strachan, *Thesauras Paleo-hibernicus*, II (Institute for Advanced Studies, Dublin, 1975), pp. 323–6.

17. The best edition of *Bethu Brigte* is that edited by Donncha Ó hAodha (Dublin Institute for Advanced Studies, 1978).

18. D. Bray, 'The Image of St Brigit in the Early Irish Church', *Etudes Celtiques*, Vol. XXIV, 1987, p. 214.

19. E. Johnston, 'Brigit: Celtic Goddess, Christian Saint?' (Course handbook for MA in Celtic Christianity, Lampeter, 1997), section A4.

20. De Paor, *St Patrick's World*, p. 96. This prints the full text of the *Confessio*.

21. Kenney, *Sources*, p. 324.

22. Bieler, *Life and Legend*, p. 115; C. Doherty, 'The cult of St Patrick and the politics of Armagh in the seventh century', in Picard, *Ireland*, p. 86.

23. Greene and O'Connor, *A Golden Treasury*, p. 65.

24. J. Stevenson, 'Literacy in Ireland: the evidence of the Patrick dossier in the Book of Armagh', in McKitterick, *The Uses of Literacy*, p. 13.

25. Aitchison, *Armagh*, p. 199.

26. H. Zimmer, *Keltische Kirche in Britannien und Irland* (Realencyklopädie für Protestantische Theologie und Kirche, Berlin, 1901).

27. Bieler, *Studies*, p. 220.

28. D. A. Binchy, 'A pre-Christian survival in medieval Irish hagiography', in Whitelock, *Ireland*, p. 166. See also Binchy's article, 'The form of St Patrick's Confession in the Book of Armagh', in Dumville, *St Patrick*, pp. 191–202.

29. Binchy, 'A pre-Christian survival', p. 168.

30. Clancy and Markus, *Iona*, p. 115.

31. Ibid., p. 149.

32. M. Enright, *Iona, Tara and Soissons: The Origins of the Royal Anointing Ritual* (Walter de Gruyter, Berlin, 1985). I discuss this further in Bradley, *Columba*, p. 93.

33. See J. O'Reilly, 'Reading the Scriptures in the Life of Columba', in Bourke, *Studies*, pp. 80–106.

34. Sharpe, *Adomnan*, pp. 210–11. This is the best and most easily accessible modern edition of the *Vita Columbae*.

35. Title of paper delivered at conference on Columba in Inverness, 31 May 1997.

36. O'Sullivan, *The Creative Migrant*, p. 88.

37. G. Markus, 'Columba: Monk, Missionary and Hi-jack Victim', *Spirituality*, No. 12, May–June 1997.

38. Henderson, *From Durrow to Kells*, p. 198.

39. R. Ó Floinn, 'Insignia Columbae I', in Bourke (ed.), *Studies*, pp. 138–9.

40. Foster, *Picts*, p. 113.

41. A. Jackson, 'Further Thoughts on Sueno's Stone', in W. O. H. Sellar (ed.), *Moray: Province and People* (School of Scottish Studies, Edinburgh, 1993), p. 94.

42. Bede, *Ecclesiastical History*, Book 3, Chapter 25. I have not specified page numbers for this source as there are several recent editions.

43. See P. Wormald, 'The Venerable Bede and the Church of England', in D. G. Rowell (ed.), *The English Religious Tradition* (Ikon, Wantage, 1992).

44. Dales, *Light to the Isles*, p. 141.
45. R. Runcie, Commemorative Lecture on the 1400th Anniversary of the Mission of St Augustine of Canterbury (unpublished MS, 1997), p. 4.
46. Bede, *Ecclesiastical History*, Book 3, Chapter 3.
47. Wormald, in Rowell, *The English Religions*, p. 16; Bradley, *Columba*, pp. 35–44.
48. Wormald, in Rowell, *The English Religions*, p. 16.
49. Ibid., p. 15.
50. Bede, *Ecclesiastical History*, Book 3, Chapter 4.
51. Wormald, in Rowell, *The English Religions*, p. 16.
52. Bede, *Ecclesiastical History*, Book 3, Chapter 27. See also the remarks on Egbert in Book 3, Chapter 4 and Book 5, Chapter 9.
53. Hunter-Blair, *The World of Bede*, p. 19.
54. O'Dwyer, *Towards a History*, p. 41.
55. Bede, *Ecclesiastical History*, Book 3, Chapter 5.
56. Ibid., Book 3, Chapter 26. On Bede's dislike of monastic opulence and nostalgia for Lindisfarne, see Hunter-Blair, *The World of Bede*, pp. 173–4, and *Northumbria*, pp. 119 and 127.
57. A. Thacker, 'Bede's Ideal of Reform', in P. Wormald (ed.), *Ideal and Reality in Frankish and Anglo-Saxon Society* (Basil Blackwell, Oxford, 1983), p. 142.
58. Henderson, *From Durrow to Kells*, pp. 115–18, 194. Bede's *Life and Miracles of St Cuthbert* can conveniently be found at the end of the Everyman edition of his *History* (pp. 286–348).
59. C. Thomas, 'Bede, Archaeology and the Cult of Relics', in *Bede and His World*, pp. 349–68.
60. Hunter-Blair, *Northumbria*, p. 222.
61. Ó Cróinín, *Early Medieval Ireland*, p. 196.
62. Kenney, *Sources*, p. 273.
63. These poems can be found in Bradley, *Columba*, pp. 61 and 86.
64. Ó Cróinín, *Sages, Saints and Storytellers*, p. 261.
65. Ibid., p. 262.
66. Ibid., p. 264. These poems can be found in Murphy, *Early Irish Lyrics*.
67. Bieler, *Life and Legend of Patrick*, p. 11.
68. D. P. Kirby, *St Wilfrid at Hexham* (Newcastle, 1974), p. 5.
69. Hale, *The Magnificent Gael*, p. 8.
70. Head, *Hagiography*, p. 287.

And win, with them, the victor's crown of gold

The appeal and appropriation of Celtic Christianity
1070–1220

Judging by the documentary sources, the first wave of interest in the early indigenous Christianity of the British Isles receded around the middle of the ninth century. Little seems to have been written about the Celtic saints and their times for the next 200 years or so. Many of the monastic communities which had survived largely unscathed since their foundation in the golden age were all but wiped out by Norse raids in the tenth century and the destruction of their libraries may explain why there is so little surviving material from this period. Less explicable is the dearth of tenth- and eleventh-century manuscripts dealing with Celtic saints in Continental monastic libraries untouched by the Vikings.

It is much more difficult to know what was happening at the level of popular devotion and oral tradition. Local saints' cults may well have persisted, and even flourished, during the period of the Norse invasions. Alan Macquarrie has suggested that the Viking raids turned the Scots in on themselves and inspired a renewed interest in native saints.[1] A significant cult of Patrick, centred on his supposed birthplace at Kilpatrick, near Dumbarton, seems to have developed from the late ninth century, and pilgrimages were made to the well where he was said to have been baptised. There is evidence that local saints' cults were encouraged by the new Anglo-Saxon rulers of Cornwall who probably felt, like the later Anglo-Normans, that this was a relatively painless way of demonstrating their attachment to local traditions and keeping in with the native inhabitants. When Aethlred created an independent Cornish diocese in 994, he established its seat at St Germans, a site associated with one of the most popular Cornish saints. In Cornwall, devotion to local saints seems to have remained strong through the tenth and early eleventh centuries and all but one of the Cornish religious houses listed in the Domesday

Book were dedicated to Celtic saints.[2] In Ireland and Wales, however, the impression given by the limited evidence that exists is of a rather lower level of enthusiasm for Celtic saints at both popular and official level between 850 and 1050 than there had been in the previous 200 years. The latter part of the eleventh century saw a significant upsurge of interest in 'Celtic' Christianity that was to continue throughout the twelfth century. At first sight, this was an unlikely time for such a revival, being the era of the Norman Conquest during which Ireland, Scotland and Wales were gradually subjugated to English rule and English influences. In ecclesiastical as in political life the dominant trends were centralisation, hierarchical organisation and supranationalism. The monastic *familia* and itinerant clergy of the Celtic churches were replaced by territorial dioceses under episcopal control and a system of parish churches. The new bishoprics were generally filled by Anglo-Norman nominees rather than native Irish, Scots and Welsh clergy. Overall, in the words of Geoffrey Barrow, 'a high degree of uniformity was imposed upon the whole of western Christendom under the authority and leadership of a revived and exalted papal monarchy. As a result the peculiarities of many regional churches of the west were ironed out'.[3] The new initiatives came from the Continent, not just in terms of ecclesiastical organisation but in the realm of spirituality and religious life where the new reformed monasticism of Cluny supplanted native insular traditions and brought further pressure to conform with Rome.

It might be thought that the only kind of revival likely to arise in such circumstances would be a last-ditch appeal to Celtic traditions by those who saw them about to be submerged by the incoming Anglo-Norman tide. Certainly there was some harking back to the golden age of the saints on the part of those in Scotland, Wales and Ireland who saw the new reforms destroying the distinctive ethos and identity of their native churches. The real architects of the twelfth-century revival, however, were those associated with the new order who displayed a surprising affection for the figures and features of the old. Anglo-Norman barons and bishops built their splendid cathedrals on the sites of old monastic settlements and eagerly appropriated Celtic saints to provide foundation legends and prove the antiquity and superiority of their particular see. New parish churches were dedicated to local saints in addition or in preference to apostles or Continental saints. Chroniclers associated with the Anglo-Norman ascendancy extolled the virtues of the native saints and Christian customs of Scotland, Wales and Ireland. Undoubtedly there was a strong element of opportunism and good public relations in this pro-Celtic approach. It cast the victors of the Norman Conquest in the role of consolidators and continuers of native tradition rather than as unfeeling aliens out to destroy all that they came across. Other factors also played a part in promoting this second wave of Celtic Christian revival. The monastic reform movement on the Continent brought a renewed interest in the eremitic life, the desert tradition and the ideal of *peregrinatio* that had been so central to the monastic communities of seventh- and eighth-century Ireland and Britain. Idealised longing for a vanished age of faith and epic journeying was also encouraged by the new emphasis on romance and imagination associated with the twelfth-century renaissance.

There are several accounts from this period of attempts to recapture the austere glories of Celtic Christianity in its golden age. One of the most striking concerns Aldwin, an English monk who was prior of Winchcombe Abbey in Gloucestershire. Prompted by reading Bede's lyrical description of the monasteries of Northumbria, he set off north in 1070 with two companions to seek a life of poverty and solitude in the land of Aidan and Cuthbert. As they toured the sites of the great Northumbrian houses, they found only roofless walls. Everything else had been destroyed by the Norsemen. At Jarrow Aldwin and his companions erected a roof of rough-hewn timber and thatch over one of the ruined outbuildings (Bede would have approved!) and lived for several years in their cold and draughty hut, fasting for long periods in imitation of the ascetic practices of their predecessors.

Another eleventh-century enthusiast for 'Celtic' Christianity was Queen Margaret of Scotland. Born in Hungary and brought up in England at the court of Edward the Confessor, Margaret, who married Malcolm Canmore, king of Scotland in 1070, and ruled jointly with him until her death in 1093, is generally portrayed as the arch-Angliciser and Romaniser of the Scottish court and church. So in many ways she was, making English rather than Gaelic the official language of the court, encouraging the cult of St Andrew by establishing a ferry-crossing across the Forth for pilgrims visiting his shrine in Fife, introducing Continental monasticism in the shape of a Benedictine community at Dunfermline and establishing the foundations for a territorial diocesan system of church government with the help of her chaplain, Turgot, a Saxon monk from Durham. Yet it is misleading to see Margaret, as many standard histories of Scotland do, as the person who almost single-handedly destroyed the remnants of an old Celtic church. It is true that she outlawed certain 'barbarous practices' found among the Scots, including laxity over marriage, irregularities in the celebration of Mass, infrequency of confession, neglect of the Lord's Day and insufficient fasting during

Lent.[4] She seems, however, to have been deeply and genuinely moved by the piety and spirituality of the surviving members of some of the old native monastic communities and to have substantially helped them at a time when they were at a low ebb.

This is the clear impression given in the account of her life written in 1093 by Turgot, who may well himself have had similar sympathies, having been a pupil of Aldwin at Jarrow. He noted:

> At that time very many men, shut up in cells apart, in various places of the Scots, were living in the flesh, but not according to the flesh; for they led the life of angels upon earth. The queen endeavoured to venerate and love Christ in them; and to visit them very often with her presence and conversation and to commend herself to their prayers.[5]

When Margaret was unable to persuade the hermits to accept a direct gift from her, she asked them to enjoin upon her some act of charity. While the queen sought to suppress monastic houses which lacked a rule and proper discipline, she actively supported and endowed 'certain monasteries of the Irish tradition'.[6] She and her husband made a substantial grant of land to a community based on St Serf's island in Loch Leven. In 1072 they visited Iona where Margaret was shocked to find a handful of monks living in some squalor in the ruins of the monastery that Columba had founded 500 years earlier. She provided money for rebuilding and to put the community on a more secure financial footing. It is interesting that the arch-Romaniser and friend to Continental monasticism did not seek to plant a Benedictine house on Columba's island but rather chose to revive the fortunes of the old Irish community and ensure that the remnants of Celtic monasticism did not wither away. Alan Macquarrie has commented: 'It may partly be to her credit that there was a thriving Celtic monastic community there in the mid-twelfth century … Not until more than a century after Margaret's death was there a serious attempt to transform Iona into a Benedictine community'.[7]

Perhaps the clearest manifestation of the new enthusiasm for Celtic Christianity in the late eleventh and twelfth centuries was the appearance of a significant number of new *Vitae*, several of which recounted the lives of Celtic saints who had not previously been the object of hagiography. This period saw a significant revival in saints' cults throughout western Christendom, apparently touched off by renewed popular concern about the need for patronage and protection and strongly promoted by the newly powerful diocesan bishops who saw the value of harnessing a popular patron saint to bolster their authority and territorial claims. The renewed interest in saints in the British Isles can be related to this wider movement but it displayed certain significant insular idiosyncracies. In Continental Europe there was a significant shift from historic to contemporary saints and a move away from local patrons towards more universal saints venerated throughout the Catholic Church.[8] This latter process was in many ways sealed and confirmed by the assumption of papal control over the whole process of saint-making by Pope Alexander III in 1170 and the formal mechanism of canonisation set up by Pope Innocent III and confirmed in the Fourth Lateran Council of 1215. Francis of Assisi was perhaps the outstanding example of a figure who effectively came to be regarded as a saint in his own lifetime. In England some of the same trends can be seen. William of Norwich became the centre of a cult just a few years after his death in 1144 and Thomas à Becket attained the status of supranational saint very shortly after his murder in 1170. However, in other parts of the British Isles both popular devotion and the cults promoted by the Anglo-Norman bishops and the new monastic orders remained firmly focused on the Celtic saints from the sixth and seventh centuries. In many cases their cults were strictly local or regional and often associated with the patronage of a particular church or diocese. This preference for local saints from the remote past at a time when the rest of Christendom was finding more recent and universal figures to venerate is a testament to the enduring appeal of the Celtic Christian golden age both to Celts themselves and to their Anglo-Norman lords and masters.

The revival in the cult of Cuthbert that took place in Durham at the beginning of the twelfth century provides a striking example of this attachment. Forced by Viking raids to abandon Lindisfarne in 875, the monks had taken with them the corpse of their beloved patron saint. It was carried round with the community on various peregrinations before finding a final resting place in Durham in 995. For the next hundred years or so Cuthbert's body lay in a shrine in the small monastic church where it attracted a steady trickle of pilgrims. Around 1100 a new *Vita* appeared illustrated with fifty-five coloured pictures and recording seven new posthumous miracles and in 1104 the saint's body was translated with great ceremony to an imposing shrine at the east end of the great cathedral which was being built as the mother church of the huge Durham diocese. Although Cuthbert was undoubtedly a much-loved figure among the people of Northumbria, this revival of his cult had very little to do with popular devotion and almost everything to do with the territorial ambitions of the Benedictine monastery established in Durham in 1083 to replace the old community that traced its roots to Lindisfarne. Throughout the 1090s the Benedictines at Durham engaged in a bitter battle to wrest back land and buildings at Carlisle, Tynningham, Coldingham, York and elsewhere which they claimed had been given to Cuthbert or his heirs and wrongfully sequestered by the Earl of Northumbria and other local noblemen. It was to further these claims that the new *Vita* was produced. Its seven posthumous miracle stories were all concerned with property disputes and five of them involved the saint cursing those who had wrongfully taken monastic land. In every case, the 'thief' was subsequently struck dead.[9] The moral was abundantly clear, as was the message when Cuthbert's incorruptible relics were installed in pride of place behind the high altar of the new cathedral that was being built adjacent to the Benedictine monastery. In the words of Peter Hunter-Blair, 'Cuthbert now possessed his own cathedral, most splendid of all that the Normans built in England ... He rapidly became the patron saint of northern England'.[10]

Cuthbert was not the only Celtic saint to be appropriated 500 years after his death by ecclesiastical power builders. The same fate befell several figures from the golden age of Celtic Christianity in Wales. Indeed, it is possible to argue that had they not been drafted in to support various political and ecclesiastical causes in the late eleventh and twelfth centuries, there would be no substantial and enduring company of Welsh saints. As we have seen, Wales largely missed out on saint-making in the first period of Celtic Christian revival. The only Welsh monks to be commemorated in early *Vitae* were those like Samson, Gildas, Maclovius (St Malo) and Winwaloe who went to Brittany and attracted Breton hagiographers between the late seventh and late ninth centuries. How widely indigenous figures like David, Teilo, Illtud, Cadog and Deiniol were venerated in the period before the Norman Conquest is very uncertain. Most of the extant references to them are confined to Breton sources and such evidence as there is from Wales itself suggests that any cults that may have existed were of a localised nature and based largely on ties of family and kinship. The church dedications which can be established with any degree of certainty in pre-Norman Wales are overwhelmingly either to major Biblical saints like Peter or Paul or to Continental ascetics like Martin of Tours. There is virtually no evidence of early dedications to local Welsh saints nor of the celebration of their saints' days or festivals.[11] Even David's tomb was reported by a monk to be crumbling, neglected and covered in briars on the eve of the Norman take-over.

This picture changes dramatically from the late eleventh century. The next hundred years saw a spate of Welsh saints' Lives, festivals and church dedications. As in Ireland four centuries earlier, the Welsh revival centred around the 'canonisation' through the medium of *Vitae* of a number of individuals, 'defined historically as ascetic clerics, monks, anchorites, missionaries, or leaders in establishing Christian foundations in the fifth through seventh centuries'.[12] Like the earlier Irish *Vitae*, the Lives of the Welsh saints cast their subjects less in the mould of the martyred saints of Continental Europe than in that of the mythological and secular heroes of their own land. They display the same formulaic quality, dealing with what one modern commentator has called 'patterned lives' based around the themes of conception and birth, childhood, miracles, monastic foundation, pilgrimage, conflict with secular rulers and death.[13]

It is no coincidence that the Welsh saints' cults emerged and flowered in the period of the Norman Conquest. In the words of Elissa Henken:

> They were the product and expression of a particular time, of the collision of the Celtic and Anglo-Norman churches and cultures. Some were written by Anglo-Norman clerics who were curious about the traditions they had inherited with their new territorial possessions, and others were produced by the Welsh who wished to defend their honour and rights of the Welsh saints against the influx of foreign saints to whom the Normans were re-dedicating the churches.[14]

In fact, I can find little evidence of Welsh churches being re-dedicated to continental saints in the twelfth century. As has been noted above, there is virtually no evidence of dedications to Welsh saints before this period. The great bulk of such dedications in fact date from the twelfth and thirteenth centuries, many of them being provided for the new parish churches established by the Anglo-Norman reforms and all presumably made with the approval of diocesan bishops.[15] Whether to further their own particular interests, or out of genuine admiration and affection, Norman incomers and local patriots equally enthusiastically invoked the memory of the early Welsh saints.

On the Norman side, we encounter once again the phenomenon of victors eulogising and romanticising the traditions of those they have conquered. William the Conqueror himself made a pilgrimage to St David's in 1081. Like Major-General Stanley in *The Pirates of Penzance*, the Anglo-Norman barons and bishops who increasingly dominated Welsh society and church in the twelfth and thirteenth century had a strong sense of propriety over their newly acquired Celtic 'ancestors'. One of the ways in which this was demonstrated was by Latinising saints' names, so that Beuno became Beunonus and Teilo Teliavus. Melville

Richards has suggested that this process was intended to identify the saints with the Roman Church.[16] It certainly led some later writers to assume that several Welsh saints had a Latin origin. In general, however, the new rulers of Wales seem to have been happy enough to accept the native saints as they were and to enlist their posthumous aid in the promulgation of their church reforms. When the bishopric of St Asaph was established in 1107 as a new-style territorial see, a foundation legend was provided associating it with the British saint Kentigern. In other places, local saints' cults were either actively promoted or allowed to flourish in the belief that they would help to reconcile the Welsh to their new Anglo-Norman masters. Elissa Henken has pointed out that 'at Llandaff, the cathedral and see which came most completely under Norman domination, the shrine which proves to be its most specific and enduring attraction was that of the three Welsh saints: Teilo, Dyfrig and Euddogwy'.[17]

For their part, the Welsh were equally keen to enlist their saints in the cause of fighting for national independence and identity. Indeed, it was in Wales that nationalism (or perhaps, more accurately, tribalism) most clearly operated as a contributory factor in the medieval revival of Celtic Christianity. Even more than their Irish counterparts, Welsh saints were portrayed both in their *Vitae* and in other written sources as having many of the characteristics of tribal chiefs and particular attention was paid to their genealogies and aristocratic lineage. One of the earliest references to David in a Welsh manuscript made him a symbol not of Christian virtue but of patriotic pride and warlike prowess. The early to mid-tenth century *Armes Prydein* (Prophecy of Britain) called on the Welsh to unite under his banner in a Celtic federation with the Irish, Strathclyde Britons, Bretons, Cornish and even the Danes of Dublin, who were counted as honorary Celts for this purpose, to expel the Saxons, and prophesied that with David as their patron they would succeed in driving out the common enemy.[18] Other early inscriptions suggest that David was also enlisted as patron and protector of the Welsh-speaking communities in West Wales seeking to protect their culture and identity in the wake of the considerable Irish incursions into this area.[19] Later it was against the English that the Welsh saints were seen as offering special protection. A Life of Bueno dating from the thirteenth or fourteenth century described how the sixth-century saint planted an oak tree on his father's grave. If an Englishman passed beneath it, a branch would crash down and kill him. A Welshman walking under its broad canopy, on the other hand, would go unharmed.

The development of territorial diocesan episcopacy in Wales engendered a squabble between different sees for supremacy in which local clergy and their new Anglo-Norman bishops and lay patrons joined to champion their own local, or adopted, diocese and the saint who was claimed as its founder. Natives and incomers were also united in wishing to assert the independence of the Welsh church from Canterbury. The claim made by Lanfranc in the 1070s that as Archbishop of Canterbury he was *de facto* Primate of all Britain inflamed the Welsh and aroused memories of Augustine's arrogant attitude towards the British bishops. It also rankled with many of the new Anglo-Norman bishops of Welsh dioceses and their powerful lay patrons as they vied with each other, and even more with Canterbury, to assert their metropolitan status.

This double agenda of vindicating the independence of the Welsh Church and establishing primacy over other Welsh bishoprics almost certainly underlay the production of the first known *Vita* of the man who was to become Wales' patron saint. Rhigyfarch's *Vita Davidi* was produced between 1093 and 1095 at a time when the bishopric of St David's had been temporarily suspended by Anselm, the newly-installed Archbishop of Canterbury who was seeking to assert his direct authority over the Welsh church. Most historians are agreed that the *Vita* reads like a response to this attack on the independence of the Welsh Church and the metropolitan status of the see of St David's in particular. Rhigyfarch's own father, Sulien, had been bishop of the diocese and, in the words of Wendy Davies, he was 'well-nigh obsessed with the claims of St David's'.[20] The Life seems to have been written to show that David was recognised as an archbishop in his own lifetime and that primacy over the Welsh Church rested with his successors in the see that he founded. To this end, he was depicted as having undergone two archiepiscopal consecrations, one by the patriarch of Jerusalem and the other by the bishops, kings and nobles of the Britons. Thus David's authority, and by implication that of his successors in the see bearing his name, was given both a Catholic and a national imprimatur.

Rhigyfarch seems to have been just as concerned to counter the claims of other dioceses to primacy as he was to assert the independence of the Welsh Church as a whole. Elissa Henken has argued that his Life of David was written to uphold the honour of the see that his father had occupied in response to a *Vita* of another early Welsh saint, Cadoc, written a year or two earlier by Lifris, son of bishop Herwald of Llandaff.[21] Significantly, no mention was made of Cadoc in the *Vita Davidi* which was otherwise keen to establish its subject's relations with other Welsh saints, especially when they could be shown to acknowledge his superiority. Later editions of the *Vita Cadoci* countered by including passages which appeared to put David in an inferior position to Cadoc. A similar tit-for-tat battle was fought out on David's behalf with two other leading Welsh saints who also had their first *Vitae* written in this period. Both Teilo and Padarn were depicted by their hagiographers as going to Jerusalem and being presented with gifts by the patriarch. In Teilo's case the gift was a bell and in Padarn's a staff and tunic. Rhigyfarch had David being presented with an altar, staff, tunic and bell. D. P. Kirby has commented, 'there can be little doubt that this passage was written to eclipse Teilo as well as Padarn'.[22] We are back to the unedifying agenda of setting saint against saint in a round of 'anything you can do I can do better'.

Rhigyfarch's *Vita Davidi* has been described as the 'last defensive cry' of the Celtic Church before it was swallowed up by the Normans.[23] In 1115, fifteen years after Rhigyfarch's death, St David's got its first Norman bishop. Its claim to primacy continued to be hotly contested by Llandaff, which in 1107 had become the first Welsh see to profess direct obedience to Canterbury. The two dioceses were involved in protracted and heated disputes over boundaries and entitlements to old monastic lands during the first three decades of the twelfth century. Llandaff ultimately secured the dominant position after some skilful playing of the Celtic card. A key weapon in its campaign was the production around 1130 of the *Liber Landavensis*, a document in many ways reminiscent of the Book of Armagh. It contained lives of five saints from the golden age – Dubricius, Teilo, Oudoceus, Elgar and Samson – and set out to prove their links with Llandaff and so demonstrate that the numerous monasteries which they were credited with founding, and the lands subsequently granted to them, belonged to that diocese. Llandaff also set out to prove entitlement to lands claimed by the newly created English diocese of Hereford, enlisting the somewhat shadowy figure of Dubricius, whose body had been brought to the new cathedral at Llandaff and enshrined there around 1120. The *Liber Landavensis* presented him as the acknowledged Archbishop of South Britain and made much of the properties that he had been granted in Herefordshire. It also took up the wider agenda found in the *Vita Davidi* and other Lives of asserting the independence of the Welsh Church, and especially its property rights, against the claims of the Norman incomers.[24]

If St David's lost out to Llandaff in terms of political power and wealth, it won in terms of the prestige and reputation of its patron saint. The factors which made David patron saint of Wales were complex and perhaps even contradictory. At one level, as we have seen, he was associated from an early period with the struggle of the Welsh, and especially the people of West Wales, for linguistic and cultural identity in the face of

Irish and Saxon incursions. At the same time, he was also taken up by the Normans and the new church establishment, as testified by the fact that almost alone among Welsh saints he became generally known by the Latinised form of his name rather than the Welsh *Dewi*. Ironically, Rhigyfrach, the great defender of Welsh church independence and the old Celtic ways, may have had a hand in selling him to the Normans as someone with whom they could do useful posthumous business. In the words of Patrick Thomas: 'Rhigyfarch tried to depict this rough-and-ready figure as a powerful territorial archbishop on the Roman pattern, whose authority would be recognized and understood by Anglo-Norman prelates'.[25] Thomas has also suggested that the strong stress on the theme of virginity in the *Vita Davidi* may reflect pressure for stricter celibacy in the Welsh Church as part of the closer conformity with Continental practice brought about through Norman influences. Whatever the reasons, David seems to have been a highly acceptable patron for the new rulers of the Welsh church. Over fifty of the new twelfth-century parish churches in Wales were dedicated to him and in a rare papal acknowledgement of Celtic sainthood he was formally canonised by Pope Calixtus II some time between 1119 and 1124.

It is easy to be cynical about the motives that inspired the twelfth-century Welsh Celtic Christian revival. Behind all the well-documented propaganda to support special interests and dreams of avarice, however, it is possible to find evidence of genuine popular devotion for the saints of the golden age and to discern dreams of a more edifying and spiritual nature. The thirty-two wells which have been identified as bearing dedications to Dewi, and the numerous others associated with lesser known local saints, testify to a high level of popular veneration. So, too, do the *cywyddau* (poems and prayers about saints often associated with their wells), the images found in churches and the development of feast days and festivals. The great majority of the cults which developed around Welsh saints were highly localised and often confined to a relatively small area. They probably reflect a fierce tribal loyalty and a strong sense of place rather than any manipulative ecclesio-political agenda. There was also probably a strong element of nostalgia for what was a vanishing rather than a vanished age. One can detect it in a *Vita* of Illtud written around 1140 by a monk at Llantwit Major and incorporated into a book on the lives of several Welsh saints produced around 1200. Here there is no attempt to advance the claims of one of Wales' oldest monasteries to hold a continuing position of pre-eminence in the contemporary Anglo-Norman church. Rather the author gazes wistfully at the Celtic crosses in the cemetery and writes fondly of the cave and well associated with the saint.[26] There are other echoes of that sense of the holiness of place which is so powerful a feature of the Welsh spiritual tradition. During the 1150s, when Powys was experiencing its final fragile period of unity and independence before English take-over, Rhirid Flaidd, a local landowner, rebuilt the church in the remote hamlet of Pennant Melangell and replaced the simple grave of the local saint with a magnificent stone shrine set up on pillars with decorated capitals. It remains to this day not just as a remarkable and rare example of a religious artefact that was almost completely destroyed in the British Isles at the time of the Reformation but also as an eloquent and moving reminder of the profound reverence felt by the medieval Welsh for their Celtic Christian ancestors, great and small.[27]

There is rather less evidence of popular native involvement in the twelfth-century Celtic Christian revival in Scotland and a greater sense of the agenda being set by rulers and reformers. This may partly be because the new Anglo-Norman church structures and Continental monasticism were introduced by Scottish monarchs rather than by outsiders. Although Columba was widely hailed as the apostle of the Scots in this period, it was only with the advent of serious tension with England following Edward I's claim of overlordship over Scotland at the tail-end of the thirteenth century that the Scots started invoking their saints in the same fiercely nationalistic spirit that the Welsh had a century and a half earlier.

Whether out of genuine affection or careful calculation, devotion to the Celtic saints, and to Columba in particular, seems to have been strong among the most staunchly pro-Norman Scottish monarchs. According to the fifteenth-century *Scotichronicon*, Queen Margaret turned in 'suppliant devotion' to Columba when she feared that she was infertile.[28] His intercessory and miraculous powers were not found wanting as she went on to produce eight children. Her three sons, who between them ruled Scotland for the first half of the twelfth century, while enthusiastically pushing forward her Romanising and reforming ecclesiastical policies, continued to revere the Celtic saints. Edgar, king of Scotland from 1094 to 1107, is said to have given the Benedictines of Durham a royal estate at Coldingham because of his devotion to Columba. Alexander I, who ruled from 1107 to 1124, founded a house of Augustinian canons on the island of Inchcolm in the Firth of Forth in 1123 and dedicated it to Columba. Later chroniclers related that he had called on the aid of the saint when he was caught in a storm in the Forth. His boat managed to reach Inchcolm where the king was looked after for three days by a hermit devoted to Columba's cult who lived in a small cell off shellfish and the milk from his cow. The Augustinian priory was apparently established as a thanks offering for Alexander's deliverance. The *Scotichronicon* adds: 'There was also the fact that he had always even from his youth revered St Columba with particular honour'.[29] David I, who ruled from 1124 to 1153 and did more than any other individual to bring about the Normanisation of Scotland and introduce the reformed Continental monastic orders into the country, also showed reverence for native saints like Mungo, Cuthbert and Columba, after whom he christened his first-born son.

Of the ten new territorial dioceses created to bring *Ecclesia Scoticana* in line with the rest of western Catholic Christendom, seven were centred on old Celtic monastic sites – Glasgow, St Andrews, Dunkeld, Dunblane, Aberdeen, Brechin and Whithorn. Many of the new parish churches created between the late eleventh and mid-thirteenth century were dedicated to Scottish saints. As in Wales, this period saw the production of a significant number of saints' *Vitae* after an apparently slack time for Scottish hagiography. Several sixth- and seventh-century monks who had not previously been written about received their first Lives. Serf, a shadowy figure who was probably a Pictish missionary active in Fife, was identified in his mid-twelfth-century *Vita* as the grandson of both the king of Canaan and the king of Arabia. Having renounced his own right to the kingship of Canaan, he was reported to have studied in Alexandria, returned to Canaan where he was consecrated a bishop and then, following the prompting of an angel, journeyed to Jerusalem where he was made a patriarch. Subsequent travels apparently took him to Constantine, Rome and across Europe, and involved him crossing both the Red Sea and the English Channel dry-shod, before he ended up in the Firth of Forth and began founding monasteries in eastern Scotland. While the main purpose of the *Vita Servani* seems to have been the usual one of providing a foundation legend for the monastery in which it was written, in this case Culross on the north bank of the Forth, it also shows the extent to which Celtic saints were acquiring an exotic and mysterious aura. The appeal of the Celtic model of sainthood is underlined by another *Vita*, recently unearthed by Alan Macquarrie and probably dating from the late eleventh century. Written by a Flemish hagiographer to provide a foundation legend for the church of Laurencekirk in the Mearns area of north-east Scotland, it tells the life of Laurence of Canterbury in a way that 'transforms the grave Italian monk Laurence into a fearsome Celtic-style miracle worker'.[30]

While the main object of the Scottish *Vitae* seems almost always to have been to prove the antiquity and property claims of a particular church or cathedral, they did not do down the saints of rival establishments with quite the same enthusiasm as the Welsh lives. The new Scottish bishoprics were not engaged in a similar struggle for supremacy. St Andrews had come to be recognised as the chief see by the tenth century and there was little attempt to challenge its pre-eminence. A bull of 1192 brought the *Ecclesia Scoticana* under the direct jurisdiction of the Pope and gave each of its ten bishops equal status so there was no metropolitan see to be fought over. However, there were still claims to monastic lands and properties to be established by the new bishoprics and this gave the *Vitae* a distinctive character so that they 'read at times almost like a collection of the title deeds of the saint's principal church'.[31]

Secular politics also played a part in promoting the cult of certain saints. This certainly seems to have been the case with Ninian who had almost certainly been the object of veneration in and around Whithorn in the centuries following his death, but had to wait until the latter part of the twelfth century for full hagiographical treatment. A Latin poem on his miracles, written by a monk at Whithorn towards the end of the eighth century, survives in a single eleventh-century manuscript preserved at Bamberg in West Germany and may have been the subject of a Life produced earlier in the eighth century which has been lost. The first extant *Vita* of Ninian, probably written by Ailred of Rievaulx around 1160, seems to have been part of a revival in the saint's cult which may at least in part have arisen out of struggles between the lords of Galloway and the Scottish crown. Both sides in the dispute enthusiastically enlisted the saint in their cause. During the reign of David I, Fergus, Lord of Galloway, the great champion of Gallovidian independence, founded a Premonstratensian priory at Whithorn which he prudently dedicated to both Ninian and Martin of Tours. The priory seems to have become known simply as St Ninian's, an indication, perhaps, of the strength of affection for the local saint. A carved figure of the saint, represented as a bishop, which is thought to date from this period, has holes through the arms, suitable for pushing poles through, and was probably carried around in processions (Plate 3).

Ailred's *Vita Niniani* seems to have been part of a concerted propaganda exercise on the part of the opposing side. It was apparently written at the behest of Bishop Christian of Galloway, a strong supporter of the Anglo-Norman cause and of the claims of the Scottish crown to rule the independent-minded inhabitants of the south-western corner of the country. Ailred had already been enlisted in the campaign against the Gallovidians and had obligingly described them as 'not men but brute beasts devoid of humanity and piety'.[32] His enthusiasm for bringing these recalcitrant rebels to heel and subjecting them to the new ecclesiastical

Plate 3. Twelfth-century wooden statue of Ninian.

discipline being imposed in the rest of Scotland (and possibly also for
keeping the see of Galloway under the direct authority of the Archbishop
of York) undoubtedly coloured and may even have directly inspired his
Life of Ninian. The *Vita* has all the usual ingredients of Celtic hagiography, with extensive coverage of the saint's miracles and a pointed
comparison between the high standards of the golden age and the laxity
of the present day: 'As I reflect upon the most saintly character of that
most holy man, I feel ashamed of our indolence and of the laziness of this
miserable generation'.[33] It lays particular stress, however, on its subject's
catholicity and connections with Rome and Continental Christianity.
Ninian is portrayed as spending several years in Rome and being consecrated bishop by the Pope who directly commissioned him to go as an
apostle to 'people in the western parts of Britain [who] had not yet
received the faith of our Saviour'.[34] On his way back from Rome, Ninian
is described as visiting Martin of Tours and later as dedicating his stone-
built church at Whithorn to the continental saint when he hears of his
death. It is this last story, almost certainly wholly apocryphal and introduced by Ailred purely to stress Ninian's continental links, that led the
foundation of Whithorn to be dated to 397, the year of Martin's death,
and made Ninian, in popular opinion, the first evangelist of Scotland
when, in reality, he is much more likely to have lived in the late fifth
or early sixth century and may even have been a contemporary of
Columba.[35]

Both secular and ecclesiastical politics probably played a significant
part in boosting the cult of another saint who was largely neglected, at
least in terms of hagiography, until this period. The two Lives of
Kentigern, or Mungo, which appeared in the latter part of the twelfth
century were almost certainly written to provide an ancient foundation
legend for and enhance the prestige of the see of Glasgow which had been
established in 1115. The first was commissioned in the 1150s by Bishop
Herbert of Glasgow and the second in the 1180s by Bishop Jocelin,
almost certainly in connection with the rebuilding of the cathedral which
was dedicated to the British saint and contained his shrine. The later
Vita, which was the work of an accomplished hagiographer, Jocelin of
Furness, pointedly located several of Kentigern's miracles in Glasgow
and also stressed his links with other saints, notably the Pictish Serf and
the Irish Columba. It recounted, for example, a meeting between Kentigern and Columba beside a river during which the two men exchanged
pastoral staffs. Alan Macquarrie has argued that the purpose of introducing this and similar stories, which are almost certainly apocryphal,
was essentially political and that they were designed to stress the links

binding the former British kingdom of Strathclyde with the rest of Pictish and Gaelic Scotland.[36]

Columba himself, as we have already seen, was a popular figure with the early twelfth-century kings of Scotland and seems to have been widely regarded as the country's patron saint. A poem which is thought to date from the reign of Alexander I asked him to be 'sword and defence of the Scots'. Later monarchs continued to regard the saint in this light. In 1178 William I entrusted the *Breccbenach* containing Columba's relics to the abbot of Arbroath with instructions that it should be used for blessing the royal troops in battle. Iona was no longer the centre of his cult and this fact, together with its remoteness, may perhaps explain why it was not chosen as a centre for one of the new episcopal sees. Despite Queen Margaret's efforts to revive it, the surviving Columban community on the island remained a shadow of its former self and seems to have petered out with the coming of the Benedictines to Iona around 1200. While the headship of what was left of the Columban monastic *familia* had transfered to Ireland, where it was disputed between Kells, Derry and Durrow, the focus of the saint's cult in Scotland presumably remained at Dunkeld, where some of Columba's corporeal relics had been taken in the mid-ninth century. There is, in fact, some evidence that they were removed to Ireland to be re-united with the rest of the saint's body towards the end of the ninth century. It is difficult to find evidence of a thriving Columban cult centred on Dunkeld in the eleventh and twelfth centuries although the saint's crosier, or *Cathbhuaidh*, remained in the cathedral's possession and is probably shown on a seal dating from around 1250.[37] There may be significance in the fact that the new diocese of Dunkeld retained little pockets of territory outside its natural geographical boundaries. Examples include Dollar in Clackmananshire and the island of Inchcolm, where there was a church or monastery dedicated to Columba.

There is some evidence that Columba was enlisted as a champion of Gaelic independence in the face of Anglo-Norman centralisation, much as David had been in Wales. He certainly seems to have been particularly popular among the Gaelic speaking Scots in the west of the country, while Andrew remained the favoured saint of the old Pictish areas in the east. It is possible that the spirit of Columba was invoked by surviving 'Celtic' monastic communities in Scotland as part of a wider appeal to their distinctive traditions as they sought to avoid being swallowed up by the newly introduced Continental orders, and especially the communities of Augustinian canons who seem to have been planted alongside them. Unfortunately, lack of evidence means that we can only guess at the nature and extent of such 'Celtic' survivals in this period. Particular uncertainty surrounds the so-called Céli Dé communities, long regarded as outposts of resistance to the onward march of Romanising influence. Some at least of the Céli Dé communities in twelfth-century Scotland appear to have been of relatively recent origin and there is considerable doubt among modern scholars as to whether they can be taken to represent a last-ditch Celtic stand against the new ecclesiastical order.[38] It is certainly the case that Céli Dé communities were located at several early monastic sites, notably Dunkeld, Brechin, Abernethy, Iona, Muthil and on St Serf's island in Loch Leven and that they were sometimes regarded as a considerable nuisance and irritant by those in the van of introducing the new Anglo-Norman church structures and reformed monasticism. Relations between Céli Dé and members of the new monastic orders seem to have been uneasy at St Andrews and Loch Leven and there was particular tension at Dunkeld where Cormac, bishop of the recently created diocese from 1114 to 1123, angered the existing Céli Dé community by his attempt to subordinate them to the newly installed Augustinian canons. Several later bishops of Dunkeld apparently based themselves at Inchcolm, which had an Augustinian priory but no Céli Dé community. Whether this move was made to avoid the hassle of Celtic obscurantism, however, must remain a matter of pure speculation.

As well as providing a rallying point for those resisting the changes being made in Scotland's political and ecclesiastical structure, Columba also remained much in demand as a founder of monasteries and churches. Numerous foundation legends, apparently dating from the twelfth century, attribute ecclesiastical establishments all over Scotland to his own personal church-planting activities. Several relate to parish churches and witness to the Scots' continuing attachment to their Celtic Christian past at a time when their church was being reorganised on a territorial parish basis. Monasteries were also keen to establish their roots in the age of the saints, not least to support their titles to property and their claims to perpetual immunity from increasing demands for feudal dues and taxes. Foundation legends involving Columba seem to have been particularly popular in north-east Scotland, a region which he is most unlikely to have visited during his lifetime. Monasteries at Aberdour and Turriff in Aberdeenshire claimed him as their founder and Gaelic notes made on the pages of a gospel book provide a touching if unconvincing account of his involvement in the establishment of Deer Abbey. They recount a visit by Columba to the local saint, Drostan, which led the two men to ask the king for land on which to build a monastery. He refused, whereupon his son was taken ill and nearly died. Columba and Drostan prayed for the ailing youth, who was miraculously restored, prompting the king to recant and grant land to the saints. The new monastery is said to have got its name when Drostan, crying because of the departure of his saintly companion, who was presumably off to found another establishment, was told by Columba to call it after his tears. The foundation legend in the *Book of Deer* is followed by charters recording grants of land made to the monastery. In two of these, dated 1131 and 1140, the name of Peter is added to those of Columba and Drostan, presumably to add some apostolic clout.[39] There were several other examples of double dedications in north east Scotland involving both local Celtic and apostolic figures – the church at Portmoak was dedicated to Monan and Stephen and the cathedral at Aberdeen to Machar and Mary – but in all cases it was the Celtic saint whose name came to be exclusively associated with the foundation while that of his Catholic rival was quietly dropped.

In Ireland, too, the late eleventh century saw an upsurge of interest in the Celtic saints. Unlike the *Vitae* written in the seventh and eighth centuries which had mostly been in Latin, many of the Lives produced in this second wave of revival were in Irish, indicating, perhaps, a new spirit of nationalism and Celtic consciousness in the face of Norse invasions and the threat of Anglo-Normanisation. While both secular and ecclesiastical politics played a part in promoting Irish saints' cults, nostalgia and romantic longing were also strong factors. As in the earlier revival, Irish monks in exile on the Continent played a major role in promoting the notion of a golden age of Celtic Christianity centred on sixth- and seventh-century Ireland. It was an Irish chronicler named Maelbrighte living in enforced exile in the monastery of St Martin at Mainz during the 1070s who seems first to have used the phrase *Hibernia, insula sanctorum* (Ireland, island of saints) in respect of this period.[40]

Much of the new hagiographical material about Celtic saints is more readily found in Continental than in Irish monasteries and may well have originated outside Ireland. The oldest manuscript sources for *Vitae* of Flannan and Mochuille, written in the 1160s by an author who had trained in southern Germany, are in monasteries in Austria and Switzerland. There are no extant copies in Ireland dating from before the fourteenth century. Twelfth-century manuscripts of a *Vita* of Coemgen found in Bavaria and a *Vita* of Ita in Austria similarly pre-date the earliest known copies of these Lives in Ireland. A fragmentary Life of Ronan, discovered in a Bavarian monastic library, has not been found in any native Irish collection. Richard Sharpe has pointed to other evidence for the considerable interest in early Irish saints which existed in this period on the Continent, much of it doubtless inspired by monks from Ireland who were leading lives of exile and based in the *Schottenkloster* in southern Germany and Austria.[41] There was also interest in England. The major *Vita* of Brigit produced in this period was the work of Laurence, Prior of Durham. Written in the 1130s, it was dedicated to Ailred of Rievaulx.

In Ireland itself, as in Wales and Scotland, reorganisation of the church along Continental lines gave an impetus to the cults of native saints. The Synod of Rathbreasail of 1111 created twenty-three territorial dioceses, several of which were centred on early monastic sites, notably Kildare, Derry, Clonmacnoise, Glendalough and Armagh. In 1152 the Synod of Kells increased the number of dioceses to thirty-seven, created four archbishoprics and established the primacy of Armagh over the whole Irish church. Several churches which had unexpectedly found themselves raised to episcopal rank busily cast around for a suitable Celtic patron to add venerability and prestige to their new-found status. Others, which had failed to make the grade, sought to press their claims by extolling the virtues of their particular saint. Disappointed that his church at Ardmore had not become an episcopal seat, Eugenius brought out a *Vita* of its patron, Declan, whom he sought to portray as the first apostle of the local district of the Déisi. His argument that Declan's see should remain the seat of the Bishop of the Déisi in perpetuity was not, however, accepted.[42]

Columba was meanwhile caught up in a more domestic dispute between monasteries vying for the headship of his monastic *familia*. Although the translation of his relics to Kells in the ninth century had made it the clear successor to Iona, Durrow and more especially Derry had begun to challenge its position. Subsequent developments owed much to the changing political fortunes of Ireland's leading clans. While the influence of the once-powerful Uí Néills, whose patronage had greatly helped Kells, declined significantly in the early twelfth century, Derry gained from its association first with the Cenel Connaill and later with the Cenél nEógain. In 1150 comarbship of the *paruchia* was transferred from the Abbot of Kells to the Abbot of Derry. At about the same time an important *Vita* of the saint was written in Irish. Where previous hagiographies, notably Adomnan's *Vita*, had concentrated largely on Columba's years on Iona, it dwelt almost entirely on his earlier activities in Ireland and portrayed him as the founder of 300 churches there. While the main aim of this *Vita* was to enhance the prestige of Derry, which it described as Columba's first and favourite foundation, it may also have had a wider agenda in presenting him as Irish missionary rather than Iona monk. In stressing Columba's Irishness, the Derry hagiographer was challenging the dominance of the Patrician cult centred on Armagh and proposing an alternative candidate for veneration as Ireland's patron saint.

Derry also seems to have been the source of a cycle of 150 poems apparently written in the twelfth century which either had Columba as their subject or were attributed to his authorship. They presented him as a heroic literary figure in the mould of the great pre-Christian Celtic bards. Indeed the Columban cycle directly parallels a cycle of poems attributed to the blind bard Ossian about the legendary Finn mac Cumaill. Columba came to be associated more closely with the *filid*, or poets, than any other Celtic saint. The Irish *Vita* included a description of his defence of the *filid* when they had come under attack at the convention of Drum Cett for over-savage satire directed against the kings of Ireland. This notion of Columba as the special friend and protector of poets became a significant feature of his cult, and of his attraction, in later medieval Ireland. So too did the image, which was also strongly propagated in the twelfth-century cycle of poems, of the exile from Ireland who longed for his homeland. Many of the poems portrayed Columba wistfully looking back to the place of his birth, Gartan in Donegal, and longing to return to his Irish monasteries, especially his beloved Derry. This was in contrast to the image presented in Gaelic poems attributed to the saint and emanating from Scotland in the same period, notably 'Columba's Island Paradise' which lyrically enthused about his life on Iona.

The theme of exile was especially marked in the mid-twelfth-century Irish *Vita* which took the form of an extended commentary on God's words to Abraham: 'Leave your country and your land, your kindred and your own patrimony for my sake, and go into the country which I shall reveal to you' (Genesis 12:1). Unlike earlier lives, it portrayed Columba as vowing never to return to his homeland and described him coming to the convention at Drum Cett with his eyes blindfolded and sods of Scottish turf strapped to his feet so that he did not technically see nor set foot in Ireland again. Máire Herbert relates this new emphasis on Columba the exile to a shift in Irish identity from the people to the land, while for James Kenney, 'it presents the saint as he appealed to the imagination of his countrymen some five centuries after his death – particularly as the exile extolling the charm of his native land. It is the earliest corpus of formally nationalist propaganda'.[43]

Romanticism as well as nationalism undoubtedly influenced the changing way in which Irish saints were portrayed in the twelfth century. David Greene and Frank O'Connor have described this as the period in which stories started to be told for their own sake and creative literature appeared. This new imaginative literature, which was still largely the province of monastic scribes, had a distinctive ecclesiastical branch – 'church history written in the manner of the old sagas' – in which:

> The saints – heroes of these pseudo-sagas – were conceded conceptions, births, and childhood adventures far more extraordinary than those of Cú Chulainn and his kind, and were recorded as destroying more enemies with their prayers and curses than the true saga heroes destroyed with their swords.[44]

This development was perhaps particularly marked in the case of Patrick who began to appear in numerous folk tales and became increasingly enmeshed in Irish mythology. *Agallamh na Seanórach* (The Colloquy of the Ancient Men), which appeared around 1200, described him meeting Ossian and his cousin Cailté, the last surviving members of the *Fiana*, the heroic warrior bands which had supposedly flourished in third-century Ireland and been associated with the legendary Finn mac Cumaill. Overcoming his initial terror, the saint sprinkled holy water on the two ancient warriors and banished the thousand legions floating over them. In some versions of the *Agallamh*, which exists both as an extended prose work and as a cycle of poems, a lively exchange followed as to the relative merits of paganism and Christianity, during which Patrick vividly evoked the terrors of hell and the fearful wrath of a judging God. Ossian and Cailté were converted to the new faith and set about recounting to Patrick the legends and stories of Ireland's pre-Christian past. Other versions portray a less confrontational atmosphere in the early stages of the meeting and describe Patrick sharing food with Ossian and Cailté and delighting in the stories which they tell in the course of a journey across Ireland.[45]

Perhaps partly because of these variations, the message of the *Agallamh* has been interpreted in radically different ways. Magnus MacLean saw it as presenting a set-piece confrontation between paganism and Christianity in which the old religion was made to look much more attractive than the new. He pointed to a poem entitled 'Ossian's Prayer' in which Ossian's question as to whether Finn was in heaven was met with Patrick's icy response: 'Finn is in hell in bonds. He is now in the house of pain and sorrow, because of the amusement he had with the hounds and for attending the (bardic) schools each day, and because he took no heed of God'.[46] The poem made Ossian the spokesman of a faith that was warm, generous and in love with life, while Patrick seemed only to offer a cold, cramped judgementalism and an attachment to pain and suffering. For MacLean this contrast ran through the entire work which he felt represented the reaction of 'monkish scribes in the twelfth century' to the increasingly narrow and world-hating brand of Christianity developed by the medieval church: 'In these dialogues paganism at its best is brought face to face with ecclesiastical Christianity, and is made to appear more just, more humane, and desirable in every way'.[47]

Other modern commentators have taken a very different view and seen the *Agallamh* as an attempt to effect a synthesis between paganism and Christianity and to show Patrick as an enthusiast for Ireland's pre-Christian mythological tradition.[48] It is certainly true that the prose version makes much of Patrick's delight in Ossian's stories and his conviction that they should be written down. It is surely no coincidence that this work appeared at a time when monastic scribes were committing to paper myths and legends which had previously only been transmitted in oral form. Was at least part of the purpose of the *Agallamh* to portray Patrick, like Columba, as the friend of poets and the man who persuaded the Irish to preserve their traditional culture for posterity? His imagined dialogues with Ossian arguably fit with the syncretist agenda of embracing elements of pre-Christian religion and mythology that has so often been associated with Celtic Christianity. One feature at least of the *Agallamh* is beyond dispute. Whether they were written to protest at the harsh exclusivity and 'churchiness' of medieval Christianity or to emphasise the closeness between Celtic saints and heathen storytellers, there can be no doubting that, in the words of one recent scholar, 'these poems bring us nostalgic memories of a perished golden age'.[49]

As well as being fondly looked back to by the Irish, Patrick was also appropriated by the country's Anglo-Norman invaders in an effort to legitimise and popularise their overlordship and the new political and ecclesiastical structures that came with it. The fullest and most influential twelfth-century *Vita* of Patrick was the work of Jocelin of Furness, the English hagiographer responsible for the Life of Kentigern. He wrote it in the mid-1180s, a decade or so after the landing of Richard de Clare at Waterford that is often taken to mark the start of the Norman invasion of Ireland. Jocelin had been brought over to Ulster by another of the early Norman invaders, John de Courcy, who had overrun County Down and established his headquarters at Downpatrick, the old monastic site associated with Patrick and widely thought to be the place where he died. An enthusiastic supporter of the movement to reform the Irish church along Continental lines, de Courcy had in 1183 granted land to the Benedictines to found a priory, with cathedral attached, at Downpatrick in place of the old Celtic monastic church. Two years later, he staged there what has been described as 'one of the most famous of all translations of Irish saints'.[50] In the presence of the papal legate and other distinguished ecclesiastics, the bones of Patrick, Columba and Brigit were placed in a magnificent new shrine. Their corporeal relics had conveniently been discovered lying in a single coffin at Downpatrick by Malachy III, Bishop of Down, following a vision in which he had seen a tomb bearing the legend: 'In Down three saints one grave do fill: Patrick, Brigit and Colmcille'.

The 'discovery' of the bones of the country's three leading saints lying side by side was a brilliant propaganda coup for Ireland's Anglo-Norman conquerors and for John de Courcy in particular. Irish hagiography had long made much of the links between these saints in life. Now here they were found to be united in death, lying in the place that de Courcy hoped would become the leading ecclesiastical and political centre of Ulster. Significantly, the translation of the relics is not mentioned in any native Irish source. It was a wholly Anglo-Norman event, enthusiastically written up by Jocelin and Giraldus Cambrensis, the great chronicler of late twelfth-century Ireland. De Courcy's overriding aim was to boost the claims of Downpatrick over those of Armagh. There was, in fact, to be another discovery and translation of the three saints' relics just over a hundred years later in what may well have been a counter-move by the anti-English party in the Irish Church. In 1293 the Abbot of Armagh enshrined what he claimed to be the bones of Patrick, Columba and Brigit after they had been found buried at Saul.

Jocelin's *Vita Patrici* was almost certainly written to accompany the Downpatrick enshrinement in 1185. It emphasised Patrick's links with other saints, introducing several stories of meetings not found in other *Vitae*, and recounted a vision of the future vicissitudes of the Irish church, apparently experienced by the saint towards the end of his life, which nicely married nostalgia for the golden age of Celtic Christianity with enthusiasm for the Anglo-Norman cause. Patrick's vision began by showing a time of glorious strength and then revealed a long period of gradual decline, almost to the point of extinction, before a great revival in the twelfth century led from Ulster by Archbishop Malachy Ó Morgair of Armagh. Jocelin repeated Maelbrighte's phrase about Ireland as the 'island of saints' and added several yet more fantastic miracles and prophecies to the substantial list with which Patrick was already credited. Indeed, he left little more to be said about the saint. As Ludwig Bieler observed: 'The legend of St Patrick, as that of other saints, had its natural growth during the Middle Ages. With Jocelin of Furness in the twelfth century it reached its limits'.[51]

Jocelin's Life of Patrick was one of the last *Vitae* to be written about a Celtic saint from the golden age. The decline of this particular hagiographical device did not, however, mean the end of the idealisation of the early native Christian communities of the British Isles. From the time of the Norman Conquest, individual *Vitae* were increasingly replaced by compilations which brought together the lives of several saints and also included poems, hymns and prayers supposedly composed in early monasteries. Among the earliest of these compilations were the *Liber Hymnorum* and the *Leabhar Na h'Uidrhe*, which probably date from the eleventh century, and the *Book of Leinster* (*c.*1150). They suggest a determination to preserve a record of early Irish culture and history in the wake of the Anglo-Norman settlement.

Several of these compilations were produced by monks who belonged to one of the new orders introduced into the British Isles during the twelfth and thirteenth centuries. On the face of it, the reformed monasticism which originated in Citeaux and Thiron-le-Gardais in the 1090s and 1100s was an unlikely patron of Celtic Christian revival. Continental in origin and temperament, its introduction is usually associated with both the Romanisation and Anglicisation of the native churches. Oliver Davies' comment that 'the Cistercian Reform of the twelfth century … marks the point of greatest influence of the norms of Catholic Christendom upon Welsh monastic life' could equally well apply to Scotland or Ireland.[52] It is certainly the case that in some areas the new monasticism did help to destroy the last surviving vestiges of the old Celtic monasticism. In Scotland, the houses of Augustinian canons planted on ancient monastic sites seem to have supplanted the adjoining Céli Dé communities. In Ireland what was left of the Columban monastic *familia* followed Derry's lead around 1220 and adopted the rule of Augustine, ending a 600-year tradition of following its founder's rule. Those in the reformed orders were by no means universally hostile to the traditions and ways of their Celtic predecessors, however. Some, indeed, especially among the Cistercians, positively admired their lifestyle and embraced their liturgy. Two of the Celtic saints' most enthusiastic twelfth-century hagiographers, Jocelin of Furness and Ailred of Rievaulx, were Cistercian monks.

The Cistercian love affair with Celtic Christianity is perhaps seen most clearly in the adulation accorded by the founder of the order to Mallachy Ó Morgair, the figure who had appeared in Patrick's vision, as recounted by Jocelin of Furness, as the saviour of the Irish church. Educated in the monasteries of Lismore and Armagh, where he became both abbot and bishop, Malachy became convinced of the need to reform Irish monasticism and enthusiastically espoused the new ideals which were being promoted on the Continent. He visited Bernard of Clairvaux, with whom he hoped to stay on as a monk. However, he was persuaded to return home, where he was instrumental in founding the first Cistercian abbey in Ireland at Mellifont, County Louth, in 1142, an event which, in the words of a recent history of early Christian Ireland, 'marked the end of the Irish monastic era'.[53] Six years later, on his way to Rome to seek the *pallium* for the Archbishops of Armagh and Cashel, he stopped off again at Clairvaux, fell ill and died in the arms of Bernard who later wrote a life of Mallachy as an example of holiness. Richard Sharpe has pointed out that this work was the most nearly contemporary *Vita* of any Irish saint. Indeed, Mallachy, the arch-reformer and Romaniser, 'whose burning desire', according to one recent Irish Protestant church historian, 'was to bring the Celtic Church under the supervision of Rome', was one of very few Irish churchmen living after the golden age of the sixth and seventh century to be widely revered as a saint.[54] Another was Laurence O'Toole, abbot of Glendalough, who in 1162 became the first (and for a long time to come also the last) Irishman to occupy the see of Dublin, in a rare departure from the practice of giving bishoprics to Englishmen. Malachy achieved widespread veneration after his death. A runic inscription dating from the latter half of the twelfth century on a stone in the Isle of Man mentions him alongside Christ, Patrick and Admomnan.[55]

Bernard of Clairvaux's admiration and affection for Mallachy was all the more striking given his generally low opinion of the Irish whom he described as 'shameless in their morals, wild in their rites, impious in their faith, barbarous in their laws, stubborn in discipline, unclean in their life. They were Christians in name, but in fact they were pagans'.[56] Undoubtedly there was an element of decadence in Irish religious life in this period. Abbots had effectively become lay lords whose family held office from generation to generation. Monasteries were now largely secular institutions with substantial land holdings and monks were reduced to the role of farm labourers. The Cistercians and other reforming orders countered this laxity with a renewed emphasis on spiritual discipline and asceticism and they found natural allies in those like Malachy who represented an older and purer Irish monastic tradition.

Many of the Cistercian ideals echoed those which had underlain sixth- and seventh-century Celtic monasticism. Richard Southern has pointed to the reaction which took place throughout Europe in the twelfth century against the overcomplexity of monasticism as it had developed under the Benedictine rule.[57] The search for a simpler and more solitary style of religious life had been prefigured in the Carthusian movement which had drawn on the desert tradition and the writings of Cassian to develop monasteries in which both cenobitical and eremitical lifestyles could flourish, as they had in the early Celtic foundations. It may well be that this affinity with some of the basic precepts and practices of Celtic Christian communities helps to explain why the Continental orders, which were largely introduced into the British Isles by the Anglo-Norman invaders, met with so little native opposition. In the case of Wales, for example, Glanmor Williams has suggested that the more rigorous and ascetical practices introduced by the Cistercians were welcomed by the indigenous population as offering a return to the ideals of the earliest Celtic monasticism.[58] For their part, the reformed orders found much in Celtic Christianity to affirm. In Wales, as in Ireland, the new monasteries collected and preserved old poems and prayers. The *Black Book of Carmarthen*, an important collection of Welsh medieval verse, which includes poems going back to the ninth and tenth centuries exploring the themes of penance and pilgrimage and casting a nostalgic glance back to the days of Merlin, was probably produced late in the thirteenth century in either a Cistercian monastery or Augustinian priory in west Wales. Oliver Davies has also argued a Cistercian provenance for the early fourteenth-century *Book of Taliesin* which contains substantial Druidic elements in its rich collection of verse and provides some of the most important early examples of that distinctive Welsh genre of 'praise poetry'.[59]

The new monastic orders enthusiastically adopted Celtic saints. In many cases this may well have been inspired by the familiar and unedifying motive of seeking to provide an ancient pedigree for a recent foundation. A *Vita* of St Buite, for example, sought to associate the sixth-century saint with the Cistercian monastery at Mellifont. There also seems to have been a genuine interest in recovering and celebrating Ireland's saintly past. The seventeenth-century historian Daniel Paperbroch directly attributed the upsurge in hagiographical activity in Ireland in the twelfth century to the arrival of Cistercians and other Continental religious orders. More recently, Richard Sharpe, following James Kenney, has argued that the new orders were perhaps keener to collect and revise existing *Vitae* than to provide new ones. One of the earliest and most comprehensive collections of Welsh saints' lives was probably compiled around 1200 by Benedictine monks in either Brecon or Monmouth. The initiative of an Irish-born Cistercian, Albinus O'Mulloy, bishop of Ferns, lay behind the production in 1230 of a composite collection of the lives of twenty-five Irish saints which were knitted together 'into a single statement that Ireland was justly to be regarded as *insula sanctorum*'.[60] Richard Sharpe has suggested that this work, which he describes as 'the crowning achievement of hagiography in Ireland', may have well have been intended 'to declare the virtues of Ireland's saintly past to its critics among the Anglo-French, English and Flemings, who had arrived in the country in the decades before and after 1200'.[61]

Native saints do not seem to have received quite the same enthusiastic endorsement from members of the new orders in Scotland that they did in Ireland and Wales. A calendar of saints produced by the Augustinian house established at Holyrood around 1130 showed a strong English bias, the only Scottish figures mentioned being Monan, Baldred, Duthac, Kessog, Constantine and Ninian, whose name had been added later. No Celtic saint was commemorated in the attached martyrology. The calendar produced at Culross, which had become a Cistercian house in 1217, acknowledged only three native saints, Serf, Felan and Fyndoca. Alexander Forbes took this calendar as a witness 'to the complete Anglicisation of the Scottish Church which took place after the epoch of S. Margaret' and argued that 'the Cistercians of Culross very much ignored what had gone before, and cut themselves off in sentiment from the old historical Church of Scotland'.[62] There is, however, one piece of evidence suggesting an attachment to things Celtic on the part of a Cistercian community in Scotland. A late twelfth-century Psalter from the Cistercian Abbey founded at Coupar Angus, Perthshire, in 1164, follows the old Irish division into three books each of which ends with a canticle and a prayer. Marginal notes refering to practices from Ireland and from the monastery of Columba suggest that the Psalter was still being used in the thirteenth century and that in this reformed community at least traditional Celtic liturgical practice had not completely given way to the ubiquity of the Sarum rite.[63]

Celtic Christianity may conceivably have provided an even more direct influence on the mendicant orders which arose on the Continent in the early thirteenth century. It has been suggested that the Dominicans, and more particularly the Franciscans, to some extent consciously modelled themselves on the itinerant missionaries and preachers of seventh- and eighth-century Ireland. It may be that Francis of Assisi visited, and was influenced by, monasteries in northern Italy which still retained some of the distinctive features and ethos of their Irish founders. There are certainly parallels in both missionary approach and asceticism between the wandering Celtic monks and the medieval Dominican and Franciscan friars, but it is difficult to establish how far the former were, in fact, a direct inspiration to the latter.

What is clear is that deep cultural currents were stirring at this time which encouraged a rediscovery and re-evaluation of what was perceived as 'Celtic' Christianity. In the final chapter of his classic work *The Making of the Middle Ages*, Richard Southern points to the subtle shifts in intellectual outlook that took place in the twelfth century. Life was seen less as an exercise in endurance, and death less as a hopeless cause, as more emphasis was put on seeking and journeying and people came to think of themselves 'less as stationary objects of attack by spiritual forces, and more as pilgrims and seekers'.[64] Reticence gave way to a greater readiness to feel and express emotion and a new tenderness and compassion. Individuals were breaking out of the constricting feudal ties of lordship and vassalage and the shackles of highly organised and centralised church structures to experience a more intense spirituality and to give greater rein to their imaginations. Significantly, Southern points to the phenomenon of Celtic revival as one of the most visible manifestations of this new mood. 'The rehabilitation of Celtic things in the twelfth century, after a long period of disfavour, is a symptom of a change of attitude towards the creations of popular imagination.'[65]

There was one particular theme which those caught up in the movement that has come to be known as the twelfth-century renaissance sought for, and found, in the Celtic tradition. The notion of the epic journey caught hold of the new romantic imagination and took on an essentially spiritual dimension. In Southern's words, 'it was not until the twelfth century that the imagery of journeying became a popular expression of a spiritual quest'.[66] Celtic mythology was full of stories about journeys. Indeed, its literature contained two highly distinctive genres dealing with this subject matter – the *immrama* or tales of voyages and the *echtrai* which dealt specifically with adventures to the other world. In Celtic Christianity, too, the theme had been central, notably in the stress on *peregrinatio* as both an inner and outer experience, a reminder of the need not to become too attached to the things of this world, to travel through it as a pilgrim and stranger and to concentrate on the journey to and beyond death. Their imaginations whetted by a mixture of romantic nostalgia and fascination with the new science of geography, twelfth-century poets and chroniclers fell on the Celtic golden age as a seemingly inexhaustible quarry of myths about journeys to the happy otherworld, fantastic voyages of adventure and discovery, apocalyptic visions of heaven and hell, and heroic quests for unattainable mysterious treasures. Where they did not find the stories or the slants that they were looking for, they cheerfully made them up. Their work of discovery and invention significantly boosted the romantic appeal and aura of Celtic Christianity and linked it indissolubly to the theme of journeying and spiritual quest.

The evermore elaborate and fanciful variations woven around the theme of Celtic wanderlust had an important precursor in the *Navigatio*

Sancti Brendani. For a long time this work was thought to be a product of
the twelfth-century renaissance, but its date of composition was pushed
back by the discovery of a tenth-century manuscript. The earliest extant
manuscripts of the *Navigatio* are to be found in the Rhineland and most
scholars are agreed that the story was probably first written down by an
Irish monk on the Continent. Whether it had any basis in fact and related
to travels undertaken by the seventh-century saint associated with
Clonfert is almost impossible to determine. Little is known about the life
of the real Brendan and although latter day voyagers like Tim Severin
have shown that he could have crossed the Atlantic in a small boat, it is
difficult to disagree with Geoffrey Ashe's conclusion that the epic of the
Navigatio came 'out of the clouds of daydream and folklore'.[67] It almost
certainly drew heavily on the Irish tradition of folktales describing
fabulous wanderings from island to island. There is debate among
scholars as to how far the *Navigatio* represents a Christianising of the
immram, and specifically of the *Voyage of Braan*, thought to date from
around 700, and how far the *immrama* are, in fact, themselves derived
from Christian legends like the *Navigatio*. There is a clear Christian
moral thread running through the work which makes it read in some
respects like a prototype for John Bunyan's *Pilgrim's Progress*. Brendan's
quest to find the land promised to saints brings him at last to the banks of
a great river too broad and deep to cross. Here a young man tells him that
God has kept him wandering for seven years to show him the mysteries
of the ocean and that the promised land will only be revealed in God's
good time after much persecution and tribulation. Some have seen the
Navigatio as an allegorical treatment of the theme of anchoritic withdrawal from the world. Whatever its provenance and purpose, it stands in
Kenney's words as 'the epic – shall we say the Odyssey? – of the old Irish
church', a literary masterpiece which rooted the perennial dream of
finding a fabulous otherworld in the golden age of the Celtic saints.[68]

The *Navigatio* seems to have been much more widely read in England
and on the Continent than in Ireland and other Celtic regions of the
British Isles. The vast majority of the 120 or so surviving Latin manuscripts, most of which date from the twelfth and thirteenth centuries,
have been found in Continental monasteries. Although the *Navigatio* was
translated into most vernacular European languages in the twelfth
century, most influentially into Anglo-Norman by Benedeit, no Gaelic
or Welsh translation exists until the late fifteenth century. Carl Selmer
points to 'the meagre representation of the story of Ireland's greatest
seafarer in his own homeland'.[69] Outside Ireland, by contrast, the story
seems to have made a considerable impact, confirming the reputation of

the Irish saints as intrepid travellers and leading medieval map makers to depict St Brendan's Isle in the outer reaches of the Atlantic.

A similar trend can be noticed in respect of two later stories which developed the motif of the fantastic journey and linked it to the golden age of Celtic saints. Significantly, both were written, like the *Navigatio*, outside Ireland. In 1149 an Irish monk in Ratisbon described a vision experienced by a knight from Cashel named Tnugdal which involved a voyage to the next world. A treatise written in 1184 by Brother H, a Cistercian monk from the abbey of Saltrey in Huntingdonshire, described the passage of another knight into the underworld by means of a cave that had been revealed by God to Patrick. While both the *Vision of Tnugdal* and *St Patrick's Purgatory* were rapidly translated into most European languages, they do not appear in Irish until a much later date and the stories are much more often found in English and Continental manuscript collections than in Ireland. Once again, we encounter the phenomenon of Celtic Christianity being presented at its most misty and romantic by and for those who are not themselves Celts. In the words of a recent study: 'It is clear that this type of literature fulfilled a deep need of adventure and a dream that somewhere in the far western region of the world the impossible becomes possible'.[70]

The development of the legend of St Patrick's Purgatory to create a major medieval pilgrimage centre shows the considerable dividends to be gained from linking a well-known Celtic saint with the popular fascination with journeying to the next world. Blending elements of the old *echtrai* mythology with the Christian message of repentance, those who created and promoted the Purgatory offered contemporary pilgrims and penitents a chance to experience for themselves a real journey to the underworld and not simply the vicarious thrill of reading about voyages there in the dim and distant past. The particular journey that Brother H described in his account had been undertaken by a knight named Owen in 1153. He identified the precise location of the cave which had been revealed to Patrick as giving access to the underworld. It was to be found on Station Island, one of forty-six tiny islands on Lough Derg in the south of Donegal. The island does not seem to have had any early association with Patrick and is not mentioned in any *Vita* of the saint. It had, however, been settled by hermits from a relatively early period and it was on the basis of this anchoritic tradition that the cult of the Purgatory seems to have developed, probably in the early twelfth century. It was supposedly mentioned in a manuscript produced in Wurzburg in 1120 but this, if it ever existed, has disappeared and Brother H's treatise of 1184 is the first surviving account of what was probably already a thriving place of pilgrimage. He presented a journey into the cave as a dramatisation of the symbolic death experienced by the recluse and offered pilgrimage to the Purgatory as a way of gaining the spiritual benefits of a long period of withdrawal from the world without the need to embark on the life of a hermit. For many of those who came to Station Island, however, it is clear that the lure had more to do with the prospect of getting a glimpse of the next world and avoiding meeting death unprepared.

A major part in promoting St Patrick's Purgatory as a pilgrimage centre was played by Augustinian canons who had been introduced into Ireland in the 1140s by Bishop Mallachy Ó Morgair and installed in a monastery on another of the islands on Lough Derg. As well as providing a lucrative pilgrim business, the Purgatory may also have served a more political role. The creation of two new archdioceses by the 1152 Synod of Kells removed the great Patrician pilgrimage centre at Croagh Patrick in County Mayo from Armagh to Tuam. The new pilgrimage to St Patrick's Purgatory provided a replacement for Croagh Patrick and gave the archdiocese of Armagh its own Patrician pilgrimage centre, strategically sited on the border of three dioceses, Raphoe, Clogher and Derry. The fact that Jocelin of Furness appears to locate Patrick's Purgatory at Croagh Patrick in his *Vita* of Patrick suggests that there was some continuing confusion, or rivalry, between two sites. By the end of the twelfth century, however, Station Island was firmly identified as the site of Patrick's Purgatory and it had become the Mecca for thousands of pilgrims annually, some coming from as far away as Hungary. While the central feature of every pilgrimage remained entrance into the cave, other penitential practices were added, including some which it is tempting to suggest were provided to add to the authentic Celtic Christian theme-park experience. Pilgrims were encouraged, for example, to plunge into Lough Derg and stand with the cold water up to their waists chanting psalms in conscious imitation of a practice associated with Columba, David, Cuthbert and Kentigern.

A rediscovered and reinvented Celtic Christianity also played a significant part in the most famous and complex manifestation of the twelfth-century fascination with journeying and spiritual quest, the legend of the Holy Grail. Yet again, the creation of this most powerful of all pieces of Celtic romance took place on the Continent and in England and was the work of outsiders rather than native Celts. In its origins, the Grail legend does not seem to have had specifically Christian overtones. *Le Conte del Graal*, written by Chrétien de Troyes in the Champagne region of France in the 1180s and usually taken to be its first significant literary expression, seems to have drawn largely on pre-Christian mythology and specifically on the Irish *echtrai* and oral traditions relating to the cauldron of rebirth and the drinking horn of plenty. It has even been suggested that the Christianising of the Grail story came about because of a misreading by monks who took Chrétien's phrase *cors benoiz* (horn of plenty) to be *cors benoit* (blessed body of Christ).[71] However, there were already stories in circulation concerning the chalice used by Christ at the Last Supper and containing drops of his blood – one, the *Translatio Sanguinis Domini*, dating from around 750, described it being given to Charlemagne and ending up at a monastery at Reichnau – and it seems more likely that these were woven into the developing Grail legend to give it a clear Christian focus. This process culminated in the production of the *Queste del San Graal*, which was probably written by a Cistercian monk from the Champagne region between 1215 and 1230. It turned what had begun as a pagan tale into a Christian allegory reinforcing Bernard of Cluny's doctrine of grace and mystical union with God. The essential qualities of epic romance and fantastic journeyings were still there – with dungeons and dragons a plenty – but they were overlaid with Christian moralising. Launcelot and Galahad were not simply embodiments of knightly virtue and chivalric honour but also shining examples of Christian manliness and devout followers of the Cistercian rule.

The *Queste del San Graal* firmly anchored the story of the Grail to the early Christian history of Britain, confirming a European 'vision of Albion' as the heartland of myth and romance which had been developed by earlier Continental authors. Robert de Borron, a Burgundian poet, in *Le Roman du Graal*, written between 1191 and 1202, was, perhaps, the first to locate the holy vessel in Britain. Drawing on a tradition which went back to the apocryphal gospel of Nicodemus, he introduced the figure of Joseph of Arimathea as its guardian. Another work emanating from France, Perlesvaus' *La Haute Escriture del Saint Graal* (*c*.1205) linked Joseph of Arimathea specifically to Glastonbury and made a further connection with the Arthurian legends which had been developed and popularised in Geoffrey of Monmouth's *Historia Regnum Britanniae* (1136). This enmeshing of the Grail legend with Arthurian material links directly with the revival of interest in Celtic Christianity. Arthur appeared in several Welsh saints' Lives from this period where he was typically portrayed granting a saint land in return for the performance of a miracle. A good example occurs in the Life of Carannog where the saint catches and tames a dragon which has been ravaging the king's lands.[72] Like so many other aspects of the twelfth-century search for romance and adventure, the development of the Arthurian legends involved much intertwining of Christian and pre-Christian material. The king's pagan wizard was even given a *Vita Merlini* by Geoffrey of Monmouth in the style of a saint's Life.

King Arthur himself was rescued from sixth-century obscurity by Anglo-Norman patronage, much as the Celtic saints had been. The Earls of Cornwall established their fortified base at Tintagel because of its supposed Arthurian connections. Ironically, the man remembered for driving the English out of Britain was adopted by the country's new Norman rulers in order to help establish the legitimacy of the expansion of England into the Celtic realms of Wales, Scotland and Ireland. Arthur was to play a key role in what has been called England's 'British project'.[73] His appeal in royal circles was shown in 1187 when Henry II named his grandson after the Celtic hero in the hope that he would one day rule as King Arthur II. Arthur was not the only early Christian monarch to enjoy a revival at this time. Alfred, the ninth-century Saxon king, who had been assiduously promoted in the eleventh century by Asser, a monk at Ramsey near Cambridge, in the interests of promoting the cause of monastic reform, was also the object of a flourishing cult.[74] It was the Celtic rather than the Saxon king who caught the popular imagination, however. His exploits, and those of the knights who gathered round his circular table, seem to have provided a compelling soap opera for the couch-potatoes of medieval Europe, as shown by the oft-repeated story of the abbot who roused a chapter of dozing Cistercian monks from somnolence by mentioning the magic name of Arthur and recounting one of the many legends about him.

Both the Arthurian and Grail legends were further linked to the wider twelfth-century revival of Celtic Christianity through the proliferation of stories suggesting that early Irish saints had visited Glastonbury. The earliest reference to the cult of an Irish saint at Glastonbury is found in a Life of Dunstan written by an Anglo-Saxon monk around 1000. Specific cults centred on Indract and Patrick may well have had their origins in the tenth century. By the twelfth century Glastonbury was famous for having been a resting place of Irish saints and a haven for wandering Celtic monks. It was also, as Michael Lapidge has pointed out, 'notorious for generating legends about its own remote antiquity'.[75] The most comprehensive catalogue of its supposed connections with the golden age of Celtic Christianity was William of Malmesbury's *De Antiquitate Glastoniensis Ecclesiae* (*c*.1129–35). It identified Glastonbury as the site of the first Christian church in Britain which had been set up by Joseph of Arimathea in AD 63 on the express orders of the apostle Philip. According to William, Patrick had come over from Ireland via Cornwall to serve as the first Abbot of Glastonbury and had died there around 472. The church had also been visited by and held the relics of Brigit, David and Aidan. At a time when relations with Rome were becoming strained, the Joseph of Arimathea story provided the English Church with a native non-Roman foundation legend. The links invented by William of Malmesbury between Glastonbury and the leading saints of Ireland, Northumbria and Wales helped to support the Norman dynasty's claims over the whole of the British Isles. In 1191 the bodies of Arthur and Guinevere were 'discovered' lying in a tomb under the Abbey floor, so establishing that the great Celtic king was buried in English soil. Glastonbury became a national shrine and the focus of a carefully nurtured myth about the continuity of British Christian kingship.

Professional chroniclers like Geoffrey of Monmouth and William of Malmesbury made a major contribution to the twelfth-century Celtic Christian revival. In many ways their work can be compared to that of travel writers and television documentary producers today. They painted colourful word pictures which were influential in forming popular attitudes towards particular places and people. While they happily pandered to, and shared, their contemporaries' taste for romance and were not above elaborating the evidence to make a better story, they were also genuinely interested in recording what was known of the past.

One late twelfth-century chronicler was especially fascinated by the early Christianity of Celtic Britain and Ireland and its survival into his own time. Giraldus di Barri was three-quarters Norman, and so in many ways his perspective was again that of the outsider, but he had been born in Pembroke and adopted the name Giraldus Cambrensis to stress his Welshness. His lifelong dream was to become Bishop of St David's. In 1176 his name was put forward by the Cathedral chapter but was rejected by the King on the grounds that he was Welsh. Presumably if he had kept the name with which he had been born, there might well have been no problem. Thwarted again when the see next became vacant in 1198, he re-wrote Rhygifarch's *Vita Davidi*, powerfully reiterating its claims for the independence of the Welsh Church from Canterbury and the primacy of St David's within it, but portraying the seat of the Pembrokeshire see in a new light as a remote haven ideal for solitary contemplation and scholarship.

In the interval between his two bids to become a Welsh bishop, Giraldus had been gripped by another aspect of the Celtic romance. In 1183 he went to Ireland as part of the Norman invasion force in which both his uncle and brother were leading figures. The main purpose of his visit, however, was to explore rather than conquer the country and particularly 'to examine the primitive origin of the race'.[76] The phrase is strongly reminiscent of that used by Dr Johnson on the eve of his visit to the Hebrides in 1773. Both men expected to find on their travels in Celtic lands the remnants of an ancient and heroic people, somewhat barbaric and primitive in their habits, untouched by modern civilisation but displaying a certain purity and simplicity of character. Giraldus at least was not disappointed. Fascinated by Ireland, he returned in 1185, 1199 and 1204.

In 1188 Giraldus wrote down his impressions of Ireland in *Topographia Hibernica*. It presented a picture of a magical and mysterious country, just as exotic as the far-off lands of the East but much more accessible and with a much more clement climate. Ireland was portrayed as a nation existing on the edge of the world with nothing beyond it to the west except boundless space. It was above all a spiritual land of miraculous happenings, holy wells and great veneration for relics such as bells, staffs and horns associated with saints, a characteristic that Giraldus noted was shared by the Welsh. He devoted most space in his topographical survey to accounts of saints from the golden age of the fifth and sixth centuries. He seems to have been especially drawn to the numerous stories involving close communion between saints and animals and wrote with considerable sensitivity and evident affection of Kevin providing a nesting place for a blackbird in his outstretched hand, Brigit taming a falcon and Colman feeding teal on a lake in Leinster.

For the ordinary Irish of his own day Giraldus had harsh words. They were wild and barbaric, treacherous, full of guile and wallowing in vice. Yet there were redeeming qualities. While their morals might have left much to be desired, the Irish were distinguished for their great music-making and poetry and for a certain spiritual energy. The Irish clergy were also singled out for special praise and commended for their chastity and their particular diligence in observing the canonical offices, singing psalms, reading and praying. Models of asbtinence and asceticism, their only fault was that they were, if anything, too monastic, devoting too much of their energy to contemplation and not enough to correcting and admonishing the people.[77] An illustration in an early thirteenth-century manuscript of the *Topographia* reinforces the scholarly image of Celtic monasticism by depicting a monk carefully copying a manuscript (Plate 4).

Giraldus Cambrensis is a key figure in the development of the notion of the Celts as a distinct ethnic group with characteristics markedly different from those of the Anglo-Saxons.[78] He is also a key figure in the development of the notion and the appeal of a distinct 'Celtic' Christianity. His *Topographia Hibernica* stands as one of the first in a long

Plate 4. Thirteenth-century drawing of a monk writing the *Book of Kildare*. (Source: Cambridge University Library Ms.Ff.1.27, f.315.)

line of books about the Celtic regions of the British Isles that read like spiritual tourist guides. Its pages list the key ingredients of the dream that many people have chased and found in Celtic Christianity – primitive simplicity, remoteness, marginality, closeness to nature, poetry and music, spirituality, monastic community and a mystical, otherworldly quality summed up in his much-quoted remark about the *Book of Kells*, 'the work, not of men, but of angels'. The *Topographia* also conveyed the message that while the golden age of the saints was long past, something of its flavour lingered – as in the sacred fire still kept alight by the nuns of Kildare – and could still be tasted by visitors to Ireland. A later work of Giraldus underlines another theme that was to contribute to the growing appeal of Celtic Christianity. In *Expugnatio Hibernica*, written in 1189, he mentioned the large number of prophecies attributed to the saints of the sixth and seventh centuries which were still in contemporary circulation in Ireland. They spoke especially of continuing war against the English. 'For instance, according to Brechan, almost all the English will be dislodged from Ireland by a king who will come from the lonely mountains of Patrick'.[79] As we have seen, much of the running in the Celtic Christian revival of *c.*1070–1220 was made by outsiders and incomers, in particular the Anglo-Normans. Yet the Celts themselves also enlisted the protection and patronage of their own saints in their struggles against the English. Over the next 500 years this was to become an increasingly dominant theme as Celtic Christianity was invoked by both Celt and non-Celt in the cause of national and denominational independence and identity.

NOTES

1. Macquarrie, *The Saints*, p. 186.
2. Payton, *Cornwall*, p. 79.
3. Barrow, *Kingship*, p. 62.
4. Anderson, *Early Sources*, p. 72.
5. Ibid., p. 76.
6. Ibid., p. 73.
7. Macquarrie, *The Saints*, p. 214.
8. Head, *Hagiography*, pp. 4, 294.
9. Abou-El-Haj, *The Medieval Cult*, pp. 51–8.
10. Hunter-Blair, *Northumbria*, p. 134.
11. Davies, *Wales*, p. 183.
12. Henken, *Traditions*, p. 3.
13. Henken, *The Welsh Saints, passim.*
14. Henken, *Traditions*, p. 5.
15. Davies, *Wales*, p. 146; Laing, *The Archaeology*, p. 119.
16. M. Richards, 'Places and Persons of the Early Welsh Church', *Welsh History Review*, Vol. 5, 1970, pp. 348–9.
17. Henken, *Traditions*, p. 19.
18. J. Davies, *The Welsh Language* (University of Wales Press, Cardiff, 1993), p. 14.
19. Thomas, *Candle*, p. 126.
20. Davies, *Wales*, p. 160. The best text of the *Vita Davidi* is in J. W. James (ed.), *Rhigyfarch's Life of St David* (University of Wales Press, Cardiff, 1967).
21. Henken, *The Welsh Saints*, p. 5.

22. D. P. Kirby, 'A Note on Rhigyfarch's Life of David', *Welsh History Review*, Vol. 4, 1968–9, p. 295.
23. N. Chadwick, *Studies in the British Church* (Cambridge University Press, 1958), p. 172.
24. On the *Liber Llandavensis*, see W. Davies, 'An Early Welsh Microcosm. Studies in the Llandaff Charters', *Royal Historical Society Studies in History*, No. 9, 1978.
25. Thomas, *Candle*, p. 127.
26. On the Life of Illtud, see Doble, *Lives*, pp. 119–35. The text of the *Vita Illtuti* can be found in A. W. Wade-Evans, *Vitae Sanctorum Britanniae* (University of Wales Press, Cardiff, 1944), pp. 194–233.
27. A. M. Allchin, *Pennant Melangell. Place of Pilgrimage* (Gwarg St Melangell, 1994).
28. Watt, *Scotichronicon*, Vol. 3, p. 111.
29. Ibid., p. 111.
30. Macquarrie, *The Saints*, p. 3.
31. Ibid., p. 2.
32. Brooke, *Wild Men*, p. 96.
33. MacQueen, *St Nynia*, p. 116. This provides the best modern translation of Ailred's Life and also of the *Miracula Ninie Episcopi*.
34. Ibid., p. 107.
35. The vexed question of dating Ninian is well dealt with in Chapter 3 of Macquarrie, *The Saints*.
36. Ibid., p. 136. The most accessible text of Jocelin's *Vita* is in *Two Celtic Saints: The Lives of Ninian and Kentigern* (Llanerch, 1989).
37. Bourke, *Studies*, pp. 173–7.
38. The standard work on the *Céli Dé* is still Reeves, *The Culdees*. See also Duncan, *Scotland*, pp. 115–16, Barrow, *Kingship and Unity*, pp. 77–8.
39. Jackson, *The Gaelic Notes in the Book of Deer* (Cambridge University Press, Cambridge, 1972).
40. Sharpe, *Medieval Irish Saints*, p. 3.
41. Ibid., pp. 27–9.
42. Ibid., p. 32.
43. Lecture on 'Columba and his successors: The early history of Irish-Scottish connections' at conference on 'Celebrating Columba: Irish Scottish Connections 597–1997', University of Strathclyde, 20 September 1997; Kenney, *Sources*, p. 441. On the Irish Life, see also J. Szoverffy, 'Some stages of the Columba Tradition in the Middle Ages' in *Across the Centuries* (Classica Folia, Boston, Massachusetts, 1988), pp. 49–76.
44. Greene and O'Connor, *A Golden Treasury*, p. 6.
45. Texts and translations of the *Agallamh* can be found in S. H. O'Grady (ed.), *Silva Gadelica*, Vol. 2 (Williams & Northgate, 1892) and W. H. Stokes and E. Windisch, *Irische Text*, Vol. 4 (Verlag von S. Hirzel, Leipzig, 1900).
46. MacLean, *The Literature of the Celts*, p. 295.
47. Ibid., p. 294.
48. See, for example, K. Scherman, *The Flowering of Ireland: Saints, Scholars and Kings* (Gollancz, London, 1981), p. 99.
49. Knott and Murphy, *Early Irish Literature*, p. 55.
50. R. Ó Floinn, 'Insignia Columbae I', in Bourke (ed.), *Studies*, p. 141.

51. Bieler, *Life and Legend*, p. 12.
52. Davies, *Celtic Christianity*, p. 10.
53. De Paor, *Early Christian Ireland*, p. 175.
54. A. Loughridge, 'Malachy', in *The New International Dictionary of the Christian Church* (Zondervan, Grand Rapids, Michigan, 1974), p. 623.
55. H. Shetelig, *Viking Antiquities in Great Britain and Ireland* (H. Aschehoug, Oslo, 1950), Part VI, pp. 202–5.
56. Bernard of Clairvaux, *Life of Malachy*, trans. A. Luddy (Cistercian Publications, Kalamazoo, 1978), p. 135.
57. Southern, *The Making*, p. 212.
58. Williams, *The Welsh*, p. 19.
59. Davies, *Celtic Christianity*, pp. 46–7, 76.
60. Sharpe, *Medieval Irish*, p. 385.
61. Ibid., p. 385.
62. Forbes, *Kalendars*, p. xxi.
63. H. M. Banister, *Specimen Pages of Two Manuscripts of the Abbey of Coupar Angus* (Danesi, Rome, 1910).
64. Southern, *The Making*, p. 212.
65. Ibid., p. 244.
66. Ibid., p. 212.
67. Ashe, *St Brendan's Voyage*, p. 62.The best edition of the *Navigatio* is J. J. O'Meara (ed.), *The Voyage of St Brendan* (Dolunen Press, Dublin, 1976).
68. Kenney, *Sources*, p. 415.
69. Selmer, *Navigatio*, p. xxxi.
70. Haren and de Pontfarcy, *The Medieval Pilgrimage*, p. 1.
71. Godwin, *The Holy Grail*, p. 91.
72. Coe and Young, *The Celtic Sources*, p. 14.
73. C. Brooke, *The Saxon and Norman Kings* (Batsford, London, 1978), p. 185; G. Ashe, *Camelot and the Vision of Albion* (Heinemann, London, 1971), pp. 210–12.
74. A. P. Smyth, *King Alfred the Great* (Oxford University Press, Oxford, 1995).
75. M. Lapidge, 'The cult of St Indract at Glastonbury', in Whitelock, *Ireland*, p. 179. See also L. Abrams, 'St Patrick and Glastonbury Abbey', in Dumville, *St Patrick*, pp. 233–42.
76. J. F. Dimock (ed.), *Expugnatio Hibernica*, Vol. V (Rolls Series, 1867), p. 351.
77. The most accessible edition of the *Topographia* is J. J. O'Meara (ed.), *Gerald of Wales – The History and Topography of Ireland* (Penguin Books, Harmondsworth, 1982).
78. See Chapman, *The Celts*, pp. 185–200.
79. A. B. Scott (ed.), *Expugnatio Hibernica* (Royal Irish Academy, Dublin, 1978), p. 233.

3

And when the strife is fierce, the warfare long

Nationalism and denominationalism 1250–1850

Fascination with the native Christianity of the British Isles in the golden age of the fifth and sixth centuries continued through the later Middle Ages. At a popular level, the Celtic saints remained the object of devotion on both a local and national scale and passed increasingly into folklore, featuring in stories explaining the origin of a particular place or phenomenon and in morality tales. The absence of fish from a Scottish river would be explained by the fact that they had been banished from its waters by Columba as a punishment when fishermen had refused to give him some of their catch. In Irish stories Patrick was portrayed as setting a mastiff on a tavern woman who failed to give full measure. Alongside this increasingly secularised popular appropriation of its leading figures, the Celtic Christian heritage was also promoted at official level by both church and state. The fourteenth and fifteenth centuries saw the development of liturgies to honour the Celtic saints, the production of compilations of Lives and the ever more enthusiastic embracing of national patron saints. Although the Reformation brought an end to official support of saints' cults, it inaugurated a new chapter in the British love affair with Celtic Christianity by presenting Columba, David and Aidan as leaders of a church that was national, independent of Rome and Protestant in all but name 900 years before the era of Calvin and Luther.

In late medieval England, romantic attachment to early 'Celtic' Christianity continued to be focused on Glastonbury, now firmly identified as Arthur's Avalon. Geoffrey Ashe notes that 'from about 1250 onwards Avalon was the pre-eminent shrine of knighthood, the holy place of the monarchy, and the accredited apostolic fountain-head of the British Church'.[1] In 1278, fresh from a campaign against the Welsh, Edward I visited Glastonbury with the Archbishop of Canterbury, who sang Mass in the Abbey somewhat to the chagrin of the local diocesan bishop. The bones of Arthur and Guinevere were briefly exhibited to public view and then entombed with considerable ceremony in front of the high altar. Edward's identification with Arthur was a vital part of his attempt to portray himself as the King of Britain and to justify his efforts to stamp out what was left of Welsh independence and claim overlordship of Scotland. Later Plantagenet kings also paid homage at Glastonbury and the thriving pilgrimage trade received a significant boost in 1367 when the body of Joseph of Arimathea was discovered and placed in a silver casket. This led to further embellishments of the legends surrounding the place and specifically to the invention of the story of the thorn which had supposedly sprouted from Joseph's staff.

A similar process of creative invention underlay the Celtic Christian revival that took place in Cornwall in the later Middle Ages. Many parish churches were rebuilt, often by Breton craftsmen, to give them a more 'Celtic' appearance, with three-stage towers and stained glass windows depicting local saints from the golden age.[2] A desire to provide Celtic Christian origins for a number of churches which did not obviously possess them led to the invention of several saints out of place names, including Kenwynus, 'discovered' as the founder of Kenwyn in 1342, Ludewanus of Ludgvan in 1319, Morvetha of Morvah in 1390 and Tallanus of Talland in 1452.[3]

In Ireland, Celtic saints continued to fulfil their double role of providing the Anglo-Norman ascendancy with a native pedigree and legitimacy while also representing Irishness to those troubled by the island's increasing Anglicisation. The great medieval Irish cathedrals were dedicated to Celtic saints, notably St Brigit's in Kildare, built in 1250, St Patrick's in Dublin (1254) and St Canince's in Kilkenny (1260). During the fourteenth and fifteenth centuries a number of books appeared which brought together the *Vitae* of several saints with other liturgical and devotional material from the 'golden age' of Irish Christianity. These compilations, which included the *Leabhar Breac*, *Liber Flavus Fergussiorum*, the *Book of Ballymote*, the *Yellow Book of Lecan*, the *Book of Lismore*, the *Codex Kilkenniensis* and the *Codex Salmanticensis*, have been seen as attempts to produce national collections of Irish saints' lives (although they often covered Continental saints as well) and reassert the distinctiveness of the 'island of saints' at a time when Irish identity and nationhood was under threat.[4]

A similar concern with national pride and tradition in the face of the increasing threat from English domination underlay the continuing appeal of Celtic Christianity in medieval Wales. It was increasingly focused on the figure of David, whose cult grew steadily with thousands of pilgrims flocking annually to his shrine in Pembrokeshire. By the mid-fifteenth century at least fifty-three churches and thirty-two wells were dedicated to the saint. A *cywydd* from this period by the Cardiganshire poet, Ieuan ap Rhydderch, one of many medieval bards to address David in verse, equated two pilgrimages to St David's with one to Rome and enthused that 'to take my soul three times to Menevia is equal to going to Christ's grave once'.[5] Glanmor Williams has shown how during the Middle Ages David's cult spread outwards from its Pembrokeshire base as he won 'an undisputed place for himself as the patron saint of the whole of Wales'.[6] In contrast to what happened to Patrick and Columba, David's increasing fame was not achieved at the expense of losing a sense of his essential humility and he was not simply elevated to the status of spiritual superman. A Life of David written in Welsh around 1350 by an anchorite whose cell was at Llanddewi Brefi made notably more of the saint's simplicity and humility than Rhigyfarch's *Vita*, which in most other respects it was content to copy. It reported his last words to his followers as a reminder to 'do the little things that you have heard me see and do'.

This stress on the importance of little things, and by implication on the significance of little and marginalised nations and peoples, was to be an important theme in the later Welsh love-affair with Celtic Christianity – indeed it has informed a more general modern perception of Celtic Christianity as being allied with the cause of the marginal and peripheral.[7] Glanmor Williams suggests that the Welsh version of David's life 'may be best understood as being as much a part of a patriotic protest against the rapidly-growing exploitation of the Welsh Church by the English state in the fourteenth century as Rhigyfarch's Latin text was against the Norman incursions in the eleventh century'.[8] Owen Glendower, the great champion of Welsh nationalism in the early fifteenth century, made much of David's prophecies that the Welsh would rout the English in battle and one of the major aims of his rebellion against Henry IV was to free the Welsh church from the jurisdiction of Canterbury and restore what he took to be its status in the Celtic Christian heyday with the Archbishop of St David's ruling over an independent province.

Nowhere, perhaps, is the link between rising nationalist sentiment and enthusiasm for Celtic Christianity in the late Middle Ages clearer than in Scotland where monastic calendars, church dedications, monarchical patronage and popular invocation testify to the strong appeal that was made to Scottish saints at a time of increased hostility towards the English. Alexander Forbes noted a distinct change of emphasis away from English and Continental saints in calendars dating from the late thirteenth century onwards in the wake of the increasingly strained relations between Scotland and England provoked by the disputed succession following the death of the 'Maid of Norway', heiress to Alexander III, and Edward I's assertion of overlordship of Scotland. In his words, 'from the time of the war of succession the tide began to turn in favour of the Scottish saints. Possibly the deep enmity against the English told in this respect'.[9] Celtic saints played a prominent role in the battle of Bannockburn (1314), with the relics of both Columba and Fillan being paraded in front of the Scottish army and fully living up to their reputation as bringers of victory over the English. As further evidence of the nationalistic purposes for which Celtic saints were enlisted, Forbes quoted a prayer used by Scottish borderers in 1379 invoking the aid of 'God and Saint Mungo' to ward off a plague raging over the border in England and cited a calendar produced in the 1450s for an unspecified cathedral which listed twenty Celtic saints, including two obscure Irish figures, Bean and Mobhi, who do not appear in any other Scottish calendar.

Unlike Wales and Ireland, of course, medieval Scotland ultimately adopted as its patron a saint who was Catholic and apostolic rather than Celtic. The triumph of Andrew over Columba was a gradual process which took place over the thirteenth and fourteenth centuries. It is tempting to portray it as a victory for the ecclesiastical establishment and it has often been seen as setting the seal on the Roman take-over of the Celtic Church. While these factors undoubtedly played a part, the ousting of Columba was a complex process which had a good deal to do with the steady shift eastwards in the centre of ecclesiastical and political gravity in medieval Scotland. Like the Celtic saints, Andrew gained in stature through his association with the cause of Scottish independence and in the saltire he provided a peculiarly powerful visual symbol of Scottish nationhood. His eventual elevation to the status of national patron saint, however, was by no means an inevitable development. For much of the thirteenth century, Columba seems to have held his place as the favoured saint of Scottish monarchs to whom he regularly appeared in visions. His appearances were not always to urge conquest and national aggrandisement. According to Norse saga, King Alexander II, bent on wresting the Hebrides from the Norwegians, was visited in a dream in 1249 by Columba and the Norse saints Magnus and Olaf who bade him turn back and give up his territorial claims. He chose to ignore their imprecations and shortly afterwards fell ill and died.[10] A seal used by his successor, Alexander III, in 1250 was imprinted on both sides with a quotation from Matthew 10: 16, '*Esto prudens ut serpens et simplex sicut*

Columba', a motto which according to a leading historian of Scotland was 'presumably chosen because it included the word Columba'.[11] It is another seal, produced by the guardians appointed to rule Scotland after Alexander III's death in 1286 and carrying the words '*Andreas dux esto Scotis compatriotis*', that is often taken to mark the beginning of Andrew's reign as official patron saint.

Even after Andrew's position as patron saint was secure, Columba remained an infinitely more popular figure among the Scottish people. He was seen in many country districts as the special protector of cattle and his name was linked to a plant, also known as St John's wort, which was much valued for its healing properties. Not surprisingly, he was especially venerated in those establishments with which he had a direct connection and which had been dedicated to him. Donald, Lord of the Isles, visited Iona in the 1410s and presented the monks with a covering of gold and silver for the hand of the saint which was on display to the pilgrims who still came to the island. During the late fifteenth century depictions of twenty-four of Columba's miracles were painted on the wall behind the high altar of Dunkeld cathedral and two statues of the saint were erected in the nave. Monks in the Augustinian priory on the island of Inchcolm continued to regard the saint as their protector and patron. Their Antiphoner, thought to date from the late thirteenth or early fourteenth century, contains the plea: 'Father Columba, glory of our national tradition, receive the prayers of your servants; save this choir that is praising you from attack by the English and assault by rivals'.[12] Their prayers seem to have had considerable efficacy, at least according to the authors of the *Book of Pluscarden*. It reported that in 1336 marauding English soldiers who had laid waste much of Fife and penetrated as far as the Ochil hills were finally halted in their tracks at Inchcolm where 'suddenly, in the twinkling of an eye, they sank in the raging waters at a very deep spot in the front of the said monastery ... This was noised abroad throughout England by the preachers as being a miraculous retribution'.[13] A later English raid on the island in 1385 was also apparently thwarted by saintly intervention. Soldiers of Henry, Duke of Lancaster, having stripped the monastic church of its ornaments, were in the act of setting fire to it when 'a strong wind blew the flames back upon them, and burnt and suffocated them almost all; and thus Saint Columba by a miracle saved his church from being burned down by them'.[14] He may no longer have been the nation's official patron saint but Columba was still second to none in his ability to protect the Scots against the English.

Medieval chronicles gave the Celtic saints a prominent role in Scotland's early history. The *Chronica Gentis Scotorum* produced between

1363 and 1385 by John of Fordun went well beyond Adomnan in claiming that Columba not only visited the Pictish King Brude but also converted him to Christianity. It established a trend that was to be followed by many other Scottish historians by claiming several Irish saints, including Columbanus, Finan, Fursey and Colman, as Scots, largely on the basis of their early identification as Scoti, the name that the Romans had used for the Irish.[15] Fordun also stated that the Scottish people were direct descendants of one of the tribes of Israel which had left Egypt at the time of Moses and come to Scotland via Spain and Ireland, bringing with them the Stone of Destiny. This origin legend, which was taken up in the campaign to refute Edward I's claim of overlordship of Scotland, seems first to have surfaced in a late tenth-century *Vita* of St Cadroe, a monk from the east of Scotland who became an abbot in Belgium and France, although Fordun claimed to have taken it from Lives of Brendan and Congal.

Much of Fordun's material was incorporated into Walter Bower's *Scotichronicon* of *c*.1440. As might be expected from an abbot of Inchcolm, Bower made much of Columba, whom he portrayed as founding the Benedictine monastery and Augustinian nunnery on Iona, staying on Inchcolm while preaching to the Picts and exchanging pastoral staffs with Kentigern during a meeting in Glasgow.[16] The *Scotichronicon* also gave an account of a meeting between Kentigern and Merlin. The apparent problems over dating such an encounter were met with the explanation: 'Do not be amazed that Merlin and St Kentigern died in one and the same year, since St Kentigern was one hundred and eighty one years old when he died'.[17] Like John of Fordun, Bower appropriated several prominent Irish saints and claimed them as Scots. He lost no opportunity to show the extent of the Celtic contribution to the Christian history of England, pointing out that large number of English kings had been baptised by Scottish bishops, that Cuthbert was an Irish-born king's son who was educated with Brigit and Columba at Dunkeld, and that Cumbria, Northumberland and Westmoreland, though now under the lordship of the English, had received the Christian faith 'through no one but the Scots'.[18] He complained at the English habit of 'stealing the Scots' glory' citing as an example Wilfrid's reference at Whitby, as related by Bede, to 'your Columba, or rather our Columba', which he took as an English attempt to claim the Celtic Christian heritage.[19]

Medieval church dedications in Scotland also bear witness to the strong popularity of Celtic saints. Predictably, Columba led the way with fifty-five dedications by the beginning of the sixteenth century. They were not confined to Argyllshire and the Hebridean islands but spread across the Highlands and into the north-east. Other Irish saints, including Brigit, Patrick, Brendan, Congal, Mirren, Finan, Ciaran, Kevin, Maelrubha and Moluag also had their names linked to churches across the country. A cluster of dedications to Fillan in central Scotland and Fife may well reflect the prominent role played by his relics at Bannockburn. British or Pictish saints like Kentigern, Drostan, Devenick, Ternan, Serf and Marnoch were also commemorated. Ninian continued to be the object of considerable veneration and Whithorn was regularly visited by Scottish kings. Robert the Bruce founded a leper hospital near Prestwick which he dedicated to the saint as a thank offering for the health-giving benefits of the water from a nearby spring. Late medieval dedications to Ninian were not just confined to south-west Scotland. There were several in the north-east, including the parish churches at Dunottar, Fetternear and Nairn. Mid-nineteenth-century restoration work at Turiff parish church revealed a brightly coloured medieval wall-painting of the Galloway saint dressed as a medieval bishop. Chapels and altars dedicated to Ninian were also established in the late fifteenth century in the cathedrals at Aberdeen, Dunkeld and Brechin and at Arbroath Abbey as well as in several large parish churches.[20]

Scottish saints became the object of increasing official commemoration in the later medieval church. A liturgical revival, itself perhaps partly inspired by the growing nationalistic mood, produced a number of quite elaborate offices used primarily in monastic churches to commemorate particular saints on their feast days. The Hyrdmanston Breviary, used in a chapel in Haddington but probably originating from Northumberland, contains an office for St Cuthbert. The Sprouston Breviary, tentatively dated to around 1300 and possibly originally intended for Glasgow Cathedral, contains an office for the feast of Kentigern, to be celebrated on 13 January, with proper texts and music for Vespers, Matins and Lauds. Nine lections from the Matins section relating to miracles performed by the saint, recently recorded on compact disc, appear to be based on material culled from the two twelfth-century *Vitae* of the saint commissioned by Bishops of Glasgow.[21] Like Ninian, Kentigern continued to be the object of special veneration throughout the Middle Ages. In 1475 King James IV of Scotland established an annual grant of 2½ stones of wax so that the lamps on his tomb in Glasgow Cathedral could be kept permanently alight.

Perhaps the most haunting and intriguing of the surviving medieval musical tributes to the Celtic saints are the chants in praise of Columba found in the Inchcolm Antiphoner. Its lauds, canticles and responses were sung by the island's monks on the eve of the saint's feast day, 9 June.

A charter of 1256 records Richard, Bishop of Dunkeld, granting twenty shillings to the Abbey of Inchcolm annually for the lighting of twenty candles on the high altar on the vigil and day of Columba. The Antiphoner provides a suitably lavish and dazzling musical accompaniment for what was clearly a major liturgical celebration. While most of the plainsong settings, as in the Sprouston and Hyrdmanston Breviaries, follow the normal style of Gregorian chant found in the Sarum rite which was in use throughout Scotland at this time, those for *Salve Splendor, O Columba Insignis Signifer, Os Mutorum, Sanctorum Piissime Columba* and *O Mira Regis* are subtly different. John Purser has pointed to the 'Celtic' characteristics of these chants, notably their similiarity in terms of interval boundaries to traditional Gaelic song and their formal patterning and interweaving which he finds reminiscent of the artwork found in the *Book of Kells* and on Pictish crosses.[22] He and others have speculated that they may go back to mid-ninth-century Dunkeld or even earlier. It is certainly true that some of the settings for the canticles and responsories celebrating Columba in the Inchcolm Antiphoner, also recently recorded on compact disc, have a quality which is altogether more ethereal and animated than the measured tones of standard Gregorian chant.[23] Whether they do, in fact, represent a genuine relic from the Celtic golden age, or as seems more likely, a later attempt to create a distinctive 'Celtic Christian' sound, these exceptionally beautiful plainsong melodies testify to the great reverence in which Columba was held in the medieval Scottish church.

It was not just in Scotland that commemoration of the Celtic Saints found its way into the official liturgies of the churches. Many of the Latin lives of the Irish saints seem to have been revised in the late thirteenth century to provide suitable readings for the celebrations of their feast days. Lections read in church on these occasions may, indeed, have played an important role in popularising and propagating the cults of several saints. Early in the fourteenth century John of Tynemouth, a Benedictine monk probably based in St Albans, produced *Sanctilogium Angliae, Walliae, Scotiae et Hiberniae*, a collection of saints' lives unusual in being compiled on a British Isles-wide basis. It seems to have been produced for reading during the offices of the church and in monastic refectories. Canons promulgated by the province of Armagh around 1400 enjoined the full observance of the feasts of Patrick, Brigit and Columba throughout the province and those of Fechin and Ronan in the diocese. In 1398 Roger Walden, Archbishop of Canterbury, ordained that David's feast day on 1 March should be observed as a major festival throughout the province of Canterbury. Within St David's diocese and in churches dedicated to the saint in Wales, his feast was celebrated weekly, probably on Tuesdays, with prayers that described him pointedly as 'champion of the Britons, the leader and teacher of the Welsh'.[24] The earliest surviving Welsh music manuscript, the Penpont Antiphonal, which is thought to date from the mid-fourteenth century, contains the offices of Matins, Lauds and Vespers for St David's Day, with its material largely being taken from Rhigyfarch's *Vita*.[25]

Developments in fifteenth-century Scotland underline the close connection between nationalist feeling and the growing liturgical interest in celebrating the feast days of Celtic saints. Despite the general adoption of the Sarum rite throughout *ecclesia Scoticana*, commemoration of Scottish and Irish saints was increasingly jostling their English and Continental counterparts out of diocesan service books. Leslie Macfarlane has noted that

> Liturgically speaking, the Wars of Independence and the anti-English feeling engendered had, by 1424, not only taken their toll of English saints but had encouraged the Scottish clergy to search back more diligently into their own past in order to re-discover the missionary endeavours of their own.[26]

Bishops, abbots and priors cultivated devotion to local saints and encouraged pilgrimages to their shrines. Archbishop Scheves, who occupied the see of St Andrews from 1448 to 1497, 'discovered' the relics of Palladius, an obscure figure, possibly of British birth, who had been sent by Pope Celestine in 431 as the first bishop to the Irish, in a dell below the church at Fordoun in Kincardineshire. He transferred them to a richly adorned shrine within the church. Robert Blackadder, Archbishop of Glasgow from 1492, built a chapel at Culross to mark the birthplace of Kentigern. William Elphinstone, Bishop of Aberdeen from 1483 to 1514, gathered a team of researchers to collect information on some eighty-seven early British, Scottish and Irish saints with a view to compiling a martyrology for his diocese and more ambitiously a national breviary for Scotland which would provide readings on all the major Celtic saints. To quote Leslie Macfarlane again: 'We surely cannot fail to see in all this historical and liturgical activity an attempt to instil into the hearts of the Scottish people a love and pride in their fatherland, a search, even, for their national identity'.[27]

Elphinstone's project, which came to fruition in 1510 with the publication of the Aberdeen Breviary, marks the culmination of late medieval Celtic Christian revivalism and confirms its close link with the rising tide of nationalism. It was strongly backed by King James IV, who recognised that a national breviary would promote the political as well as spiritual unity of his kingdom. Scotland's first printed book, the Aberdeen Breviary was modelled on the Sarum Breviary but removed most of its English saints and substituted in their place local figures or Northumbrians like Cuthbert and Colman who had Scottish missionary connections. Altogether, eighty-one Scottish saints appeared in the calendar attached to the Breviary. Elphinstone's team of researchers followed John of Fordun and Walter Bower in claiming as Scots a number of figures who were almost certainly Irish. Finbarr, for example, was given a Scottish pedigree and presented as the son of a Caithness nobleman, presumably to tie in with his veneration at Dornoch in Sutherland. The short *lectiones* provided for each saint and intended to be read on his or her feast day were culled from twelfth-century *Vitae*, local legends and other compilations. Alan Macquarrie has described the Breviary as 'by far our greatest cornucopia of Scottish hagiography' providing 'a tantalizing glimpse of what must have existed in a nation proud of its saintly traditions'.[28] Leslie Macfarlane points to its status as a work 'which was the first of its kind in Europe: a national breviary'.[29]

Produced at the beginning of a century that was to witness the ending of the Middle Ages and the coming of the Reformation, the Aberdeen Breviary stands in some ways as the last glorious swansong of the medieval fascination with Celtic Christianity which had given birth to a host of myths and legends and been sustained by a mixture of romantic nostalgia, popular piety, ecclesiastical power politics and nationalism. There are signs in the early 1500s of a reaction setting in against the excesses of Celtic Christian revivalism. A generation or more before the Protestant Reformers demanded the abolition of saints' cults and relic worship, the church authorities were trying to curb some of the grosser fabrications and fraudulent claims associated with the Celtic saints. In 1497 complaints by a disillusioned Dutch pilgrim prompted the Pope to order the closure of St Patrick's Purgatory. The complainant, an Augustinian canon, had reported that he had been forced to pay large sums of money to the diocesan bishop and the prior of the monastery on Station Island in order to gain access to the island. When he eventually reached the cave, he was let down into it by rope but despite spending twelve hours there he 'had seen nothing, had heard nothing and had suffered no inconvenience nor distress'.[30] Despite Rome's efforts to close the place down, pilgrims continued to come to Lough Derg and in 1503 the Archbishop of Armagh petitioned the Pope to revoke his closure order and grant indulgences to those who made the pilgrimage. Later attempts to stamp out the pilgrimage proved equally unsuccessful but the

Pope was not the only person to have misgivings and St Patrick's Purgatory never again attracted the huge numbers that had flocked there in its medieval heyday. Cynicism over the claims made about Celtic saints' powers was also creeping in at a more popular level. When plague broke out in Caputh, 5 miles from Dunkeld, around 1500, George Brown, Bishop of Dunkeld, sent people in the infected village jars of water in which Columba's bones had been dipped. While it was faithfully reported that those who drank the water were spared the plague and those who refused to do so took ill and died, one local villager asked: 'For what does the bishop send us water to drink? I could wish he had sent us some of his best ale'.[31]

Despite the sceptics, pilgrimage sites associated with Celtic saints were still enjoying considerable patronage through the sixteenth century, not least from royalty. James IV, King of Scotland from 1488 to 1513, made annual pilgrimages to Whithorn, visited the tomb of St Mirren at Paisley and venerated the head of Fergus at Scone and the relics of St Winning at Kilwinning. His successor James V, who ruled from 1513 to 1542, visited the Isle of May in the Forth to venerate the relics of Adrian, for which he provided a new gold reliquary. He also paid for a new shrine to house the relics of Mo Fhécu, an Irish saint associated with Lesmahagow, and in 1539 he wrote enthusiastically to the Pope about the constant stream of pilgrims to Ninian's shrine at Whithorn and the almost daily miracles occurring there. Queen Mary Stuart founded a chapel to St Ninian at Roscoff in Brittany, possibly as a thank offering for a prosperous voyage from Scotland. Soon after his accession as king of England, Henry VII showed his Welsh Tudor pride by making a personal allowance to ensure that St David's Day was celebrated in style at court.

The invention of printing provided new opportunities to promote stories and figures from the golden age of Celtic Christianity. An edition of the *Navigatio Sancti Brendani* produced in Augsburg in 1476 had wood-cut illustrations of some of the more fantastic episodes from Brendan's voyage (Plate 5). Among the first *Vitae* to be printed were Cogitosus' Life of Brigit (Milan, 1486) and Jocelin's Life of Patrick (Antwerp, 1514). New saints' Lives were still appearing on the very eve of the Reformation. In 1532 a Donegal chieftain, Manus O'Donnell, published what was effectively an encyclopaedia on Columba, the result of years of work by a team of researchers who had explored folklore and local stories about places as well as more conventional hagiographical sources. In the preface O'Donnell declared that he had produced the book for 'God's honour, the raising up of Colum Cille's name, the profit of the people who read or listen to it … and the dishonour and destruction of the devil'.[32] It also had

Plate 5. Fifteenth-century woodcut of the Voyage of St Brendan. (Source: *Sankt Brendans Seefahrt* (Augsburg, 1476).)

a strongly nationalistic theme, with one of the 150 poems it attributed to Columba beginning 'I would rather die in Ireland than live for ever in Alba'.

The Protestant Reformers viewed saints' cults and their associated devotional apparatus of relics, shrines and pilgrimages with a mixture of horror and disapproval. They were particularly scathing about the 'monkish legends' which had built up certain figures into miracle workers and spiritual supermen. Protestants were not without their own hagiographers but they tended to eulogise recent martyrs rather than saints of long ago. John Foxe's *Acts and Monuments of these Latter and Perilous Days*, first published on the Continent in 1554 and in England in 1563, provided a whole pantheon of contemporary Protestant 'saints'.

The initial impact of the Reformation was in many places destructive of the Celtic Christian heritage. In Wales, William Barlow, the first Protestant Bishop of St David's, proposed in the late 1530s that his see be moved to Carmarthen to rid it of the 'ungodly image service, abominable idolatry and popish pilgrimage' associated with the veneration of the Welsh patron saint.[33] This was resisted but Barlow successfully removed the saints from their place in the liturgy of the Welsh church and put an end to pilgrimages and veneration of relics. In England, the great national shrine to Celtic Christianity at Glastonbury was sacked and pillaged following the hanging of the Abbot and two of his monks on

Glastonbury Tor in 1539. Twelve years later the surviving Abbey buildings were turned into an industrial settlement for Huguenot weavers
from Flanders. During Elizabeth I's reign a puritan zealot attempted to
cut down the twin trunks of the thorn tree supposedly planted by Joseph
of Arimathea. He severed the larger one but as he aimed at the smaller
one, the axe rebounded, hurting his leg and sending a splinter of wood
into his eye. He abandoned his attempt and the surviving thorn remained
a major tourist attraction until a second more dextrous puritan felled it
during the Civil War, though not before a number of cuttings had been
taken by those anxious to keep this particular piece of Celtic tradition
alive.

In Ireland, the relics of saints received similarly rough treatment.
During the Elizabethan conquest of Gaelic Ulster many were removed
from their traditional locations and sent as curios to Dublin, mainland
Britain and the Continent. In 1584 the English Deputy in Ireland, Sir
John Perrot, sent a jewelled cross associated with Columba to the Queen's
Chief Secretary, Lord Burleigh, with the message:

> I send him unto you that, when you have made some sacrifice unto
> him, according to the disposition you bear unto idolatry, you may,
> if you please, bestow him upon my good Lady Walsingham, or my
> Lady Sydney, to wear as a jewell of weight and bigness.[34]

Roman Catholics enlisted the aid of the Celtic saints to resist the
onward march of Protestant ideology and iconoclasm. Those involved in
the rising in 1536 known as the Pilgrimage of Grace and associated with
opposition to the dissolution of the monasteries gathered in York under
the banner of Cuthbert. A late sixteenth-century Irish poem, *Fada
h-éisteacht a Mhuire*, called on Mary to 'awake Colum and Patrick' to
prevent the extinction of Catholic Christianity.[35] Set-backs to the
Protestant cause were hailed, on both sides, as evidence that the saints
had not been deaf to these pleas. When an explosion in the ammunition
store of the English garrison in Derry killed over thirty people in 1566,
English soldiers were heard to cry out 'the Irish god Columba killed us
all'.[36] Such incidents were few and far between, however, and it must have
looked to many as though the Reformation would brutally suppress the
native Celtic tradition in British Christianity and replace it with the alien
Continental doctrines and practices of Wittenberg and Geneva.

In the event, however, the propagandists and apologists for the new
Protestant faith were to prove just as susceptible to the lure of Celtic
Christianity, and just as aware of its potential to reinforce their cause, as
the medieval hagiographers had been. They found the Celtic Church to

be a Protestant institution in all but name, characterised by evangelical purity and wholly independent of Rome. Far from bringing in new-fangled Continental principles, as its opponents claimed, they argued that the Reformation represented a return to the values of indigenous British Christianity in its golden age.

The process of rewriting history to give it a new Protestant spin was begun by William Tyndale. In *The Obedience of a Christian Man* (1528) and *Practice of Prelates* (1530), written in exile in Holland, he presented a picture of an independent British Church which had steadily succumbed to the shackles of Roman domination during the Middle Ages. Tyndale's particular hero from the Celtic golden age was Gildas, the sixth-century British monk, whom he portrayed as a prophetic figure sent by God to rebuke his countrymen for having deserted the Scriptures. His strongly pro-Roman sympathies conveniently overlooked, Gildas became for many of the apologists of the Reformation a proto-Protestant prophet calling his countrymen to repentance and preaching the true gospel.[37]

Tyndale's pioneering efforts to find a precedent for Protestantism in early British Church history were taken up and developed by John Bale, a former Carmelite friar who had decisively rejected Catholicism in the late 1530s. His most important work, The *Actes of Englysh Votaryes*, written during a period of exile in Antwerp in the early 1540s, presented an idyllic picture of a pure and primitive British Church uncontaminated by Rome. Picking up the Glastonbury legends, he located the conversion of Britain in apostolic times and specifically in the mission of Joseph of Arimathea in AD 63. Like many Reformers, Bale had a detestation of clerical celibacy and stressed the fact that Joseph was a married man. The notion that this was the route by which Christianity had first come to the British Isles was to remain a major plank in Protestant history and propaganda for the next 150 years or so. Catholics pointed rather to a mission undertaken in the late second century by two monks who had been sent to Britain by Pope Eleutherius in response to a letter from King Lucius. The historicity of this mission, for which there was little evidence outside the writings of Geoffrey of Monmouth, was also accepted by some Protestants who predictably played down the Pope's involvement in it and portrayed the two missionaries involved, Fagan and Damian, as simple evangelists. John Foxe, for example, saw the Christian faith arriving in Britain 'not with any cross or procession, but only at the simple preaching of Fagan and Damian'.[38] Several leading figures in the post-Reformation Church of England, notably Matthew Parker and John Jewel, enthusiastically took up the notion of Lucius as the first Christian king of Britain and argued that it showed the British Church to have been from the first a national institution in which the initiative and leadership came from the monarch rather than the Pope. Those of a more Presbyterian disposition, however, were uneasy about the Lucius–Eleutherius story because of the precedents it created both of Papal intervention and a royally-founded episcopate.

Whatever their differences about how and when the faith had arrived here, there was agreement among Protestant historians that the British Church had originally been independent and free of Roman influence. The fatal contamination had occurred in 597 when Augustine had been sent by Pope Gregory the Great with authority over the existing British bishops to establish a new hierarchy based in Canterbury. Catholic historians, not surprisingly, took Augustine's mission as marking the beginning of the true Church of England, a point notably made by Thomas Stapleton in his preface to a new translation of Bede's *History* in 1565. On the Protestant side, Bale set the anti-Augustine agenda with a vigorous denunciation of the Italian monk, whom he described as a man 'not of the order of Christ as was Peter, but of the superstitious sect of Benedict, there to spread abroad the Romish faith and religion, for Christ's faith was there long afore'. Bringing a 'new Christianity, for neither was it known of Christ nor of his apostles, nor yet even seen in England afore',[39] Augustine set out, according to Bale, 'to prepare Antichrist a seat here in England' and to that end introduced 'candlesticks, vestments, surplices, altar cloths, singing books, relics' and other papish abominations.[40] In sweeping away these idolatrous images, the Protestant Reformers were returning the church to the puritan simplicity of the fifth and sixth centuries.

Vilification of Augustine became a marked feature of Protestant Church history throughout the later sixteenth and seventeenth centuries. In his influential *Apologia Ecclesiae Anglicana* (1562) John Jewel, Bishop of Salisbury, added banners and holy water to Bale's list of the Italian monk's abominable innovations and blamed his 'heaps of novelties and superstitions' for perverting the Christian faith which had hitherto been 'universally received and perfectly rooted in this realm'.[41] Apologists for the Reformation made much of Bede's account of Augustine's stubborn refusal to stand and greet the seven British bishops who met him to discuss differences of usage between the Celtic and Roman churches. They also pointed to his complicity in the massacre of 1,200 British monks at Bangor by Aethlred, King of Northumberland. A statement in Bede's history that Augustine had died before the massacre had taken place was dismissed by Jewel as a later interpolation 'violently thrust into the text by a guileful parenthesis'.[42] Led by William Fulke, Protestant historians preferred to follow Geoffrey of Monmouth's account of the massacre which suggested Augustine was involved. Bale saw the slaughter of the British monks, and posterity's neglect of them, as a prime example of Roman oppression and distortion of truth. The Bangor monks went into Protestant martyrology. Edmund Spenser's *Fairie Queen* of 1590 portrayed the 'massacred martyrs' of Bangor as victims of the 'ambitious will of Augustine' and John Milton gave a full account of the massacre, which he blamed on Augustine, in his *Outlines for British Tragedies*.[43]

Although most of those rewriting early church history from a Protestant perspective were especially concerned with the English Church, they were generally keen to stress its British character and to portray the native Celtic people – Irish, Scottish and British – as heroes, and the Saxons, Angles and Normans as 'baddies'. John Bale is the earliest author I can find to use the word *Celtae* and so by implication to suggest a distinct Celtic (and British) Christian identity defined over and against Roman (and Continental) Christianity. Robert Runcie has described him as 'one of the first to build up a myth of the kindly and easy-going Celtic clergy being dragooned by the pitiless, bureaucratic-minded Romans'.[44] Bale even cited Merlin's prophecy that the descendants of the ancient Britons would one day be restored to their primeval and rightful position in the island and suggested that it had been fulfilled by the ending of Roman domination brought about by the Reformation. The Britishness of the early English Church was a major theme of *De Antiquitate Britannicae Ecclesiae*, written in 1572 by Matthew Parker while Archbishop of Canterbury.

Parker was greatly helped in his historical research by a number of Welsh scholars who had an added reason for stressing the Britishness of the early church and pushing an anti-Saxon and anti-Norman as well as an anti-Roman line. The most prominent was Richard Davies, Bishop of St David's from 1561 to 1581 who in 1567 published an 'Address to the Welsh Nation' in the form of a preface to his Welsh translation of the New Testament. In it, he set out to show that Anglican Protestantism, far from being the religion of the Angles and Saxons, in fact represented the restoration of the faith of the ancient British (and, therefore, of the modern Welsh) people.

> There was a great difference between the Christianity of the Britons and the false Christianity which St Augustine of Canterbury gave the Saxons. The Britons kept their Christianity pure and

immaculate, without admixture of human imaginings. Augustine's Christianity veered rather from the matchless purity of the Gospel and was mixed in with much superficiality, human opinions and vain ceremonies, which did not accord with the nature of the kingdom of Christ.[45]

Davies even adduced evidence, on the basis of an unidentified chronicle, that while the Welsh had been happy enough to traffic with the Saxons while they were heathens, they would have nothing to do with them after their conversion, so great was their abhorrence of the superstitions introduced by Augustine.

Davies' work was clearly designed to counter the Catholic claim that Protestantism was an alien English innovation being imposed on the people of Wales. Rather he set out to show that it was Roman Catholicism that had been the alien creed introduced first by Anglo-Saxon and then by Norman invaders. In Glanmor Williams' words, 'he felt confident of being able to prove that at the apogee of the ancient British kingdom its religion had been firmly grounded on the Protestant rock of scriptural authority'.[46] The notion of Protestantism as the native Welsh religion, developed by Davies and others in the later sixteenth century, was to be enormously important in promoting the appeal of Celtic Christianity in the principality over the next 300 years. Welsh Anglicans and Nonconformists alike enthusiastically embraced the notion of a Celtic church distinguished for its national independence and evangelical purity as well as its attachment to the Welsh language.

In Scotland, too, Reformers were enthusiastically constructing a new model early church which was both distinctively Celtic and Protestant. George Buchanan's *Rerum Scotiarum Historia*, published in 1582, is generally taken to be a pioneering work in the identification of the Celtic origins of the peoples of the British Isles. Struck by the similiarity of place names in Scotland, southern Britain, Gaul and Spain, Buchanan, a leading humanist scholar and lay moderator of the General Assembly of the Church of Scotland, posited the notion of a single race, which he named Celts or Gauls. He argued that the modern Irish, Scots and British descended from this people, who had spread westwards across Europe in the millennium or so before the birth of Christ, rather than from a lost tribe of Israel or the Phoenicians as medieval origin legends had suggested.[47] While Buchanan is widely lauded among scholars of Celtic studies for being the first to make this discovery, he also deserves a prominent place in the historiography of the Reformation for his work in promoting the notion of a distinct Celtic Church, characterised by beliefs and structures which were essentially Protestant and nationalistic. Specifically, he set out to show that in its origins the Scottish Church was completely independent of Rome. He also claimed that until the arrival of Palladius in the mid-fifth century (like so many of his contemporaries he took the Roman word Scotia to mean Scotland rather than Ireland and so believed that Palladius had come to the former rather than the latter country), it was non-episcopal: 'The Church unto that time was governed by Monks without bishops, with less pride and outward pomp, but greater simplicity and holiness'.[48] Thus was born that particularly Scottish notion that the Celtic saints were good Presbyterians.

During the early decades of the seventeenth century Scottish Presbyterians built on Buchanan's work and found further evidence from the Celtic church's primitive golden age of their favoured form of ecclesiastical government. The most significant work to issue from this camp was almost certainly the *History of the Kirk of Scotland* written by David Calderwood following his return to Scotland in 1625 after a period of exile for attacking monarchical interference in the forms of worship of the Kirk. Having followed Buchanan in tracing the descent of the Scots from the 'Celtick Gaules', Calderwood presented an idyllic picture of early Scottish Christianity in which a pure and essentially Protestant faith was taught by itinerant priests with no bishops or 'monkish superstitions' to contaminate or impede them. He singled out the Culdees as 'holie and religious men, exercised in teaching, prayer, meditation and reading ... They were not bound by the vow of obedience to ridiculous rules, nor of chastitie to a single life'.[49] He rejected the story of Andrew's relics being brought to Fife with the observation that 'no doubt, a monkish writer hath devised this fable' and described it as highly improper that Palladius, as the Pope's emissary and the man who had brought bishops to the country, should be called the Apostle of the Scots.[50] In contrast to these Roman-inspired figures, native Celtic clergy received Calderwood's unqualified praise. Columba was lauded for his strict life and great authority and for the fact that his monks on Iona were 'farre different frome the monkes which arose after in corrupter times'.[51] Calderwood could not resist pointing out that Columba was 'a presbyter, not a bishop' and cited Bede to show that in the Celtic Church bishops were subject to abbots.[52] Bede was also drawn on to provide a flattering portrayal of Aidan and a description of the Synod of Whitby which left no doubt that the heavy hand of Roman bureaucracy had crushed the native church.

It was not just Presbyterians who found much to affirm and approve in the doctrines and practices of the early Celtic Church. Those Scottish reformers who favoured the episcopal system of church government were

equally enthusiastic, as can be seen from the writings of John Spottiswoode, Archbishop of St Andrews from 1615 to 1638. His *History of the
Church of Scotland*, published posthumously in 1655, is a fascinating
mixture of revisionism, romance and anti-Irish nationalism. While the
book's main aim was to trace the history and establish the supremacy of
the see of St Andrews, it had a substantial opening chapter dealing with
the early Scottish church which contained flattering portraits of its
founding fathers, Ninian, Columba, Kentigern and Aidan. Augustine
received much less sympathetic treatment although, true to his critical
and revisionist spirit, Spottiswoode left open the question of his complicity in the Bangor massacre. Although Spottiswoode was keen to strip
away the 'many lying miracles' and 'legends of monks' that had gathered
around the Celtic saints, he still found them heroic figures and cited Bede
to show the veneration in which they were held.[53] Spottiswoode gave his
history a distinct Protestant 'spin'. Discussing Ninian's foundation at
Whithorn and its dedication to St Martin, for example, he pointed out
that the habit of 'denominating churches by the names of Saints
departed' was practised in this period simply to preserve the memory of
the saints' virtues 'and incite others to the imitation thereof' and not to
erect tutelary saints 'which in after-ages, when superstition prevailed,
was the conceit of the people'.[54] He dismissed St Patrick's Purgatory as
the invention of a ninth-century monk at Glastonbury Abbey and noted
that it was wholly inimical to the spirit of the Celtic Church: 'The
opinion of a fiery Purgatory, in which the souls are tormented after their
going forth of the body, was not then known among Christians; nor did
the ancient Irish believe any such matter'.[55] While distancing himself
from the more excessive aspects of the medieval Catholic appropriation
of Celtic Christianity, however, he was also keen to condemn extreme
Protestant interpretations of the early Celtic Church. Buchanan was
taken to task for suggesting that it was originally ruled by monks rather
than bishops.

Overall, Spottiswoode's *History* conveyed a picture of a golden age
of Scottish Christianity existing in the fifth and sixth centuries. 'The
condition of this Church in those times was most happy, all the care of
preachers being to win souls unto Christ; Avarice and Ambition, the two
main pests of the Church, had not yet seized upon them.'[56] His work also
showed a strongly patriotic quality. Following in the tradition of the
medieval chroniclers like John of Fordun and Walter Bower, Spottiswoode wished to claim for Scotland virtually the whole panoply of Celtic
saints, and certainly all the most important ones. Despite the lack of
conclusive evidence as to Patrick's birthplace, he was firmly identified in

the *History* as 'a Scotchman, born upon the River of Cluid, not far from Glasgow'.[57] Rather more controversially, Brigit was described as being born in Caithness. Spottiswoode bitterly attacked Irish historians and churchmen for claiming as Irish those saints described in early sources as Scoti and insisted that they should be counted as Scots. He was particularly indignant about the claim that Columba had died in Down and was buried there alongside Columba and Brigit.

Irish as well as Scottish saints appeared in the Kalendar attached to the Scottish Prayer Book of 1637. In a letter to the Scottish Privy Council Charles I had specified that:

> In their Kalendar they should keep such Catholic Saints as were in the English, such of the Saints as were most peculiar to that kingdom (especially those which were of the Blood Royal and some of the most holy Bishops) being added to them; but that, in no case, St George and St Patrick be omitted.[58]

In the event, the Kalendar retained the saints preserved in the Church of England's Book of Common Prayer and included in addition a good company of Celtic saints, including Mungo, Colman, Patrick, Cuthbert, Gilbert, Serf, Columba, Palladius, Ninian, Adomnan and Drostan, as well as Queen Margaret and King David. The appearance of several of their favourite Celtic presbyters in the Kalendar seems to have done nothing to diminish Presbyterian outrage over the high church nature of the Prayer Book and its imposition on the Kirk.

The general enthusiasm for Celtic Christianity among seventeenth-century Protestants even extended to Ireland. The new Protestant cathedral built in the colonial city of Londonderry between 1628 and 1633 was dedicated not to St Paul or St George, as its London patrons might have been expected to favour, but to Columba. The argument that the ancient Celtic Church had been in all essentials Protestant was taken up with particular alacrity by James Ussher, Archbishop of Armagh from 1625 to 1641. Of Anglo-Irish merchant stock and one of the first graduates of the new Protestant foundation of Trinity College, Dublin, Ussher made it his lifetime's work to prove that the Anglican Church of Ireland conformed both with the New Testament idea of a church and also with the church founded by Patrick in the fifth century. He bought up old manuscripts and commissioned researchers to comb through libraries throughout Ireland and across for Europe for material that would sustain this thesis. In *A Discourse of the Religion Anciently Professed by the Irish and British*, published in 1631, he reported that his research had revealed beyond any doubt that:

The religion professed by the ancient bishops, priests, monks and other Christians in this land, was for substance the very same with that which now by public authority is maintained therein, against the foreign doctrine brought in thither by the Bishop of Rome's followers.[59]

Following Buchanan's lead, Ussher stressed the close similarities both in structure and belief between early Irish, Scottish and British churches and saw these as providing evidence of a distinctive 'Celtic' Christianity in the British Isles which was much closer both doctrinally and liturgically to Protestantism than to Roman Catholicism. He argued that the Celtic Churches had no concept of purgatory or transubstantion, and took a similar line to the Reformers on the doctrines of predestination, judgement and grace. He quoted Patrick, Columbanus and Samson to show that Eucharistic celebration in the early British Church resembled Reformed rather than Roman practice.[60] Like other Protestant apologists, he made much of the existence of married clergy in the early British and Irish Church and contrasted the self-sufficient and ascetic Celtic monks with the mendicant friars of medieval Europe who lived parasitically off society: 'Our monks were religious in deed, and not in name only; far from the hypocrisy, pride, idleness and uncleanness of those evil beasts and slothful bellies that afterward succeeded in their room'.[61] He devoted a whole chapter of his book to the Easter controversy 'which the Britons, Picts and Irish maintained against the Church of Rome' and gave a highly coloured account of the debates at the Synod of Whitby.[62]

The crux of Ussher's thesis was contained in a chapter which he entitled 'Of the Pope's spiritual jurisdiction; and how little footing it had gotten at first within these parts'.[63] There he set out to show that not one of the holy men who had given Ireland its name the 'island of saints' had received any solemn canonisation from the Pope until the time of Mallachy of Armagh and Laurence of Dublin. The sixty-five bishops said to have been ordained by Patrick had been consecrated without any consultation with the see of Rome. The same was true in Wales. It was monarchs rather than popes who had appointed the bishops and archbishops in the early Irish and British Church. In establishing national state churches under monarchical governorship, the British Reformation was restoring the erastian principles found in the golden age of Celtic Christianity.

Ussher's work exemplifies another aspect of the new approach to the early Christian history of the British Isles brought in by the Reformation. Although his primary purpose was polemical, Ussher was also a scholar and together with other Protestant historians he brought a critical approach to the study of ancient sources and legends about the Celtic saints and their times that had been largely lacking throughout the Middle Ages. He carried out original research on manuscript sources, the fruits of which appeared in two significant academic studies, *Veterum Epistolarum Hibernicarum Sylloge* (1632) and *Brittanicum Ecclesiarum Antiquitates* (1639). The latter work was a meticulously researched study of the origins and early history of Christianity throughout the British Isles. Its seventeenth chapter provided what Ludwig Bieler has called 'the first truly critical account of St Patrick's life' and became a standard work used by both Catholic and Protestant historians.[64] The first complete edition of Patrick's *Confessio* was edited by Ussher's pupil, James Ware, in 1656. In keeping with his scholarly interest, and despite his own virulent anti-Catholicism, Ussher corresponded and collaborated with Roman Catholic scholars who were also working on the lives and times of the Celtic saints. He maintained a lengthy correspondence with David Rothe, Bishop of Ossary and Vicar-General for the absent Catholic Bishop of Armagh. Such was the sensitive nature of the contact that both men used pseudonyms. Ussher was also in touch with several Irish Roman Catholic scholars based on the Continent who were working on the Lives of the Irish saints.

There was, in fact, considerable Catholic interest in the Celtic saints in the first half of the seventeenth century. In part this arose from a desire to stress the Catholic heritage of the British Isles in the aftermath of the Reformation. It was an aspect of that wider Counter-Reformation celebration of saints which inspired the great Bollandist project associated with the Antwerp-based Jesuits, Herbert Rosweyde and Jean Bolland, both of whom were themselves deeply interested in the Irish saints. Other motives also inspired Irish Catholic scholars working in this field. As in earlier periods, many of those who developed a particular interest in the early Irish saints were themselves exiles on the Continent. Driven out of their homeland by religious persecution and intolerance, they looked back wistfully to the island of saints and felt a need to assert its native Gaelic and Catholic heritage in the face of the increasingly dominant English and Anglo-Irish Protestant presence there. Nor was it just English and Protestant influences that constituted a threat to the vision of Ireland as the land of saints. Perhaps the most explicit agenda behind the writings of seventeenth-century Irish Catholic historians was to counter the erroneous propaganda of the Scots. They were particularly incensed about the work of a Scottish Roman Catholic, Thomas Dempster, who had claimed that most of the Irish saints were, in fact, Scots. National pride was stronger than denominational loyalty and the Irish scholars were determined to claim back their misappropriated saints and show that 'through the nine Christian centuries and more the name Scotia, whether used by Christians or pagans, Irish or foreigners, applied only to Ireland'.[65]

Among the first exiled Irish Catholics to research the Irish saints with a view to rehabilitating their country's reputation as *Insula Sanctorum* were two Jesuits, Henry Fitzsimmons and Stephen White. Fitzsimmons, who lived in France and Italy between 1604 and 1630, produced a catalogue of the Irish saints which was first published in 1611 and was expanded to include over 400 saints in 1619. White, who held academic posts in Spain and Germany between 1593 and 1629, made important discoveries of early manuscripts of Adomnan's *Vita Columbae* and Cogitosus' *Vita Brigitae*. He regarded his work on the saints as a 'joyful and untiring labour' which would 'advance first the glory of God and, next, the glory of our most beloved Ireland' and described his task as being:

> To draw forth from a few and widely separated dark caverns of antiquity, and place in the light of day … the history of the ancient Scots or natives of Ireland, the Island of Saints, who were once so celebrated at home and abroad for holiness of life, literary culture, and bright deeds in war and peace.[66]

Both Fitzsimmons and White contributed to a vindication of the Irish saints published in 1624 by Thomas Messingham, Rector of the Irish College in Paris, under the title *Florilegum Insulae Sanctorum*. Their pioneering work was taken up by a group of Franciscans associated with the Irish College of St Anthony at Louvain in the Spanish Netherlands. Hugh MacCaghwell, Hugh Ward, Francis Matthews and Patrick Fleming spent the 1620s and 1630s searching through libraries across Europe in order to recover and preserve early Irish *Vitae* and liturgies which might otherwise have perished. Michael O'Clerigh, a fellow Franciscan who was sent as a 'fieldworker' to Ireland to copy and collect ancient manuscripts, produced a *Calendar of the Saints of Ireland* in 1630 and was largely responsible for the *Annals of the Four Masters*, produced in the Franciscan Friary at Donegal between 1632 and 1636, which chronicled the history of Gaelic Ireland from the creation to the seventeenth century.

Much of the work done by these men did not come to fruition in their own lifetimes. A major study by Patrick Fleming on Columbanus, for example, which brought together many early sources, was not published until 1667, thirty-six years after his death. The task of collating their research and bringing it to publication fell to another Louvain Franscican, John Coglan. He planned a six-volume work on the Irish saints but a shortage of funds meant that only two volumes were published. The first, *Acta Sanctorum Veteris et Maioris Scotiae seu Hiberniae, Sanctorum Insulae*, which appeared in 1645, dealt with those saints whose feast days fell in the first three months of the calendar year and the second, *Triadis Thaumaturgae Acta* (1647) concentrated on Ireland's three patron saints, Patrick, Brigit and Columba.

Despite its incomplete nature, the Louvain project had a considerable impact. Joseph Leerssen has written that:

> It helped to redefine Gaelic national pride primarily in terms of its ecclesiastical history ... it also implied that Catholic, anti-English Ireland is equated increasingly with Gaelic Ireland: Old English recusancy is absorbed and swamped by this general identification between Gaelic culture and Irish sanctity.[67]

We can see here, perhaps, another stage in the making of the myth of the 'Spiritual Gael' that was to be so important a feature in both the nineteenth- and twentieth-century's love-affairs with Celtic Christianity. More immediately, the work of the Franciscan scholars successfully rehabilitated those Irish saints who had been hi-jacked by the Scots. Indeed, the tables were turned. Richard Sharpe has observed of this period that 'so great was the impact of the Irish on European ideas of sainthood that it became a common motif in hagiography to ascribe to almost any little known saint an Irish birthright'.[68]

It was perhaps on the Continent that the writings of the exiled Irish Catholics about the Celtic saints had most impact. Leerssen suggests that they were designed to enlist the sympathy and support of Catholic Spain, Italy and France for the cause of Gaelic Ireland and to counter English attempts to defame the Irish character by portraying it as lazy, barbarous and uncouth. Several compilations of saints' Lives seem to have been written specifically for a European readership to promote an image of Ireland not just as a deeply Catholic country but also one with a rich spiritual and cultural heritage. *De regno Hiberniae sanctorum insulae commentarius*, a tract published in 1632 by Peter Lombard, a former Archbishop of Armagh who resided in Rome, seems to have been aimed largely at the Italians. Another exposition of Ireland's saintly heritage, *Historiae Catholicae Iberniae Compendium*, published in 1622 by Philip O'Sullevan Beare, an Irish nobleman who had been banned from his native Kinsale and spent most of his life in Spain, was designed, in Leerssen's words, 'to obtain Spanish sympathy for the anti-English cause by representing it as a battle of suffering Catholics against heresy'.[69] Accepting Buchanan's thesis that the Gaels were descended from the Spanish, Beare went on to divide the population of Ireland into *Iberni Ibernici*, or *Veteres Iberni*, who were the 'real' (i.e. Gaelic) Irish, and the *Ibernici Anglici* or *Novi Iberni* who included the old English Catholic recusants as well as the more recent Protestant settlers. For him, Irish identity was primarily ethnic rather than religious. Specifically, it was Celtic and anti-English. When Beare published a scholarly account of the life and work of Patrick in 1629, he vehemently attacked the work not just of James Ussher but also of Richard Stanihurst, an English settler in Dublin who had converted to Catholicm and published a biography of Patrick in 1587. The trouble was, of course, that Stanihurst was English – a worse crime than being a Protestant. Ironically, Stanihurst had also been fiercely attacked by a fellow Anglo-Irish Palesman, Barnaby Rich, a Protestant, for being too sympathetic towards Irish Catholicism. One wonders what Beale made of *St Patrick for Ireland*, a play written around 1640 by the English Roman Catholic dramatist, James Shirley, which, in the words of Owen Dudley Edwards, 'exhumes Patrick as a type of British civilisation who converted the native Irish to Christianity and, in so far, as it was possible, Briticism'.[70]

In England and Wales, too, Protestants and Catholics continued to appeal to Celtic Christianity to promote their own particular agendas while discretely abandoning some of the more implausible stories about how the faith had arrived in Britain. In his 1670 *History of Britain* John Milton expressed considerable scepticism about the historicity of the mission initiated by Lucius. On the Roman Catholic side, an alternative origin legend was initiated by Richard Broughton whose *True Memorial of the Ancient, most Holy and Religious State of Great Britain* (1650) argued that St Peter himself had initiated the first Christian mission to the British Isles. Protestants countered by proposing Paul as the true apostle of Britain. This notion was taken up by Edward Stillingfleet, Bishop of Worcester, in his *Origines Britannicae* (1685), one of the first major studies of Christian origins in Britain to abandon the story of Joseph of Arimathea which had become increasingly difficult to sustain. From now on the scarcely more credible notion of a direct Pauline mission became a standard feature of Protestant accounts of early British Church history.

The idea of a pure and independent Celtic Church continued to exert an especially strong appeal in Wales. The thesis originally propounded by Richard Davies was developed with considerable Arthurian embellishments by Charles Edwards, an itinerant Puritan preacher in Denbigh-

shire, in his *Hanes y Ffydd Ddiffuant* (1671) and Theophilus Evans, who
held various rural benefices in mid-Wales, in his *Drych y Prif Oesoedd*
(1739). While virtually all the material written on this subject in Wales
was fiercely Protestant and anti-Catholic in tone, some of it also
attempted to establish the episcopal nature of the Celtic Church to
counter the claims of Presbyterians and Independents. In 1703 William
Lloyd, Bishop of Worcester and formerly Bishop of St Aspah, brought
out *The History of the Government of the Church as it was in Great Britain
and Ireland When they First Received the Christian Religion* to refute the
widespread notion that 'the ancient Scottish Church was a Church
formed without Bishops'.[71] He described the notion that this church had
been governed by presbyters as 'a monkish dream' and associated it
particularly with a gross over-estimation of the importance of the
Culdees, whom he seems to have felt were largely an invention of
Giraldus Cambrensis. Hailing Ninian and Columba as the bearers of
'diocesan episcopacy' to Scotland and Oswald as the one who introduced
it in Northumberland, Lloyd sought to show that there were bishops in
the British Isles before there were monasteries. Strong though it was, his
episcopalianism was ultimately subordinate to his Protestantism. He
attacked Augustine for shattering the 'primitive liberty' of British
Christians and applauded their courage for telling him plainly 'we will
not be thy subjects'.[72]

The keenest Welsh exponent of the proto-Protestant nature of the
Celtic church was almost certainly Thomas Burgess, Bishop of St
David's from 1803 to 1825. His *Tracts on the origin and Independence of the
Ancient British Church; on the Supremacy of the Pope, and the Inconsistency
of All Foreign Jurisdiction with the British Constitution; and on the Differences between the Churches of England and Rome*, published in 1815, were
designed to counteract 'Popish delusions' and demonstrate that 'the
British Church, founded by St Paul, was in its origin, and for many
centuries, wholly independent of the Church of Rome.'[73] The Pauline
origins of what he called 'the Church of Britain' were particularly important to Burgess because they proved that it had actually been in existence
for longer than the Church of Rome. Burgess cited Bede to show both the
'primitive plainness and simplicity' of the early Celtic Church and the
brave fight which its bishops had put up against Augustine's attempt
to submit it to papal supremacy. From the end of the sixth century, the
British Church had taken on a new character: 'We see her, not only
an Apostolical and independent, but also a PROTESTANT Church,
distinguished by her rejection of the Pope's authority, and of all communion with the Church of Rome'. Burgess' conclusion was simple: 'The

Church of Britain was a Protestant Church nine centuries before the days of Luther'.[74] The Reformation represented a restoration of its original condition and an ending of 'the popery [that] constitutes the middle ages of the British Church'.[75]

Thomas Burgess exemplified another of the factors that helped to promote the appeal of Celtic Christianity in the eighteenth and early nineteenth centuries. As well as being an ardent Protestant, he was a considerable patriot, particularly proud of his country's cultural and linguistic heritage. In 1819 at Carmarthen he presided over the first of the new provincial *eisteddfodau* which were an important manifestation of a new assertion and celebration of Welsh identity. It was perhaps in Wales that patriotic nationalism was most clearly linked to the rediscovery and reinvention of the Celtic Christian tradition. Without native patron saints, the celebration of England's and Scotland's national identity was focused on recent secular figures like John Bull and Robert Burns. Columba was still remembered and written about in Scotland – Thomas Innes, a Catholic priest, produced a new life in the 1720s and in 1798 John Smith, minister of Campbeltown in Argyllshire, wrote the first English life of the saint – but he was less of a national icon than he had been in the Middle Ages. Patrick continued to remain the personification of a certain kind of Irishness and was first associated with the shamrock in a book published in 1727. However, the complex ethnic and religious undercurrents in his adopted land perhaps inhibited his emergence from the world of folklore to become the standard-bearer for Irish patriotism and cultural identity.

In Wales, however, David had no serious competitors and increasingly took on this role. He was first taken up by the Welsh patriotic societies established in the eighteenth century and largely made up of exiles from the homeland. Welsh societies in London, like the Society of Ancient Britons set up in 1715 and the Honourable Society of Cymmrodorion founded in 1751, celebrated St David's Day with a church service, a sermon and a large dinner. Many of the Welsh emigrants across the Atlantic also made the patron saint the focus of devotion to their country. The first recorded St David's Day celebration in America took place on 1 March 1729 when members of the Welsh Society of Philadelphia met for a banquet and traditional singing. Virtually all of the hundred or more Welsh societies which flourished in America in the eighteenth and nineteenth centuries incorporated the saint's name in their titles. By the end of this period celebrations of St David's Day had also become common in Wales itself, where they typically took the form of a church service followed by a dinner at which toasts would be proposed to the King and

Church, the Principality of Wales and the immortal memory of the saint.[76]

Remembering David in this way did not necessarily, of course, betoken any special interest in or fondness for the church in which he had played a leading part. His association with Celtic Christianity was, however, stressed and reinforced by both Anglican and Nonconformist clergymen. Thomas Price, an incumbent in Breconshire in the early nineteenth century, strongly supported the celebration of David both for its Christian basis and because it 'offered an opportunity for Welshmen to meet together to nurture patriotism and to support those practices and institutions that tend to the honour of our native country'.[77] Similar sentiments were expressed in 1816 by David Peter, a Nonconformist minister from Carmarthen, in his *Hanes Crefydd yng Nghymru*. As Glanmor Williams has pointed out, David had a particular appeal to Welsh Nonconformists: 'His ascetic self-restraint, his reputation as a drinker of water, and his emphasis on hard and regular work seemed to fit in admirably with the Nonconformist ethic of sobriety, moral fervour and self-improvement'.[78]

The antiquarian movement which began in the later seventeenth century also brought a new interest in the Celtic Christian era. Ussher was not alone in having a fascination for ancient monastic manuscripts, early liturgies and saints' Lives. Libraries started forming collections of this material. Trinity College, Dublin, acquired the *Book of Kells*, or the *Book of Colum Cille* as it was then entitled, in the early 1660s. Edward Lhuyd, keeper of the Ashmolean Museum, Oxford, in the 1680s and 1690s spent five years in his native Wales recording and transcribing early Christian memorial stones. A strong Welsh patriot, he developed George Buchanan's theories about the common basis of the native languages of the British Isles, demonstrating in his *Archaeologia Britannica* of 1707 that Welsh, Cornish, Breton, Scottish and Irish Gaelic all belonged to same linguistic family which he called Celtic.

Lhuyd probably did more than anyone to promote the term 'Celtic' and to give it British rather than Continental associations. Hitherto, the Celts had been thought of as a European people who belonged to Gaul, Spain and regions further afield. From the beginning of the eighteenth century they came to be thought of primarily as the original indigenous inhabitants of the British Isles, there before the Romans, Saxons, Angles, Vikings and Normans. The fact that the Celts themselves had once been invaders was conveniently forgotten. At home, the notion of a primeval and pure Celtic Britain chimed in with the values of Protestant patriotism. On the Continent, where much of the serious research on Celtic languages was pursued, it reinforced the idea of Celts as primitive yet deeply spiritual outsiders. Across the whole of Europe, Britain included, an idealised Celticism became one of the chief constructs of the rising tide of romanticism. As Leerssen has pointed out:

> The construction of the Celt takes place roughly from 1650 to 1850. That means that it coincides with developments such as the invention of the Sublime, the cult of Nature and the idea of the Noble Savage ... The construction of the Celt documents the revolt against rationalism and against the Enlightenment.[79]

It was pagan rather than Christian Celtic culture which was perhaps given the greatest boost by the romantic movement. Its devotees felt that they had uncovered a truly European civilisation which rivalled those of Greece and Rome. In the early 1760s James Macpherson announced that he had discovered a great cycle of heroic poems which revealed the blind third-century bard Ossian to be as great a poet as Homer. The Ossianic cult spread through Europe, catching Victor Hugo, Napoleon, Goethe and Schiller in its grip. In 1771 John Macpherson, minister of Sleat in Skye (and no relation of James), published an *Introduction to the History of Great Britain and Ireland* which placed Gaelic-speaking Celts in Scotland four centuries or so before their actual arrival and portrayed them as the native Caledonians who resisted the Romans. As the Scots traced their ancestry back to heroic warriors whose exploits had been celebrated in myth and epic poem, the Welsh celebrated their heritage of Druids, bardic poetry and song and made the harp a national symbol alongside St David's leek.[80]

The particular appeal of pre-Christian Celtic religion and mythology in the wake of the romantic movement had an important bearing on the way that the Celtic approach to Christianity was perceived. It was during this period that the idea developed of Celtic Christianity as being much closer than other inculturations of the Christian faith to the values of pagan and primal religions. This syncretist agenda fitted with the broad, deist outlook of the eighteenth century. It was initially put forward on the basis of the similarities between Druidism and early British Christianity. In one of the first studies of the ancient stones of Britain, *Stonehenge, a Temple restor'd to the British Druids* (1740), William Stukeley, a Lincolnshire clergyman, argued that the Druids, who had come over to Britain soon after the Flood, 'had a religion so extremely like Christianity that in effect it differ'd from it only in this: they believed in a Messiah who was to come into this world, as we believe in him that is to come'.[81] His book presented an attractive vision of a broad and non-dogmatic patriarchal religion, practised in both pre- and early Christian Britain, which appealed to many of his fellow clerics. Stukeley, who called the Britons Celts, floated another idea that was to gain wide currency and enhance the syncretist flavour of Celtic Christianity when he suggested that the notion of the Trinity was a Celtic invention. His book portrayed the Druids as gentle, cultured, tolerant figures very much in the mould of eighteenth-century Latitudinarian Anglican divines. There was little or no reference to the sacrifices and darker side of pre-Christian Celtic religion. John Ogilvie, minister of Midmar in Aberdeenshire took a similar line in his poem, *The Fane of the Druids* (1787), which portrayed the priests of pagan Britain as pure, upright figures clad in flowing white robes and leading heroic and virtuous lives.

From this it was but a short step to suggest that early British Christianity had in fact absorbed much of the ancient religion. In 1766 John Cleland argued that Druidism so successfully permeated early Christianity with its doctrines that the Mass took its name not from the phrase Missa est but from mistletoe. Edward Williams, a Glamorgan stonemason who moved to London and adopted the pen-name Iolo of Glamorgan, claimed in 1794 that the Welsh medieval poems of Taliesin 'exhibit a complete system of DRUIDISM' and that 'by these writings it will appear that the Ancient British CHRISTIANITY was strongly tinctured with DRUIDISM'.[82] In two books written in the first decade of the nineteenth century, *Celtic Researches on the Origin, Traditions and Language of the Ancient Druids and Mythology of the British Druids*, Edward Davies, curate of Olveston in Gloucestershire, suggested that much had been carried over from the old to the new faith. He described Iona as 'a great asylum of the Northern Druids' and pointed out that 'the early Christians did often erect their churches upon the ruins of heathen temples'. He also expressed the view that Drudisim 'was removed but a few paces further from the religion of Noah than popery' and was indeed a good deal closer to 'the faith, purity and simplicity of the Gospel' than some other modes of worship 'denominated Christian'.[83]

Other facets of the romantic movement enhanced the appeal of the more specifically Christian aspects of Britain's Celtic past. Perhaps the most influential was its fascination with ruins. The Reformation played its part in creating this particular cult. The dissolution of the monasteries, like the Viking raids seven centuries earlier, inspired a wistful nostalgia for a lost golden age of simple piety and devotion. Travelling through England in 1622 the poet Michael Drayton gazed on the ruins of 'great Arthur's tomb and holy Joseph's grave' at Glastonbury and asked, 'Did so many kings do honour in that place, For Avarice at last so vilely to deface?'.[84] The ivy clad remains of hermits' cells and remote monastic settlements became tourist sites, visited by increasing numbers of travellers in search both of sublime and picturesque scenery and of spiritual uplift and atmosphere. The fact that so many of the Celtic monastic sites were in wild, rugged places far away from civilisation made them all the more appealing to those who had turned their backs on the classical ideal of ordered beauty and sought rather the wilderness experience and the noble savage. Samuel Johnson and James Boswell embarked on their tour of the Scottish highlands and islands in 1773 hoping 'to find simplicity and wildness, and all the circumstances of remote time or place, so near our native great island'.[85] Although they found that they had come too late to see 'the people of peculiar appearance and the system of antiquated life' they had hoped for, they were not disappointed by the 'ruins of religious magnificence' which stood as 'melancholy memorials' to a long lost age of faith.[86] They were especially moved by the Celtic Christian sites of the Inner Hebrides, first on Inch Kenneth where 'it was not without some mournful emotion that we contemplated the ruins of religious structures' and then on Iona, 'that venerable seat of ancient sanctity; where secret piety reposed, and where fallen greatness was reposited'.[87] Both men were deeply affected by the sight of 'those illustrious ruins' which provoked Johnson's famous observation that 'that man is little to be envied … whose piety would not grow warmer among the ruins of Iona'.[88]

Numerous travellers followed in the wake of Boswell and Johnson and made pilgrimages to the sacred sites of Celtic Christianity. Artists produced romantic engravings and watercolours of deserted hermits' cells, half-ruined round towers and high crosses. Poets, too, drew inspiration from these sites and imagined and idealised those who once lived there. In 1814 William Wordsworth, visiting Loch Lomond, was moved to take up his pen by the sight of 'a beautiful ruin' on one of the islands which had been 'a place chosen for the retreat of a solitary individual'.[89] In his poem, 'The Brownie's Cell', he described the hermit in terms that might have come straight out of Macpherson's 'Ossian' as the 'Proud Remnant of a fearless race' and idealised the call of Celtic monasticism:

> To barren heath, and quaking fen,
> Or depth of labyrinthine glen;
> Or into trackless forest set
> With trees, whose lofty umbrage met;
> World-wearied Men withdrew of yore, -
> (Penance their trust, and Prayer their store;)

And in the wilderness were bound
To such apartments as they found;
Or with a new ambition raised;
That God might suitably be praised.[90]

During the first half of the nineteenth century the influences of antiquarianism, patriotism, Protestantism and the romantic movement combined to produce a growing interest in early Celtic Christianity and an increasingly idealised view of its nature and character. Artefacts which had been smashed and buried at the time of the Reformation were dug up and put on display again. In 1822 Henry Duncan, the minister of Ruthwell in Dumfriesshire, described by his son as having 'an ingenious and sentimental turn of mind', exhumed and repaired the shattered pieces of the eighth-century Ruthwell Cross and re-erected it in the garden of his manse.[91] Later it would be installed in the parish church. In England, numerous parish churches returned to the practice of adopting saints' names which they had dropped after the Reformation. Recent research by Nicholas Orme has suggested that in the process they often either invented or mistakenly appropriated Celtic saints in preference to the Catholic or Anglo-Saxon figures to whom their churches had originally been dedicated. In Wales, David continued to exert an ever more powerful appeal. In 1822 Bishop Burgess' dream of a theological college dedicated to the patron saint came to fruition with the founding of St David's College, Lampeter. Fourteen years later, in a popular book on *The Saints of Wales*, Rice Rees, another Anglican clergyman, called for David to be honoured above all Welshmen as a model of heroic sanctity.

In England, the leading figures in the Oxford Movement had a somewhat lukewarm attitude to the Celtic saints. Their appropriation by militant Protestants and their apparent ambivalence over the authority of bishops made them rather unappealing role models for Tractarians. E. B. Pusey, preaching in 1838 on the theme that most national apostles had been bishops, was forced to concede that 'one remarkable exception to this trend was Columba, the converter of the North Picts, who preferred going out as an Abbot', a fact that had been 'seized on by the adversaries of Episcopacy'.[92] He hastened to assure his hearers that Columba had a bishop in each of his monasteries. Most Tractarians preferred to invoke the example of the early Fathers and the founding figures of eastern Christianity rather than the Celtic saints.

In Presbyterian Scotland, by contrast, the Culdees were idealised as heroic figures who had practised an essentially Protestant form of the Christian faith and valiantly resisted the onward march of Romish influence for as long as they could. In a highly influential study which first appeared in 1811 and was still being reprinted in 1890, John Jamieson, minister of a small secessionist congregation in Edinburgh, suggested that they had particularly close links with Iona and with the Druids who had preceded them. Arguing that they also had a special attachment to St John's Gospel, Jamieson portrayed the Culdees as non-monastic clergy who formed colleges and chose an abbot or president from among themselves. Among 'the errors of the Church of Rome' which they 'vigorously opposed' were territorial episcopacy, auricular confession, idolatry, celibacy, works of supererogation and the doctrine of the real presence.[93] Despite their ruthless suppression by medieval bishops and the Augustinian canons sent into their strongholds as agents of the 'Romish church', Jamieson found evidence that they had lingered in some places until the Lollard movement of the fourteenth century and felt that the adoption of Presbyterianism as the dominant form of church government following the Scottish Reformation was in some measure due to their influence. Their survival through the Middle Ages was, he felt, 'a singular proof of the providence of God in preserving the truth in our native country, even during the time that the Man of Sin was reigning with absolute authority over the other nations of Europe'.[94] The fact that the Celtic Church had allowed married clergy was especially emphasised by Protestant writers. Verses written by the Scottish poet Thomas Campbell in 1824 about Reullura, the wife of Aodh, the last Culdee of Iona, looked back to a golden age of Scotland's ecclesiastical history 'long ere her churchmen by bigotry/were barred from holy wedlock's tie'.[95] Others pursued more esoteric theories. In 1844 Algernon Herbert suggested that the Culdees practised secret mysteries, including human sacrifice, and that Scottish freemasonry originated on Iona.[96]

    In Ireland, too, much was made of the Culdees by Protestant propagandists. In a tract published in 1822 and directed at Roman Catholics, Henry Mason identified them as the original monks who had come to the island a century or so before Patrick and who were closely linked with Egyptian and Greek Christianity. He emphasised that these first Christians in Ireland 'did not look up to the Pope, or to any other foreign person, as their spiritual head' and read the Scriptures in their native language rather than in Latin.[97] Mason also pointed out to his Catholic readers that 'St Patrick, St Columbkill, and all the saints of their times, on account of whom the island got the name of the Island of the Saints, professed the religion of the Bible, and one very different from that which you are now taught by your priests'.[98] In a less polemical spirit, scholars and antiquarians were taking an increasing interest in the literary and archaeological remains of Ireland's early Christian past. Important pioneering work in this area had been done in the eighteenth century by Charles O'Conor, a Catholic priest who edited the Irish manuscripts gathered by the Duke of Buckingham and housed at Stowe and by a quartet of Church of Ireland clergymen who produced significant historical studies: William Nicholson (editor of the Irish Historical Library, 1724), Mervyn Archdall (*Monasticon Hibernicum*, 1786), Thomas Leland (*A History of Ireland*, 1773) and Edward Ledwick (*Antiquities of Ireland*, 1790). In 1772 the Dublin Society formed a committee to make enquiries on Irish antiquities and ten years later a meeting of Trinity College graduates led to the foundation of the Royal Irish Academy which published its first volume of transactions in 1787.

   In the early decades of the nineteenth century this growing antiquarian interest merged with the rising tides of romanticism and nationalism to create a Celtic revival movement in Ireland. That the Christian aspects of the country's Celtic past received considerable prominence in this movement was in large part due to the particular enthusiasms and activities of the man described in a recent study of Irish cultural nationalism as the 'linchpin of the Celtic revival'.[99] Like so many of those attracted to Celtic Christianity, George Petrie was an outsider, the son of Scots parents who had settled in Dublin. A landscape painter, he developed a particular interest in Ireland's early ecclesiastical remains while directing the historical section of the Irish Ordnance Survey in the 1830s. He was also instrumental in acquiring thousands of early manuscripts for the library of the Royal Irish Academy, including the important *Annals of the Four Masters*. Petrie had a strong romantic streak and, influenced by Wordsworth's pantheistic poetry and sense of presence, he found in the old Celtic Christian sites an almost tangible expression of the Irish soul. He would go again and again to gaze at the high crosses of Monasterboice and the ruined monastery at Clonmacnoise, scene of his most famous painting 'The last round of pilgrims at Clonmacnoise' (1828). There, in 'the most interesting spot that our island affords', he found an atmosphere 'altogether lonely, sublime and poetic'.[100] Among the pilgrims visiting the site, he observed 'an abstract intensity of feeling that takes the mind back to remote times, and a rapturous expression of devotion and holy love'.[101]

   The enthusiasm of the staunchly Protestant and Unionist Petrie for these remnants of Ireland's Celtic Christian past was in contrast to the unease that they engendered among the country's Roman Catholic bishops. In 1829 an attempt was made to abolish pilgrimages to saints' wells and more closely supervise what was going on at Lough Derg.[102]

Petrie felt that the golden age of the saints should be affirmed because of its eirenic spirit. He argued that Roman Catholics and Protestants might be brought closer together by acknowledging their common Celtic Christian heritage. Above all, he wanted to assert the deeply Christian nature of Irish national identity, conceived in terms of the gentle, scholarly monastic culture of the fifth to tenth centuries, against attempts by the English to dismiss the Irish as stupid barbarians and post-Enlightenment portrayals of them as representing heroic pagan virtues. This agenda underlay his important work on the round towers found at so many Celtic sites, which won the prize in a competition set in 1832 by the Royal Irish Academy for the most convincing explanation of the origin and purpose of these distinctive features on the Irish landscape. His essay, published in 1846 as *The Ecclesiastical Architecture of Ireland*, took issue with those who argued that the towers dated from pre-Christian times, were associated with the worship of natural manifestations of divine energy and anticipated the symbolism of freemasonry. Petrie sought to prove that they were wholly Christian in origin and belonged to the monastic culture he so much admired (Plate 6).

Petrie was not alone in his idealised vision of Celtic Christianity as a moral, educative force that might heal the divisions between Catholics and Protestants and ease the problems of early nineteenth-century Ireland. It was shared by many of those involved in the Young Ireland Movement of the early 1840s, not least its leader, Thomas Davis, a half-Welsh, half-Irish Protestant who was fascinated by the noble example set by the Celtic saints, Aidan especially. Like Petrie, he sought to recover the memory and values of the golden age and believed that a return to its high-minded, chivalric Christianity and learned culture would go a long way towards solving Ireland's social and political tensions.

In the event, the potato famine of 1845–7 put paid to these hopes and gave birth to a very different kind of Irish nationalism which emphasised political power and physical force rather than gentle evocations of the Celtic spirit. If Celtic Christianity lost its appeal as a solution to the Irish problem, however, it remained enormously popular with the new breed of spiritual tourist who flocked to ancient monastic sites. One of the reasons for the foundation of the Irish Archaeological Society in the early 1840s was to protect the country's ancient monuments from the damage inflicted by visitors who roamed over them and sometimes took away souvenirs. To cater for this new variation of the medieval pilgrim trade, popular guidebooks were produced, like W. F. Wakeman's *Archaeologia Hibernica: A Handbook of Irish Antiquities, Pagan and Christian, especially of such as are easy of access from the Irish Metropolis* (1848), illustrated by

KILLREE TOWER.

DOORWAY OF KILLREE TOWER.

Plate 6. Engraving of Killree Tower by George Petrie. (Source: M. Stokes, *Early Christian Architecture in Ireland* (1878).)

Plate 7. Engraving of the Cross of Muiredach, Monasterboice. (Source: W. Wakeman, *Irish Antiquities* (3rd edn, 1903).)

romantic engravings of the ivy-clad remains of hermits' cells and pious virgins kneeling in prayer at the foot of high standing crosses (Plate 7). The stage was set for the romantic high noon of late nineteenth-century Celtic Christian revivalism.

NOTES

1. Ashe, *King Arthur's Avalon*, p. 241.
2. Payton, *Cornwall*, p. 115.
3. N. Orme (ed.), Nicholas Roscarrock's *Lives of the Saints: Cornwall and Devon* (Devon and Cornwall Record Society, Exeter, 1993), p. 35.
4. Maher, *Irish Spirituality*, p. 117.
5. Williams, *Religion*, p. 117.
6. Ibid., p. 115.
7. Thomas, *Candle*, pp. 127–8.
8. Williams, *Religion*, p. 116.
9. Forbes, *Kalendars*, p. xxiii.
10. Anderson, *Early Sources*, Vol. 2, p. 557.
11. Duncan, *Scotland*, p. 556.
12. Booklet accompanying CD 'Columba, Most Holy of Saints' (Academy Sound and Vision, London, 1992).
13. Skene, *Book of Pluscarden*, Vol. 2, p. 213.
14. Ibid., p. 245.
15. W. F. Skene (ed.), *John of Fordun's Chronicle of the Scottish Nation* (Edmonston & Douglas, Edinburgh, 1872), Vol. 2.

16. Watt, *Scotichronicon*, Vol. 1, p. 189; Vol. 2, p. 81.
17. Ibid., Vol. 2, p. 87.
18. Ibid., Vol. 6, p. 149.
19. Ibid., Vol. 3, p. 19.
20. Mackinlay, *Ancient Church Dedications*, passim.
21. 'The Miracles of St Kentigern', CD Gau 169 (Academy Sound and Vision, London, 1997).
22. J. Purser, *Scotland's Music* (Mainstream, Edinburgh, 1992, pp. 39–45.
23. 'Columba, Most Holy of Saints', CD Gau 129 (Academy Sound and Vision, London, 1992).
24. Williams, *Religion*, p. 115.
25. O. Tudor Edwards, 'The Earliest Monument in Welsh Music', *Welsh History Review*, Vol. 14, No. 4, December 1989, pp. 553–73; O. Tudor Edwards, *Matins, Lauds & Vespers for St David's Day* (D. S. Brewer, Cambridge, 1990).
26. Macfarlane, *William Elphinstone*, pp. 233–4.
27. Ibid., p. 234.
28. A. Macquarrie, 'Lections for St Constantine's Day in the Aberdeen Breviary' in *The Society of Friends of Govan Old Fifth Annual Report*, September 1995, p. 25; Macquarrie, *The Saints*, p. 10.
29. Macfarlane, *William Elphinstone*, p. 243.
30. De Pontfarcy, *The Medieval Pilgrimage*, pp. 191–2.
31. Mackinley, *Ancient Church Dedications*, p. 41.
32. Lacey, *Colum Cille*, p. 94.
33. Williams, *Religion*, p. 118.
34. Lacey, *Colum Cille*, pp. 95–6.
35. O'Dwyer, *Towards a History*, p. 170.
36. Lacey, *Colum Cille*, p. 95.
37. Von Maltzahn, *Milton's History*, p. 123.
38. Williams, *Reformation Views*, p. 57.
39. Ibid., p. 39.
40. L. P. Fairfield, John Bale, *Mythmaker for the English Reformation* (Purdue University Press, West Lafayette, Indiana, 1976), p. 95.
41. Williams, *Welsh Reformation*, p. 211.
42. Von Maltzahn, *Milton's History*, p. 163.
43. Ibid., p. 163.
44. R. Runcie, Commemorative Lecture on the 1,400th Anniversary of the Mission of St Augustine of Canterbury (unpublished, 1997), p. 7.
45. R. Davies, '*Epistol at y Cembru*', in G. Hughes (ed.), *Rhagymadroddian 1547–1659* (University of Wales Press, Cardiff, 1951), p. 18.
46. Williams, *Welsh Reformation*, p. 211.
47. Buchanan, *History*, p. 75.
48. Spottiswoode, *History*, p. 7.
49. Calderwood, *History*, Vol. 1, p. 39.
50. Ibid., p. 41.
51. Ibid., pp. 41, 19.
52. Ibid., p. 42.
53. Spottiswoode, *History*, p. 11.
54. Ibid., p. 7.

55. Ibid., p. 8.
56. Ibid., p. 8.
57. Ibid., pp. 8,12.
58. Forbes, *Kalendars*, p. xliii.
59. *The Whole Works of the Most Rev. James Ussher* (no publisher or date), Vol. 4, p. 238.
60. Ibid., pp. 278–9.
61. Ibid., pp. 299–300.
62. Ibid., p. 336.
63. Ibid., p. 319.
64. Bieler, *Life and Legend*, p. 13.
65. Sharpe, *Medieval Irish Saints*, p. 58.
66. Ibid., p. 58.
67. Leerssen, *Mere Irish*, p. 308.
68. Sharpe, *Medieval Irish Saints*, pp. 4–5; see also pp. 40–74.
69. Leerssen, *Mere Irish*, p. 313.
70. O'Sullivan, *The Creative Migrant*, p. 92.
71. W. Lloyd, *The History of the Government of the Church as it was in Great Britain and Ireland when they first received the Christian Religion* (Charles Brome, London, 1703), p. 3.
72. Ibid., p. 64.
73. Burgess, *Tracts*, p. 83.
74. Ibid., p. 143.
75. Ibid., p. 279.
76. Williams, *Religion*, pp. 120–2.
77. Ibid., p. 123.
78. Ibid., p. 123.
79. J. Leerssen, 'Celticism' in Brown, *Celticism*, p. 5.
80. P. Morgan, 'From a Death to a View: The Hunt for the Welsh Past in the Romantic Period', in E. Hobsbawm and T. Ranger (eds.), *The Invention of Tradition* (Cambridge University Press, Cambridge, 1984), pp. 43–101.
81. Piggott, *Ancient Britons*, p. 145.
82. Piggott, *The Druids*, p. 171.
83. E. Davies, *Mythology of the British Druids* (printed for the author, London, 1809), pp. 479, 497.
84. Ashe, *King Arthur's Avalon*, p. 278.
85. J. Boswell, *Journal of A Tour of the Hebrides* (Heinemann, London, 1963), p. 3.
86. Johnson, *A Journey*, p. 46.
87. Ibid., p. 120; R. W. Chapman (ed.), *Letters of Samuel Johnson* (Clarendon Press, Oxford, 1962), Vol. 1, p. 322.
88. Johnson, *A Journey*, p. 124.
89. C. H. Ketcham (ed.), *Shorter Poems, 1807–1820, by William Wordsworth* (Cornell University Press, Ithaca, 1989), p. 130.
90. Ibid., p. 131.
91. P. Meyvaert, 'A New Perspective on the Ruthwell Cross', in B. Cassidy (ed.), *The Ruthwell Cross* (Princeton University Press, 1989), p. 99.
92. E. B. Pusey, *The Church: The Convertor of the Heathen* (J. H. Parker, Oxford, 1836), p. 5. I owe this reference to Dr Gavin White of St Andrews.

93. J. Jamieson, *A Historical Account of the Ancient Culdees of Iona* (T. D. Morison, Glasgow, 1890), pp. 146–55.
94. Ibid., p. 231.
95. Sharpe, *Adomnan*, p. 95.
96. See Reeves, *The Culdees*, pp. 67–77.
97. H. M. Mason, *The Catholic Religion of St Patrick and St Columb. Kill and the Other Ancient Saints of Ireland truely set forth* (Dublin, 1822), p. 25.
98. Ibid., p. 6.
99. Hutchison, *Dynamics*, p. 79.
100. Ibid., p. 82.
101. Ibid., p. 82.
102. Maher, *Irish Spirituality*, p. 137.

4

O blest communion, fellowship divine

Celtic Christian revival in the later nineteenth century

Alongside their well-known enthusiasm for medievalism and classical antiquity, the Victorians also had a fascination for the culture of the ancient Celts. The Celtic revival that took place in the later nineteenth century may not have been quite as spectacular in its effects as the earlier Gothic revival but it had a significant impact on architecture, art, music and literature. In all these areas specifically Christian themes and motifs from the golden age of the sixth and seventh centuries played an important role. More academic Celtic studies boomed with archaeological sites being properly investigated and important early texts being translated and published for the first time. As in earlier revivals, the concept of Celtic Christianity was also taken up to serve particular denominational and national interests and a heavy dash of romanticism added considerably to its appeal.

Not all Victorians were in love with the Celts. This period also witnessed a considerable upsurge of interest in Britain's Anglo-Saxon heritage which confirmed many in their opinion that it was more significant than the Celtic legacy. A Scottish provincial newspaper reflected in 1851 that:

> Ethnologically the Celtic race is an inferior one, and attempt to disguise it as we may, there is naturally and rationally no getting rid of the great cosmical fact that it is destined to give way – slowly and painfully it may be, but still most certainly – before the higher capabilities of the Anglo-Saxon.[1]

It was against such notions that Celtophiles sought to champion the claims of a marginalised and peripheral people. In the event, that very marginality came to be perceived as one of the Celts' most attractive features.

Victorian enthusiasm for the Celts, and indeed the whole modern concept of 'Celticity', are often attributed to the writings of two men, the French historian of religion, Ernest Rénan, and the English poet and critic, Matthew Arnold.[2] While this may underplay the contribution made by others, it is certainly true that many prevailing popular notions of the distinctive character of Celtic Christianity can be traced to their writings. Rénan, who came from Brittany and was originally destined for the Roman Catholic priesthood, published in 1854 a study of *La Poésie des Races Celtiques*. As the title implies, it portrayed the Celts first and foremost as a poetic people, essentially feminine in character and distinguished for their intuition, imagination and sensitivity. Rénan also portrayed them as instinctively religious: 'That gentle little race was naturally Christian'.[3] In marked contrast to the tardy and grudging acceptance of Christianity by the Teutonic people, the Celts had taken easily to Christianity. There had been no disjunction from their Druidic paganism but rather an easy transition from the old religion to the new. Rénan wrote approvingly of the 'half-bardic, half-Christian schools of St Cadoc and St Illtud' in Wales.[4] He was an enthusiastic subscriber to the notion of a golden age of Celtic Christianity:

> When we seek to determine the precise moment in the history of the Celtic races at which we ought to place ourselves in order to appreciate their genius in its entirety, we find ourselves led back to the sixth century ... Few forms of Christianity have offered an ideal of Christian perfection so pure as the Celtic Church of the sixth, seventh and eighth centuries'.[5]

For Rénan the most distinctive characteristic of the Celts was their pursuit of impossible dreams. He found this to be particularly marked in some of the early manifestations of Celtic Christian revivalism, notably the legendary voyage of St Brendan which he saw as 'the most singular product of this combination of Celtic naturalism with Christian spiritualism' and the account of Knight Owen's journeys into St Patrick's Purgatory. He felt that these and similar stories epitomised the spirit of a race that:

> has worn itself out in taking dreams for realities, and in pursuing its splendid visions. The essential element of the Celt's poetic life is the adventure – that is to say, the pursuit of the unknown, an endless quest after an object ever flying from desire. It was of this

that St Brendan dreamed, that Knight Owen asked of his subterranean journeyings. This race desires the infinite, it thirsts for it and pursues it at all costs, beyond the tomb, beyond hell itself.[6]

Matthew Arnold's *Study of Celtic Literature* was published in 1867, having been delivered in lecture form at Oxford University over the previous two years. He took as his starting point a visit to an *eisteddfod* at Llandudno where the 'spell of the Celtic genius' had been destroyed for him by the triumph of 'the prosaic, practical Saxon'.[7] The speeches had been in English, the proceedings dull and lifeless and the atmosphere ruined by the 'miserable looking Saxons' who arrived on the Liverpool steamer.[8] In short, the philistinism of the English had been allowed to prevail over the poetic sensitivity of the Welsh. So it was in Britain as a whole which Arnold characterised as a country having 'a vast obscure Cymric base with a vast visible Teutonic superstructure'.[9] His experience at Llandudno led him into a long disquisition about the differences between the Anglo-Saxon and Celtic races which was highly flattering to the latter. While the Saxon temperament was steady-going, prosaic, plodding and materialistic, the Celtic temperament was sensitive, visionary, poetic, spiritual, mercurial and given to melancholy. Picking up Rénan's phrase about the '*infinie délicatesse de sentiment qui caractérise la race Celtique*', Arnold identified 'sentiment' as 'the word which marks where the Celtic races really touch and are one; sentimental, if the Celtic nature is to be characterised by a single term, is the best term to take'.[10]

Arnold's generalisations about the Celtic temperament were based on a relatively small range of sources from the golden age of the sixth and seventh centuries and its immediate aftermath. He drew heavily on early Irish, Scottish and Welsh religious poetry, and especially on a single eighth-century epitaph to Angus the Culdee, while making virtually no reference to post-medieval Celtic literature. Like Rénan, he saw no great discontinuity between pagan and Christian Celtic religion and argued that pre-Christian themes and images permeated Celtic Christianity. In the poetry of Taliesin, for example, he found clear echoes of Druidism and pagan mythology as well as a characteristically Celtic closeness to nature and fascination with the supernatural. Although, like Rénan, Arnold portrayed the Celts in some sense as outsiders, standing at the edge and defined in terms of their 'otherness', he was also struck by their essential Britishness: 'Of the shrunken and diminished remains of this great primitive race, all, with one insignificant exception, belongs to the English empire; only Brittany is not ours; we have Ireland, the Scotch Highlands, Wales, the Isle of Man, Cornwall'.[11]

Arnold's specific aim in his *Study of Celtic Literature* was to awaken his countrymen, and especially academics, to their neglect of this part of their national heritage. The Celts, he wrote:

> are a part of ourselves, we are deeply interested in knowing them, they are deeply interested in being known by us; and yet in the great and rich universities of this great and rich country there is no chair of Celtic, there is no study or teaching of Celtic matters; those who want them must go abroad for them.[12]

He was particularly incensed by the philistinism and Anglo-Saxon prejudice that had greeted Sir Robert Peel's proposal in 1849 that the early Irish manuscripts amassed at Stowe be bought for the British Museum. The Museum's trustees, led by Lord Macaulay, had turned down the suggestion on the grounds that there was nothing in the Stowe collection worth having apart from some correspondence on the American war. As a result the manuscripts had been bought by a private collector who allowed no one to consult them.

Arnold's characterisation of the Celts as a peculiarly spiritual, poetic and sensitive people was to have much more impact in Britain than his call for them to be the subject of proper academic attention. Celtic studies, whether in the fields of archaeology, philology or literary and textual criticism, remained much more advanced on the Continent. The pioneering archaeological work begun at Hallstat in 1848 and La Tène in 1856 was followed by important linguistic studies in France and Germany through the 1860s and 1870s. The first academic journal dedicated exclusively to Celtic subjects, the *Revue Celtique*, was established in Paris in 1870. The second, *Zeitschrift für Celtische Philologie*, was founded in Germany in 1896.

Although Celtic scholarship in the British Isles was much more amateurish, significant advances were made during the later nineteenth century in the knowledge and understanding of the Celtic Christian era, especially through the work of archaeologists. In Wales the Cambrian Archaeological Association, founded in 1846, pioneered field-work on early Christian sites and published detailed studies of Welsh crosses in its journal, *Archaeologia Cambrensis*. Important work on the inscribed stones of Wales and Scotland was done by John Rhys, whose election as the first Professor of Celtic at Oxford in 1877 answered one of Arnold's specific pleas in *A Study of Celtic Literature*. Rhys, who occupied the chair for nearly twenty years, was also a distinguished philologist and published on early Welsh, Irish and British history. The distinctive Celtic crosses in Wales were studied by J. Romilly Allen, a civil engineer from Pembrokeshire, who published his findings in *Archaeologia Cambrensis* at the end of the century. In Scotland pioneering work was undertaken by Joseph Anderson, who published *Scotland in Early Christian Times* in 1881 and later collaborated with Romilly Allen to produce the first comprehensive study of *The Early Christian Monuments of Scotland* (1904). Ireland continued to receive extensive archaelogical attention, reflected in Henry O'Néill's *The Most Interesting of the Sculptured High Crosses of Ancient Ireland* (1857) and Margaret Stokes' *Early Christian Architecture in Ireland* (1878), both lavishly illustrated with engravings which squeezed every ounce of spiritual atmosphere and melancholy melodrama out of the ruined remains (Plate 8).

Works of art from the golden age of Irish Christianity were also becoming the focus of increasing interest. The Royal Irish Academy began collecting early antiquities in the 1840s with a view to forming a national collection. Around 1850 George Waterhouse, a jeweller who had recently moved to Dublin from Sheffield, acquired a brooch which had been discovered on the shore near Drogheda. Cashing in on the growing enthusiasm for Celtic folklore, he decided to name it after the sacred hill associated with Ireland's high kings and to market facsimile copies. Among the first to buy a reproduction of the Tara Brooch, which he exhibited in the 1851 Great Exhibition at the Crystal Palace, was Queen Victoria. Her well-publicised enchantment with it helped to promote a craze for reproduction Celtic jewellery and made the Tara Brooch something of an icon for the Celtic revival in Ireland. The original was acquired in 1868 by the Royal Irish Academy along with the Ardagh Chalice, which had been dug up during a potato harvest. The interlacing knotwork and distinctive zoomorphic designs found on early Celtic metal-work and high standing crosses were taken up by artists and craftsmen. As a result, what had begun as ecclesiastical art forms lost their religious connotations and came to be prized for their decorative value alone, ending up in jewellers' windows and arts and crafts exhibitions in a move described by one art historian as being 'from liturgy to Tiffany's'.[13] Owen Jones' popular *Grammar of ornament* (1856) provided pages of patterns taken from sculptured crosses, metalwork and illuminated manuscripts 'with elements isolated as if they were botanical specimens' and Christopher Dresser's *Studies in Design* (1876) further promoted Celtic knotwork as a pattern to be taken up and used by artists and designers.[14]

The distinctive calligraphy and ornamentation found on early Irish illuminated manuscripts had a similar appeal. In 1843 John Westwood, an entomologist who became fascinated by the tiny representations of animals and birds in early monastic manuscripts, brought out the first

Plate 8. Drawing of the Way of the Cross, Skellig Michael, by Margaret Stokes. (Source: M. Stokes, *Early Christian Architecture in Ireland* (1878).)

of a series of illustrated studies of *Palaeographia sacra pictoria*. In 1861 Margaret Stokes designed a title page based on an illustration from the *Book of Kells* for an edition of Samuel Ferguson's poem *The Cromlech of Howth*, in what was perhaps the first example of the use of early Celtic Christian design for purely decorative purposes. In the 1870s the new technique of photozincography was used to produce a four-volume facsimile of the most important early Irish illuminated manuscripts. The content of the manuscripts was also coming under increasing scrutiny. The texts must often have seemed rather heavy-going in comparison with the illustrations and ornamentation that surrounded them – Alexander Forbes described his meticulously researched compilation of the *Kalendars of Scottish Saints* (1872) as 'dull as last year's fillet or a presbyterian sermon' – but they attracted the attentions of a number of dogged amateur scholars, most of whom, like Forbes, were clergymen.[15] William Reeves, Dean of Armagh and later Bishop of Down, brought out an important critical edition and translation of Adomnan's *Vitae Columbae* in 1857. Seven years later he produced a revisionist study of *The Culdees of the British Isles* which questioned many prevalent assumptions and remains the standard work on the subject today. It demonstrated that the term *Céli Dé* did not come into use until the late eighth century (i.e. during the first Celtic Christian revival) and could not properly be applied to the clergy on Iona during Columba's time. Reeves was also responsible for the first critical editions of the twelfth-century Lives of Ninian and Kentigern, published in 1874. Another Irish clergymen, James Todd, who had been instrumental in founding the Irish Archaeological Society and combined parochial duties in Dublin with the presidency of the Royal Irish Academy, wrote a life of Patrick in 1864 which stripped away many of the legends surrounding the saint. He also translated and edited a number of early hymns and poems, including Columba's *Altus Prosator* and *In Te, Christe*. William MacIlwaine, incumbent of St George's Church, Belfast, published an important collection of early Irish religious poems, *Lyra Hibernica Sacra*, in 1878. In Scotland significant work on early Gaelic texts was done by Alexander Cameron, a Free Church minister, who edited the *Scottish Celtic Review* and in 1892 produced a two volume collection of *Reliquae Celticae*.

The dissemination of Celtic Christian material was greatly facilitated by the emergence of a number of antiquarian societies dedicated to publishing early texts. The Irish Archaeological and Celtic Society, the result of a merger between two smaller groups in 1853, published the *Book of Hymns of the Irish Church* in 1869. In the same year the Spalding Club, which had been set up in Aberdeen in 1839 to publish manuscripts relating to the history of north-east Scotland, brought out an edition of the *Book of Deer*. The Henry Bradshaw Society, founded in 1890 for 'the editing of rare liturgical texts', produced the first printed editions of the *Antiphonary of Bangor* (1895) and the *Liber Hymnorum* (1898).

The Royal Irish Academy was also active in this field, publishing facsimile editions of *Lebar na hUidre* (1870), *Leabhar Breac* (1872–6), the *Book of Leinster* (1880), the *Book of Ballymote* (1887) and the *Yellow Book of Lecan* (1896). This period also saw the appearance of a number of multi-volume compilations of saints' lives, most again the work of clergymen. They included *Lives of the Cambro-British Saints*, edited by W. J. Rees and published in 1853, Sabine Baring-Gould's *The Lives of the Saints* (1872–7) and John O'Hanlon's *Lives of the Irish Saints* (1875). The Scottish Text Society began publication of a series of volumes on the *Legends of the Saints* in 1887. In the same year John Patrick Crichton-Stuart, third Marquess of Bute, financed the publication of an edition of the *Acta Sanctorum Hiberniae* from the *Codex Salmanticensis* which had been prepared by two Bollandists. A two-volume edition of *Lives of the Scottish Saints*, published in 1889, included much previously untranslated material and was supplemented in 1895 by W. M. Metcalfe's *Ancient Lives of Scottish Saints*.

None of this work was done, as it would be today (and as it was then on the Continent), in a university context. The nearest that Victorian Britain had to professional scholars working in this area were two trained lawyers. Whitley Stokes, A Dublin-born barrister who spent twenty years in India as the legal member of the Viceroy's Council, translated and edited a number of important early Irish ecclesiastical documents, including the *Tripartite Life of Patrick*, the *Book of Armagh*, the *Book of Lismore* and several saints' Lives. William Skene, an Edinburgh writer to the Signet who in 1881 became Historiographer Royal in Scotland, edited a number of early medieval Scottish and Welsh chronicles. His major work, *Celtic Scotland: A History of Ancient Alba* (1876–80) ran to three volumes, one of which was devoted entirely to the 'history of the old Celtic Church'. In his preface, Skene deplored the fact that the history of the early church in Scotland 'has become the battle-field on which Catholic and Protestant, Episcopalian and Presbyterian, have contended for their respective tenets' and promised that his own work would be free of all ecclesiastical bias.[16] In the event, however, he took the standard Protestant line, portraying the Celtic Church as a proud and independent entity locked in conflict with Rome and the Culdees as a heroic remnant who bravely tried to resist alien Continental ways. His book ended with a flourish of romantic nostalgia:

> Thus the old Celtic Church came to an end, leaving no vestiges behind it, save here and there the roofless walls of what had been a church, and the numerous old burying grounds to the use of which people still cling with tenacity, and where occasionally an ancient Celtic cross tells of its former state.[17]

A similar note of regret for a lost age of innocence and purity sounds through much of the work of the Victorian scholar clerics. Alexander Forbes, who rejoiced in the preface to his edition of the *Kalendars of the Scottish Saints* that 'the nineteenth century, an age of reconstruction ... has nobly avenged the scepticism of the preceding age which scoffed at everything', quoted approvingly the observation of a recent 'devout writer' that 'the lives of the Saints ... are like the ruins of their own monasteries, lonely and melancholy fragments, which are but indications of a beauty which has passed away from the earth'.[18] Not all those who wrote about the subject of Celtic Christianity in the later nineteenth century were prone to such romanticism, however. When the eighth Duke of Argyll penned a little volume on Iona in 1870, he might have been expected to wax lyrical about the sacred isle which was in his personal possession. Instead, he chose to berate those who had turned Columba's church into a denominational football.

> It is vain to look, in the peculiarities of the Scoto-Irish Church for the model either of Primitive practice, or of any modern system. As regards the theology of Columba's time, although it was not what we understand as Roman, neither assuredly was it what we understand as Protestant.[19]

Few ecclesiastics chose to heed this layman's warning. For them much of the attraction of Celtic Christianity, and the reason for writing about it, was the support that they felt it offered for their own particular churchmanship and denominational persuasion. Several of those whose work we have already noted displayed a clear denominational bias. William Skene was to be accused of starting 'a chain of error in Scottish history' through his deliberate misquotation of sources to suggest an anti-Roman agenda on the part of early Irish missionaries (see p. 177). James Todd's book on Patrick came in for criticism in the early twentieth century from the German scholar Ludwig Bieler who noted 'unfortunately, the author approached his subject with a biased mind: he laboured to make St Patrick a precursor of the Established Church, of which he himself was a minister'.[20] More immediately, Todd's work triggered off a Catholic response in the form of several Lives of Patrick written in the 1870s which underlined his Roman connections and credentials.

The appropriation of Celtic Christianity to serve denominational ends can be clearly seen in four works produced during the 1850s by members of the dominant churches in each of the four constituent nations of the United Kingdom. The English contribution came from William Bell

Scott, a painter and poet who, although born in Edinburgh, spent most
of his life south of the border. While running the government school of
art in Newcastle, he developed a fascination with the Northumbrian
Christian heritage and with Bede in particular. Although apparently an
agnostic, he was a very Anglican agnostic and had no doubt that were
Bede to return to life, he would find his spiritual home in the Church of
England. In 1852 he expressed this conviction in a poem which was
apparently provoked by the invocation of Bede's name by Cardinal
Wiseman, Roman Catholic Archbishop of Westminster, when opening
Hartlepool Roman Catholic Church. Scott imagined Bede being resusci-
tated in response to this invocation and finding little to commend in the
Cardinal's religion:

> Man clad in scarlet, who art thou?
> The whiff of death comes out of thee.[21]

One glimpse of Wiseman and his brand of religion was enough for Bede
who cried out 'Lay me again beneath the sod'. Scott's poem shows how
Britain's Celtic Christian inheritance was harnessed to anti-Catholicism
in Victorian England.

A study published in 1855 by Duncan McCallum, Church of Scotland
Minister of Duirnish on Skye, also played on anti-Roman prejudices
and plugged the familiar theme of the Protestantism of the Culdees,
describing them as the 'ancient British clergy' who originated in Gaul
and came to Britain in the late second and third century to escape
Roman persecution.[22] Insisting that they were not 'monkish' in any way,
McCallum linked the Culdees with Iona and identified Columba as one
of their number who 'was not in the least tainted by the errors of the
Church of Rome'.[23] He portrayed them as crypto-Presbyterians who had
no truck with bishops and had more in common with Druids than with
Roman priests, favouring the common tongue over Latin and preferring
simple, provisional huts to splendid and imposing buildings for worship.
Although they managed for many centuries to go on living 'in the primitive simplicity of the fathers' while those around them were succumbing
to superstition and idolatry, they were finally brought under the yoke of
'the clergy of the Romish persuasion' in the twelfth century.[24]

From Wales a tract on *The British Kymry, or Britons of Cambria* (1857),
presented the Welsh as 'the primogenital family of mankind' and Arthur
as 'the great Christian conqueror of the pagan hordes who overthrew the
Roman Empire'.[25] The author, R. W. Morgan, Vicar of Tregynon, was in
no doubt that 'the Roman Catholic Church has no pretensions to being
the primitive or apostolic church of Britain. It came in so late as a century

and a half after the Saxon, and four centuries after the establishment of the native British church'.[26] He ended his testament to Welsh Protestant manliness on a contemporary note with a stirring tribute to the heroism of the Royal Welsh Fusiliers at the siege of Sebastapol in 1855.

Ireland's contribution to this quartet of fiercely partisan interpretations of Celtic Christianity came from the Catholic side. Thomas Walsh's *History of the Irish Hierarchy, with the monasteries of each county and biographical notes of the Irish Saints* was published in New York in 1856 and had a reassuring message for the many Catholic emigrants who had settled in America in the wake of the great famine:

> The Irish Catholic, who has sought a home in this land of the West, will be gratified to find the chain of the Episcopal Succession of Ireland unbroken and unsevered from that Apostolic rock, which has protected the Irish Church in all her vicissitudes, and that apostolic bond, with the see of Peter, kept up in its integrity to this present hour.[27]

It was in Ireland that the battle between different denominations as to who represented the true Celtic Christian inheritance was fiercest. Roman Catholic and Church of Ireland apologists engaged in a lively pamphlet war, with each side claiming that its bishops stood in an uninterrupted line of descent from those consecrated by Patrick. Presbyterians made occasional forays to point out that the early Irish church had not been particularly keen on bishops of any kind. Typical of the Church of Ireland's contribution to the debate was a pamphlet published by the National Protestant Union in 1869 and specifically designed to refute the argument contained in Thomas Walsh's book. W. H. Hardinge's *Narrative and Proof of the Uninterrupted Consecrational Descent of the Bishops of the Church of Ireland from the Bishops who in the year* 1536 *represented the Bishops of the Early Irish Church* noted that 'the primitive Apostolic "Ecclesia Hibernica" lasted for seven centuries; the Roman Catholic usurpation lasted two centuries and a half; the revived and still subsisting Apostolic Catholic Reform Church has lasted three centuries and a half'.[28] The Presbyterian position is well represented in *The Celtic Church in Ireland*, written in 1898 by James Heron, Professor of Ecclesiastical History in the Assembly's College, Belfast, which set out to show not just that the early Irish Church was Protestant – Heron took that as axiomatic and even cited Cardinal Newman who had described it as 'vehemently opposed' to the Roman Church – but also that it was nonepiscopal and non-hierarchical in its form of government.[29] Its real rulers were abbots and not the Celtic bishops who bore no similarity at all to the prelates of the Tudor Church. Heron could find no evidence whatsoever to support the claim made by Anglicans that 'the Church set up by Henry VIII, Edward VI and Elizabeth was a continuation of the early Irish Church, and substantially identical with it'.[30] No early Irish king had ever claimed to be supreme head or governor of the Church. The Tudor sovereigns had created church structures out of expediency and to suit their own political purposes and not out of some quaint antiquarian attachment to Celtic models and practices. 'The very last thing that they dreamed of was to revive the early Irish church.'[31]

Inevitably, Patrick was dragged into the controversy. Protestants followed Ussher in playing down his Roman connections. Richard Murray, Dean of Armagh, in his *Outlines of the History of the Church in Ireland* (1845) rejected as groundless claims that his mission had been directly inspired by Rome and in his 1864 Life of the saint, James Todd made much of the fact that Patrick did not mention Rome in his *Confessio*. On the Catholic side, Dr Moran, Vice-Rector of the Irish College in Rome, published a pamphlet in 1864 which adduced what he claimed to be incontrovertible evidence 'to show that our apostle derived his authority from Rome, and founded our Church with the sanction of Christ's Vicar on earth'.[32] He was contemptuous of Anglican attempts to claim the Celtic saint:

> Though it cannot be said that they have manifested much respect for the name or labours of St Patrick, yet they have occasionally claimed him as their own; and in order to show that his views were conformable to theirs, they have not hesitated to assert that he received no sanction for his mission from Rome, and that he established a church in Ireland something like the Irish Anglican Church, hostile to, or at least independent of, the Prince of the Apostles.[33]

Moran felt it relevant to point out that the last resting place of Patrick had been profaned at the Reformation, with his remains being disturbed and his crosier burned. 'Irish Catholics, on the other hand, like loving children, cherish with unbounded respect the name of their father in faith, and have erected innumerable churches under his invocation at home and abroad'.[34] Rejecting the British sites for his birthplace generally favoured by Protestants, Moran opted for Armorica and suggested that following his years as a slave and escape from Ireland, Patrick had gone back to Gaul. There he had been educated at the monastic school presided over by Germanus of Auxerre, an institution which 'was not as Cambridge or Trinity College [Dublin], or some other such establishment of the British crown' but rather 'a school of saints'.[35] From there Patrick had hastened to Rome where 'he represented to the Holy Father the spiritual darkness which hung over our distant island'.[36] Having been selected by Germanus of Auxerre to go as a missionary to Ireland, he had immediately secured the blessing of Pope Celestine for his endeavours. Moran quoted from Patrick's prayers to show his 'faith in the supremacy of the See of Peter' and also cited evidence that the Patrician Church in Ireland taught the Catholic doctrines of the real presence in the Blessed Sacrament, the sacrificial nature of the Mass and the veneration of the Blessed Virgin.[37]

Columba, too, was hailed as both a proto-Protestant and proto-Catholic. In Scotland he was claimed as a founding father by Episcopalians, Presbyterians in the established Church of Scotland and even by figures in the more evangelical Free Church like Thomas M'Lauchlan whose book, *The Early Scottish Church* (1865) contrasted 'the ambitious, grasping spirit' of Augustine and his companions, 'covetous of place and power', with the humility of Columba and the missionaries of Iona and Lindisfarne who were 'covetous of exalting Christ, but crucifying self'.[38] Roman Catholics also claimed him, perhaps none more vigorously than the aristocratic French controversialist, Charles de Montalembert. In the third volume of his *Les Moines d'Occident* (1860–7), which was dedicated to those who had brought the faith to the British Isles, he noted 'the absolute conformity of the monastic life of Columba and his monks to the precepts and rites of the Catholic Church in all ages' and specifically cited their practice of auricular confession, invocation of the saints, prayer for the dead, the sign of the cross, fasting and abstinence.[39] His notes on Columba, published in English as a separate book in 1868, portrayed the saint in dramatic terms as an austere ascetic who 'from his island rock swooped down to preach, convert, enlighten, reconcile, reprimand princes and peoples, men and women, laics and clerics' and concluded that 'the assumption made by certain writers of having found in the Celtic Church some sort of primitive Christianity not Catholic crumbles to the dust'.[40] Protestant apologists remained unconvinced, however. William Ross, a Presbyterian minister, maintained in 1885 that it had been established:

> beyond the power of reasonable contradiction, that no worship of the Virgin, or of saints, was sanctioned by Columba; that he gave no countenance to the doctrine of Purgatory; that Extreme Unction formed no part of his creed; and that, although some doubtful phrases do occur in reference to the Lord's Supper, communion at Iona was in both kinds.[41]

Geographical as well as denominational rivalries were reflected in the appropriation of the Celtic Christian tradition. Anglicans outside England found it very helpful for showing that their origins were British rather than English. G. T. Stokes, Vicar of All Saints, Blackrock in Dublin, made much of this point in his *Ireland and the Celtic Church* (1886): 'English Christianity, the Christianity of the Angles and of the Saxons, dates from Augustine and was derived from Rome. British Christianity was the Christianity of the Britons; it existed here before Augustine, and must have been derived immediately from Gaul'.[42] The Britishness of the English Church, derived from its Celtic past, was especially emphasised by Anglicans in the north of England who took up Bede's assertion of a distinct and, by implication, superior northern 'Celtic' brand of Christianity, altogether stouter and more British than the effete southern kind. In a series of sermons gathered together in a volume entitled *Leaders in the Northern Church* and published in 1887, Joseph Lightfoot, Bishop of Durham from 1879 to 1889, eulogised the Northumbrian saints for being the true founders of the Church of England. Lightfoot was warm in his tribute to Columba, noting that 'Iona stepped in where Rome had failed' but his greatest praise was reserved for Aidan to whom he accorded 'the first place in the evangelisation of our race. Augustine was the apostle of Kent, but Aidan was the apostle of England'.[43] Lightfoot was clear that 'Northumbria bore the chief part in the making of the English Church'.[44] He was equally clear that 'Rome neither initiated, nor controlled, these Celtic missions. The missionaries owed allegiance, not to the Bishop of Rome, but to the Presbyter-Abbot of Iona'.[45] He made a special point of the fact that they did not take their orders from the south of England. Lightfoot's pride in the distinctive Celtic heritage of northern England and his feeling that the Church of England as a whole had sprung from these roots was shared by many of his clergy. To mark the tenth anniversary of his consecration as Bishop of Durham, they presented him with a pastoral staff decorated with portraits of Aidan, Hilda and others 'the great makers, not only of the Church of England, but likewise of the polity and civilisation of England'.[46]

It was not only in the north of England that Anglican clergymen cast approving glances back to their Celtic forebears. In his rectory in the decidedly Saxon parish of East Mersea near Colchester, Sabine Baring-Gould toiled for many hours through the 1870s on his fifteen-volume *magnum opus* on *The Lives of the Saints*. In the preface he wrote of the difficulties of treading 'in the romance world of Irish hagiology, where the footing is as insecure as on the green bogs of the Emerald Isle'.[47] His own approach was romantic enough, however, perhaps reflecting his birth on the Devon-Cornwall border in another part of Celtic Britain. There, too, there were stirrings of revival in the latter part of the nineteenth century. Cornwall's claim to be regarded as the county of saints was reinforced by antiquarian researchers and by a new wave of hagiography in the wake of the Tractarian revival. R. S. Hawker, the famous Vicar of Morenstow from 1824 to 1875 who is credited with the invention of the harvest festival, invoked the spirit of the Cornish saints in opposition to the county's increasingly Nonconformist, utilitarian and industrial culture. Anglo-Catholic clergy like W. S. Lach-Szyrma, Vicar of Newlyn, flew the flag of St Piran over their churches and Celtophiles like Robert Hunt encouraged a sense of the Cornish people as peculiarly spiritual and imbued with the 'inner life'.[48] When Cornwall was given its own diocese in 1877, many hoped that the cathedral would be sited at one of the county's major Celtic Christian sites like St Germans or St Columb.

Anglicans were generally the most enthusiastic proponents of Celtic Christian revival in the latter part of the nineteenth century. Leaders of the Scottish Episcopal Church were particularly keen to claim the Celtic mantle and saw themselves as standing in a tradition which had been strongly spiritual and liturgical while remaining independent of Rome. A new church established near Edinburgh Castle in 1846 was dedicated to Columba and the cathedral built in Perth in 1850 to serve the united diocese of St Andrews, Dunkeld and Dunblane was dedicated to Ninian. Several Scottish bishops actively promoted the Episcopal Church's rediscovery of its Celtic roots, notably Alexander Ewing, Bishop of Argyll and the Isles from 1847 to 1873, Alexander Chinnery-Haldane, who occupied the same see from 1883 to 1906, and John Dowden, Bishop of Edinburgh from 1886 to 1910. Dowden, an Irishman who hailed from Cork, was especially active in the field of liturgical revival, composing prayers based on Columba's *Altus Prosator* and on material in the *Book of Deer* which were later incorporated into the Scottish Liturgy of 1912. He also wrote a study of *The Celtic Church in Scotland* (1894) which included a chapter devoted to showing that the Celtic Church had been Episcopalian rather than Presbyterian in government.

Scottish Presbyterians were perhaps not quite so enthusiastic about things Celtic but there were some notable Celtophiles in their ranks. When a new outpost of the Kirk was established in the fashionable West End of London in 1884, the decision was made to dedicate it to St Andrew. However Donald MacLeod, its first minister, who was a Highlander, insisted it be St Columba's 'for the sacred isle of Iona possessed his heart'.[49] He was later commemorated by a rose-shaped window designed by Douglas Strachan showing Columba sitting at his desk and laying down his pen for the last time. Stained glass windows featuring Celtic saints were installed in several other Church of Scotland churches. There is a particularly fine one, dating from the 1880s and depicting Ninian and Patrick alongside King Solomon, Nehemiah and St Peter, in the old Barony Church in Glasgow (now the great hall of Strathclyde University). Some Scottish Presbyterians were anxious to claim that their distinctive traditions expressed continuity with the outlook and practices of the old Celtic Church. Donald Masson's *Vestigia Celtica* (1882), for example, pointed to the special reverence accorded to the Psalms in both early Celtic and contemporary Presbyterian worship and quoted from the Gaelic Psalter to show a living embodiment of the Celtic language of devotion.[50]

In Wales Celtic Christian revivalism continued to run in tandem with nationalism and enthusiasm for the Welsh language. There was some unease in Anglican circles in the middle of the century that the Celtic card was being played by Nonconformists opposed to the 'Saxon bishops' of an alien church. One commentator complained in 1853 that agitators were seeking to rouse 'the dormant jealousy of race, and stirring up the passions of Celt against Saxon'.[51] Henry Richard, ex-Congregational minister and MP for Merthyr Tydfil, who led the campaign for Welsh church disestablishment in Parliament, frequently appealed to the Celtic legacy which he felt Nonconformists represented much more faithfully than Anglicans. Several Welsh Anglicans, troubled by their alien English image, sought to make their church more Celtic. Henry Edwards, Dean of Bangor, argued for the appointment of more 'bishops of Cymric blood' and suggested that only if the Church in Wales acquired a more Celtic feel would Nonconformity lose its grip on the principality.[52]

It was in Ireland that Anglicans most obviously sought to re-create the distinctive features of the early Celtic church. The Church of Ireland was in the van of the movement to incorporate ancient Irish hymns into contemporary worship. 'St Patrick's Breastplate' had first been translated into English by George Petrie in 1839, and appeared in new verse translations in both Todd's *St Patrick* and MacIlwaine's *Lyra Hibernica Sacra* but it was a translation made for a St Patrick's Day service in 1889 by Cecil Frances Alexander, the hymn-writing wife of the Bishop of Derry and Raphoe, that really established it as a popular hymn. New Anglican cathedrals were given dedications to Celtic saints, notably St Fin Barre's in Cork (1870) and numerous Church of Ireland parish churches were dedicated to St Patrick. Some new ones were even built in the style of the ancient monastic churches, notably St Patrick's, Jordanstown, County Antrim, designed by William Henry Lynn from 1865–8, which was given a round tower in conscious imitation of the one at Clonmacnoise and chancel windows depicting Patrick, Brigit, Columba and Comgall. The fashion for reproducing the distinctive motifs of early Celtic ecclesiastical architecture even extended to secular buildings. The English architect E. W. Godwin incongrously perched a replica round tower on the battlements of Dromore Castle in County Limerick in the late 1860s.

Some new Roman Catholic churches were dedicated to Celtic saints, like St Colman's Cathedral in Cobh, begun in 1868, but on the whole the nineteenth-century Irish Catholic Church looked more to Rome and to Continental influences than to its Celtic roots. J. J. O'Riordain has rightly pointed out that it was both less 'Irish' and less 'Catholic' in this period than at any other time in its history.[53] Certain individual priests were conscious of the native Celtic tradition. Anthony Cogan, parish priest in County Meath throughout the middle decades of the century, hankered after the primitive age of lost innocence. However, he identified more with the fugitive priests of the seventeenth and eighteenth centuries than with the sixth- and seventh-century saints.[54] Possibly the early Celtic period did not appeal to nineteenth-century Irish Catholics because it had not produced martyrs and did not chime in with the siege mentality of a church that felt itself isolated and persecuted. Perhaps they cold-shouldered the Celtic tradition simply because it had been so effectively and enthusiastically taken over by the rival Church of Ireland.

The Anglican enthusiasm for Celtic Christian revival in nineteenth-century Ireland was part of a wider assertion of a distinct Anglo-Irish identity by the descendents of the Protestant settlers of the seventeenth century. Like those earlier settlers who had come in the wake of the Anglo-Norman invasions in the twelfth century, they sought to identify themselves with native traditions. In some respects, indeed, like many incomers, they became almost more Irish than the native Gaels, developing a particular fascination with local history and topography and even in some instances claiming kinship with the aristocratic Finnian warriors whose deeds were recorded in epic literature. John Hutchison has pointed out how members of the Anglo-Irish Protestant ascendancy resented being treated condescendingly by the English as colonial cousins and reacted by reasserting Ireland's distinctive contribution to European civilisation and its links with other Celtic cultures. 'Protestants were thus the chief supporters for most of the modern period of antiquarian, archaeological and philological research into the Celtic past, notably through the Royal Irish Academy.'[55] While they could never fully identify with the native Irish, they could venerate a mythical and unhistorical Irish past of mysterious Druids, sturdy peasants and pure, primitive Christians.

As in Wales, Celtic revival in Ireland was also bound up with growing nationalist sentiment in which Protestants as well as Catholics played a part. The golden age of Celtic Christianity was drawn on to provide iconic symbols for the new movements of cultural and political nationalism. Henry MacManus, a member of the Young Ireland Movement, showed a dramatic painting of *The Introduction of Christianity to Ireland* at the 1853 Dublin Exhibition. An accompanying note in the exhibition catalogue contained a lengthy passage about Patrick's association with the shamrock and with Druids. When a competition was announced in 1864 for a public monument to the nationalist leader Daniel O'Connell, one of the entrants, James Cahill, submitted a design for a statue with an octagonal base and radiating pedestals in which Patrick would take his place alongside figures from the pre-Christian era like Ossian. Irish writers called on artists to produce more pictures of Patrick as a national hero and specifically to depict him preaching to the high king at Tara. Although this subject does not seem to have been taken up, the saint's baptism of the King of Munster proved a popular scene with both painters and sculptors. George Mulvany depicted it on canvas in 1845 and forty years later W. H. Byrne carved it on a gravestone in the Catholic cemetery at Glasnevin, Dublin. This particular cemetery seems to have led the trend for using the characteristic Celtic ringed cross as a funerary monument. By the end of the century cemeteries in Scotland as well as Ireland contained many headstones in that style.[56]

In Scotland, Columba was a popular subject for painters and poets and exerted a similar appeal as national hero rather than just as Christian monk and missionary. Romantic portrayals of the saint in the 1870s and 1880s included Robert Gibb's *Columba in Sight of Iona* and *The Death of Columba* and Robert Herdman's *Columba Rescuing a Captive*. John Stuart Blackie, one of the chief promoters of Celtic revival in Victorian Scotland and the moving spirit behind the establishment of the country's first university chair in Celtic at Edinburgh in 1882, fostered the notion of Columba as romantic Gael and cultural icon. His *Lays of the Highlands and Islands* (1872) contained two poems about the saint which described him bringing culture as well as Christianity to the Picts and Scots, having left his native 'land of learning' to converse 'with uncouth people'.[57] This theme was taken up by Robert Brydall's *History of Art in Scotland* (1889) which noted in its opening paragraph that when Columba landed on Iona 'the first symptoms of the dawn of art with that of civilisation began to appear in Scotland'.[58]

The popular appeal of Celtic Christianity was boosted by the growth of interest in folklore. The image of the Celts as a peculiarly spiritual people with a strong feel for the supernatural was confirmed by the publication of collections of tales about fairies, visitations from the other world and manifestations of the second sight. The most assiduous Victorian collector of Gaelic folklore was John Francis Campbell, the Eton-educated laird of Islay, whose *Popular Tales of the West Highlands* (1860–2) and volume of poems about Finn mac Cumaill and other legendary heroes, *Leabhar na Feinne* (1872), both sold well. He inspired others to mine the rich vein of oral Gaelic folk tradition, most notably Alexander Carmichael, who travelled around the Highlands and islands of Scotland between 1855 and 1899 collecting prayers, poems, chants and incantations. The results of his labours, the six volumes of *Carmina Gadelica* published between 1900 and 1971, will be considered in the next chapter. Both Campbell and Carmichael were fired by an almost evangelical enthusiasm to show that the Gaels were not the barbaric savages that they were so often portrayed as being in the predominant Anglo-Saxon culture but rather a highly cultivated and sensitive people. In their understandable desire to right the imbalance they perhaps over-romanticised their subjects and set up idealised models of the spiritual Gael and the visionary Celt. These images inevitably coloured popular perceptions of Celtic Christianity, giving it a more mystical quality, reinforcing the sense that it was closely interweaved with older pagan mythology and generally increasing its romantic aura and appeal.

The Victorian Celtic revival reached its apogee in the 1890s. Although much of its focus was on recovering the myths and legends of the pre-Christian period, Christian themes were also taken up, especially by practitioners in the decorative arts. The distinctive motifs found on illuminated manuscripts and high standing crosses had long been popular among those involved in the arts and crafts movement – William Morris used Celtic initials and interweaving snakes on a cabinet in 1861. In Ireland there was a major revival of Celtic Christian artwork, thanks largely to the activities of two designers, Edmond Johnson and Archibald Knox. Johnson, who came of a long line of Dublin jewellers and silver-smiths, had first become fascinated with the genre when he was given the task of restoring the Ardagh Chalice in 1868 (Plate 9). Struck by the intricacy and novelty of its design, he started making replicas of the most important pieces of early Celtic metalwork, copying old techniques of construction and producing multiple copies for sale. He showed his work

Plate 9. Engraving of the Ardagh Chalice. (Source: M. Stokes, *Early Christian Art in Ireland* (new edn, 1932).)

at the 1892 exhibition of the Arts and Crafts Society of Ireland and the following year at the World's Columbian Exposition at Chicago he exhibited nearly 200 facsimile reproductions of bells, crosiers, Gospel book shrines, chalices and reliquaries, including shrines for Patrick's tooth and Lachtin's arm. The reproductions were on sale in the department stores of Chicago and New York as well as in Dublin and were particularly popular with Irish Americans.

Archibald Knox's interest in Celtic art derived from his upbringing on the Isle of Man which was blessed with a particularly fine group of high standing crosses, catalogued in 1887 by P. M. C. Kermode. He was also deeply influenced by a visit in 1890 to the newly opened National Museum of Ireland in Dublin where the sizeable collection of Celtic artefacts assembled by the Royal Irish Academy was put on permanent display. In the mid-1890s Knox was taken on by the London firm of Liberty and Co. and for the next fifteen years he supplied hundreds of Celtic designs, based on motifs found on crosses and illustrated manuscripts, for Liberty's fabrics, pewter and silverware. His designs appeared on bowls, inkstands, cigarette boxes, mirrors, lampstands, cutlery, clocks and on leather handbags. They were complemented by another Celtic range, known as the 'Cymric line', which was produced in Birmingham.[59]

Celtic Christianity was now chic. Detached from their original ecclesiastical contexts, its distinctive symbols had been secularised and domesticated. Motifs that properly belonged on high standing crosses or liturgical vessels were turning up on dressing tables and in drawing rooms. One of Edmond Johnson's best-selling items was a sugar bowl modelled on the Ardagh Chalice and furnished with tongs suitably decorated with Celtic knotwork. A series of volumes published during the early 1890s on *Celtic Ornament from the Book of Kells* presented Celtic Christian art in the style of the coffee-table books of the later twentieth century, as something to be appreciated more for its aesthetic quality than its deeper theological and spiritual significance. The influential architectural magazine, *The Builder*, carried articles on Celtic ornamentation throughout 1893 and devoted an entire issue to the Celtic crosses on the Isle of Man. It is from this period that the fashion dates of wearing jewellery based on Celtic designs, and especially of pendants and necklaces in the form of Celtic crosses. One of the earliest and the finest of these pendants, now displayed in the Ulster Museum in Belfast, was made in Glasgow in 1893 with a border of shamrocks and interlacing picked out in gold on a cross made of Connemara marble. The most distinctive icon of Celtic Christianity had become a fashion accessory.

Those involved in the literary side of the 1890s Celtic revival drew less inspiration from the Christian tradition. Although they almost all came of Anglo-Irish Protestant stock, several of the most prominent Celtic revivalists eschewed orthodox Christian belief in favour of various forms of mysticism, occultism and nature worship. Their main focus was on recovering pre-Christian and pagan folklore. Indeed, it was a collection of such material culled from old peasant tales and published in 1893 by W. B. Yeats that gave the movement its name, the 'Celtic Twilight'. His latest biographer has encapsulated Yeats' conception of the Celtic tradition as 'non-English, anti-materialistic, anti-bourgeois and connected to Theosophical and Rosicurian symbolism, via Blake and Swedenborg'.[60] Druidism, fairy lore and pre-Christian heroes loomed much larger in this scheme of things than monasteries, hymns and saints. John Hutchison remarks that 'for Yeats the Celtic ideal was personified, above all, by the pagan aristocratic warrior Cuchulain – the man of passions and ungovernable will'.[61] Yeats' first major published work, *The Wanderings of Oisin* (1889) portrayed the legendary meeting between Patrick and Ossian in terms which left no doubt as to where his own sympathies lay. After visiting three magic lands, Ossian returned to an Ireland which, thanks to Patrick's missionary activities, had been diminished and robbed of its joy by the life-denying austerity of Christianity. When Yeats announced in 1897 that 'in an impending annunciation, Celtic spirituality would redeem the world' he was not thinking in Christian terms but rather of the primitive, pastoral paganism of the ancient Irish who had sat watching golden sunsets on primeval evenings, communing with nature in a seer-like trance of inspiration.[62] Although he took themes from the quest for the Holy Grail and the Arthurian legends into his writings, notably in *The Speckled Bird*, it was not their Christian aspects that appealed to him but rather their wider spiritual mystery. Yeats found his spiritual home in esoteric occult movements like Rosicurianism, theosophy and the Hermetic Order of the Golden Dawn which practised ritual magic and sought enlightenment. He was strongly attracted to a heresy associated with a twelfth-century prophet, Joachim of Fiore, who prophesied a New Age, or third reign of heaven on earth, and looked to a new order of Children of the Holy Spirit who would reveal the hidden substance of God. It was artists, poets and other visionaries who would form this new order, not priests and monks from the old world of the church. Indeed, Yeats wrote eagerly of the coming battle 'between the Church and the mystics'.[63]

Others prominently involved in the Celtic Twilight movement also tended to draw more inspiration from Ireland's pagan past than its Christian golden age. Lady Augusta Gregory was more interested in Cuchulain than in Patrick and wrote about *Gods and Fighting Men* rather than about saints. When George Russell wrote under his usual pseudonym of AE in 1895 that Ireland was 'long ago known as the sacred isle', it was the fact that 'the Gods lived there' that he had in mind rather than the more usual association with saints.[64] The quasi-religious Celtic Order set up in 1897, which included Yeats, Russell, Edmund Hunter and Fiona MacLeod, alias William Sharp, among its founder members, did not model itself on the severe penitential disciples and rigorous austerity of Irish monasticism but looked rather to the visionary experiences of the pre-Christian poets, the holiness of the Irish landscape and the heroism of the mythical figures from pagan times.

Not all of those involved in the Celtic revival were interested in esoteric religion and magic. Douglas Hyde, whose *Beside the Fireside: a Collection of Irish Gaelic Folk Stories* (1890) is often taken as marking the beginning of the Irish literary renaissance, remained true to the Anglican faith of his clergyman father. Yet he too was predominantly interested in the mythical pre-Christian folklore of Ireland. His overwhelming concern, expressed in his famous speech in Dublin in 1892 calling for the de-Anglicising of Ireland and the establishment of the Gaelic League in the following year, was with preserving the distinct linguistic and literary culture of Ireland. He was less exercised by the more specifically spiritual qualities of Celtic Christianity. Eoin MacNéill, Hyde's principal ally in the foundation of the Gaelic League, was perhaps more obviously attracted to and influenced by the Christian aspect of the Celtic tradition. He was unusual among the Celtic revivalists in being a Roman Catholic, although like most of them he was not a native Gaelic speaker. His books included a study of Patrick which portrayed the saint in highly idealised terms as the man who by pacifying and uniting the warring tribes and fusing Christian and Celtic culture had brought into being the Irish nation and established the unique blend of sanctity and learning which marked the golden age of Irish civilisation.

Although they were not primarily concerned with recovering and promoting Celtic Christianity, those involved in the Celtic Twilight movement in Ireland did play a significant role in influencing the way that it was perceived. Their writings considerably reinforced existing popular perceptions of Celtic Christianity as being peculiarly susceptible to and interweaved with pagan motifs and as having a special regard for and closeness to the natural world. Hyde's *Literary History of Ireland* (1899) made much of the good relations that existed between Christian saints and Druids. He pointed out that Columba's first teacher had been a Druid and that it was a Druid who prophesied Brigit's birth. Following this syncretist agenda, he hailed the Celtic saints alongside pre-Christian bards as enthusiastic environmentalists and lovers of nature, writing in his *Story of Early Gaelic Literature* (1895) that 'Columkille like Ossian and the Pagan Irish was enthusiastically alive to the beauty of Nature'.[65] MacNeill similarly noted in a study of the characteristics of Irish literature that 'love of nature' had always been a prominent theme, running through early Christian verse as much as pre-Christian poetry.[66]

A similar note was struck by the leading figures in the Celtic Twilight movement in Scotland. As in Ireland, their main focus was on the pre-Christian Celtic tradition but their approach embraced and encouraged a romantic perception of Celtic Christianity. The pan-Celtic consciousness championed by Patrick Geddes, founder of the briefly lived *Evergreen* magazine, had no specifically Christian dimension. However, it made a strong appeal to Protestants as a way of detaching Celticism from Catholicism and presenting it as a kind of north European, or British, movement which in some senses prefigured the Reformation. William Sharp was much more interested in fairy runes and pagan myths than old Christian *lorica* and prayers. His own religious sympathies were shown in the *Pagan Review* which he founded in 1892, and to whose one and only issue he was the sole contributor. He was, however, happy to include poems associated with the Celtic saints, especially those which tended towards pantheism and nature worship, in anthologies of Celtic verse. The enormously popular *Lyra Celtica* which he and his wife put together in 1896 printed 'The Rune of St Patrick' and two of the poems of exile attributed to Columba alongside 'The March of the Faerie Host' and 'The Death Song of Ossian', strongly reinforcing the impression of Celtic Christianity as syncretist in nature and possessing a dreamlike, almost fey character.

The 1890s also saw a renewed interest in Celtic Christianity among many churchmen. Undoubtedly stimulated by the romanticism of the Celtic Twilight movement, this had a more practical side as well. In a development that was to be even more characteristic of Celtic Christian revival in the twentieth century, the Celtic Church came to be seen as a model for the contemporary church to follow. This mixture of romanticism and restorationism can be seen clearly in two developments that took place during the decade in Wales. During work on St David's Cathedral a wooden casket containing two sets of bones was discovered set into a wall. Despite some scepticism among his colleagues, the Dean, William Williams, insisted that they must belong to David and Justinian. He was particularly excited to find David's bones, which had been lost since the Reformation, and put them on prominent display in the Cathedral. Carbon-dating carried out in 1997 has revealed that the bones in fact date from only the eleventh or twelfth century but in the mood of the 1890s they were enthusiastically accepted as belonging to Wales' patron saint.[67] A book published in 1897 shows the other side to the appeal of Celtic Christianity. Annoyed that virtually all histories of the church in the British Isles 'regard the question from the Latin, none from the Celtic, point of view', John Willis Bund, a Worcestershire barrister and amateur historian, wrote *The Celtic Church of Wales* to provide a detailed account of Christianity in Wales before 'the subjugation of the country by the Latin Church'.[68] He put a new spin on the conflict between Celtic and Latin Christianity, which he regarded as a much more 'deadly fight' than that between Christianity and paganism.[69] Essentially, it reflected a struggle between a tribal and an imperial church. The Anglican Church in Wales had opted for the Latin imperial model. Unless it wished to sink into oblivion, Willis Bund advised it to switch to the Celtic tribal model pretty quickly.

Willis Bund was not uncritical of the Celtic fathers. He was uneasy about their apparent flirtation with paganism and noted that the story of Columba invoking the Druids and using pagan incantations at the battle of Culdremne 'brings out the worst side of Celtic Christianity'.[70] In general, however, he admired the slightly anarchic autonomy of the Celtic Church, its resistance to Roman imperialism and its closeness to the people. Its clergy provided a model for Anglican clergy in Wales who needed to 'sink the Church and ecclesiastical theories and become as much one of the villagers as the old Celtic tribal priest had been'.[71] The more that the Church in Wales went on about establishment and its rights and privileges, the more it would drive the Welsh into the arms of Nonconformity which 'comes far nearer the old tribal idea of Celtic Christianity than anything else'.[72] The modern Anglican establishment in Wales was 'not the church of David and Teilo, but of Elizabeth and Laud'. If it wished to survive, it should return to the essentially decentralised, laicised, tribal model of the early Celtic Church in Wales, 'the only independent church, independent of all foreign control, Papal or Royal, that survived in Western Christendom'.[73]

In Scotland, too, there was a rediscovery and celebration of the tribal nature of Celtic Christianity. In many ways it was part of a more general idealisation of the Highlands and their inhabitants. The influence of Macpherson's 'Ossian', the writings of Rénan and Arnold and the Celtic Twilight movement had all played a part in changing the popular perception of the Highlander from half savage barbarian to heroic warrior and sensitive spiritual Gael. More directly, agitation by the crofters for basic rights of security of tenure and fair rents during the early 1880s had won much sympathy for the Highlanders' cause and greatly increased their romantic appeal. Several of those who were prominent in the Celtic revival movement, notably John Blackie and Alexander Carmichael, had given active support to the crofters' campaigns and had their enthusiasm for Celtic culture greatly stimulated in the process. Although the re-discovered (or newly invented) figure of the 'spiritual Gael' had a good deal of pre-Christian heroic mythology in his make-up, there was also an attempt to give him an impeccably Presbyterian pedigree and to suggest that there was, in fact, a distinct Celtic strand running through Highland Christianity from the time of Columba to the present day. One of the first works to develop this thesis was *The Literature of the Highlands*, published in Inverness in 1892 and described by its author, Nigel MacNeill, a Scot in exile in London where he was minister of Bedford Church, as 'the child of the peaceful Highland revolution on which the political and Christian genius of the Right Hon. W. E. Gladstone stamped imperial sanction and approval in the Crofters Act of 1886'.[74]

Rather in the manner of the Celtic revivalists in Ireland with their distinct Anglo-Irish perspective, MacNeill announced himself to be 'an advocate of the just rights and claims of a noble race and an obscure literature' while at the same time remaining 'a lover of the great English people'.[75] He also showed himself to be a true disciple of Rénan, asserting that 'the Celt has been generally very religious'. His most original observation, however, took him away from the romantic syncretism of the Celtic Twilight school. 'The religion of the Gael of Scotland,' he pointed out, 'like that of the Kymry of Wales, whether in ancient or in modern Christian times, has always flourished in an atmosphere of deep severity'. Perhaps because of the 'hard life at a distance from enervating centres of civilisation' experienced by its practitioners, Gaelic religion was characterised by sternness of doctrine and 'earnest heartiness'.[76] MacNeill argued that to some extent Calvinism had its roots in Celtic Christianity and he traced a distinct line of succession from Patrick and Columba to modern Gaelic evangelical bards like Dugald Buchanan in the eighteenth century and Peter Grant in the nineteenth.

MacNeill saw the modern Free Church as being closer to the spirit of the Celtic Church than the established Church of Scotland. Piercing through 'that belt of ecclesiastical darkness which Papal Rome wove round the body of our national life during the four centuries which preceded the Reformation', he found that 'from the days of Ninyas, in the beginning of the fifth century, to the accession of the "Sair Saint", King David, in 1124, a Free Church, comparatively evangelical and aggressive, existed in Scotland for a period of 700 years'.[77] The purity of this golden age of evangelical Christianity had not been fully restored at the Reformation:

> With all the advantages attendant on post-Reformation times, large tracts of our country, once aglow with gospel life, remained practically heathen until the lost ground began to be reconquered and reclaimed by the modern Free Church of Scotland. In all this there is much to humble, instruct and encourage us.[78]

MacNeill was not alone in claiming that the Free Church of Scotland, created after the 1843 Disruption, was the true heir of the Celtic Church. A history of the Free Church published in 1893 made the same point and claimed Columba as its founding father.

A group of Scottish churchmen of a very different persuasion was also looking to the Celtic Christian heritage as a model. In 1895 the Scottish Church Society, recently founded by those on the 'Scoto-Catholic' wing of the established church, held a conference on 'The Divine Life in the Church' in which two prominent Celtophiles gave papers on 'The Celtic Inheritance of the Scottish Church'. Duncan MacGregor, a noted liturgist and Gaelic scholar who hailed from Fort Augustus in the heartland of Gaeldom but ministered at Inverallochy near Fraserburgh in Pictish north-east Scotland, argued that the Celtic Church offered liturgical

riches that the modern Church of Scotland with its rather bare and im-
poverished forms of worship would do well to draw on. In his lecture, he
singled out regular observance of the Scriptural hours of prayer, weekly
celebration of the Eucharist, guidelines for the devotional life of the
clergy and the provision of a native liturgy as characteristics of the
devotional life of the Celtic Church which had been lost in the eleventh
century. Among other elements of the 'sacred deposit' of Celtic Christianity that the national church should now recover he particularly commended the office of soul friend which was 'on the whole, free from the
elements which render the office of Confessor in certain churches offen-
sive to many intelligent and pious people'.[79] MacGregor further suggested that his fellow Presbyterians might derive spiritual benefit from
such Celtic practices as early rising, daily cold baths (he did not specify
whether these should be in the sea in the manner of Cuthbert, Kentigern
and David), frequent genuflections, fasting, abstinence from meat and
intoxicating drink and 'frequent seasons of solitude and silence'. He suggested that the Celtic monastery offered a model of seminary, missionary
institute, collegiate church, hospital, hotel and almshouse and felt that
there was much to be said for the Celts' habit of sending out missionaries
in groups rather than alone. He even felt that there were lessons to
be learned from the Celtic Church's approach to miracle-working but
accepted that 'the mind of the Church is not at present prepared to discuss a subject so abstruse and mysterious'.[80]

MacGregor emphasised the continuity between the Celtic Church and
the contemporary Church of Scotland:

> The modern Kirk of Scotland, whatever be her faults and de-
> ficiencies, is by historic descent, by national position, by actual
> office, the very same church that was founded by St Ninian and
> built up by Saints Buide, Kentigern, Columba, Barehan, Calmonel,
> Marnoch, etc. in precisely the sense in which the river Clyde at
> Glasgow is the same river Clyde that passes Lanark.[81]

Just as all Scotland's Christian inhabitants in the time of these saints
had belonged to a single church without denominational divisions, so
MacGregor felt that in his own time:

> All Scots who receive the gospel should belong to one National
> Scottish Church, and ought not to separate from it on any ground
> whatever, even though they think that in some things it is wholly in
> the wrong. So all English Christians should belong to the historic
> English Church, not because it has this or that kind of government
> or doctrine, but because it is the English Church.[82]

This vision of national ecumenical churches which would end denominational divisions was shared by the other main speaker at the Edinburgh Conference, James Cooper, who was Minister of the East Church of St Nicholas in Aberdeen and a native of north-east Scotland. According to his friend and biographer, Henry Wotherspoon, Cooper underwent a spectacular 'conversion' to Celtic Christianity, which he had previously regarded as 'a barbarous muttering', after becoming Professor of Ecclesiastical History at Glasgow University in 1898. His 'translation from the severe Scandinavianism of Aberdeen to the more Celtic atmosphere of Strathclyde' opened Cooper's eyes to the vitality of the Celtic tradition and 'the exigencies of his Chair of Church History sent him to a thorough study of the Celtic Church and made him conscious of its spiritual splendour and of its extraordinary importance in the evangelisation of Europe'.[83] Wotherspoon also suggests that visits to Ireland, friendship with Celtic enthusiasts like Duncan MacGregor and the influence of the Highland students at Glasgow played a part in effecting Cooper's 'conversion' which was so complete that he forsook the Borders as a holiday resort in favour of Lorn and Badenoch.

In fact, Cooper's address to the 1895 Conference indicates that his enthusiasm for things Celtic pre-dated his move to Glasgow. The theme of his lecture was the Church of Scotland's neglect of the Highlands and Islands, that Celtic region to which it owed such a great debt. Peripheral and poor as they were, the Celts had been the founders not just of Scottish but of British Christianity. Like MacGregor, Cooper called on the modern Church of Scotland to draw much more on its Celtic inheritance, especially in the area of liturgy. He specifically suggested that contemporary use should be made in both public and private worship of Patrick's *Confessio*, Columba's hymns and the Antiphonary of Bangor and mentioned that he had himself translated and used the office of communion of the sick in the *Book of Deer* and celebrated the Liturgy of Dunkeld every Friday in his previous church at Broughty Ferry. He too felt that revival of Celtic Christianity would lead to 'the healing of the divisions in Scottish Christianity on Catholic lines'.[84] Indeed, Cooper's ecumenism went even further than MacGregor's. He was passionately committed to the cause of reuniting the fissured churches in Scotland and set up a Scottish Reconciliation Society to promote that aim. For him, however, this was just the first step in a much bigger scheme of what he called imperial reunion in which all the churches of Great Britain and the Empire would join together on the basis of their common Celtic heritage. In pursuit of this dream, he lobbied a number of Anglican bishops, some of whom were happy to accept the validity of Presbyterian orders, but his call for a union between the established Churches of England and Scotland was never taken seriously by either body.

Cooper had some other rather idiosyncratic suggestions as to how the contemporary church might model itself more closely on its Celtic predecessor. He argued that acting in the spirit of Columba, it should draw more on those of high rank and noble birth and use 'the gifted sons of our nobles and chiefs' to provide both leaders and additional lay helpers to assist parish clergy. He also called for the creation of a network of memorials to Celtic Christianity in the form of replica high crosses which he proposed should be erected in 'the numerous spots which are consecrated by saintly memories' as well as in churchyards and by the wayside:

> There is no fear now of superstition connecting itself with them. They would simply be silent preachers – reminders to the lonely wayfarer of the Saviour's lonelier conflict on the Tree, of His all-victorious love, and of His call to us to be crucified with Him.[85]

Perhaps his most impassioned plea was for the restoration of the Abbey buildings on Iona as a living embodiment of the whole Celtic Christian tradition. He had a vision of it being developed as a theological college, retreat house and school of Celtic art and music. Wotherspoon commented that Cooper's new-found affection for Celtic Christianity came to be focused on his dreams as to what might happen on Columba's isle: 'Iona excited him, and when he talked of it ... the fire burned'.[86]

In reality, Iona symbolised nothing so much as the divided state of the church. Although the Duke of Argyll allowed visiting clergy from both the Epsicopalian and Roman Catholic churches to celebrate services within the walls of the ruined Cathedral, this was strongly opposed by many Presbyterians in the Church of Scotland and Free Church of Scotland who had the only churches on the island. After a visit to Iona in 1869 a Catholic priest lamented that 'no altar was there for the eucharistic sacrifice ... the poor people from the cradle to the grave were living without graces and dying without the blessing of true religion'.[87] In 1888 on the occasion of another Catholic pilgrimage, a reporter from the *Glasgow Daily Mail* noted from his soundings of local opinion that 'it would be safe to say that a plebiscite of the resident population would not have supported the permission given by the Duke of Argyll to hold a service within the ruined walls of the Cathedral'.[88] Episcopalians fared little better. The island's Free Church minister had to be forcibly restrained when Bishop Ewing ended an open-air service in the ruins with a Latin prayer. An islander later challenged the Bishop to say how his ceremonies differed from those of the Papists. Ewing's response 'If you had attended to my prayers you would have perceived a vast difference' was met with the retort 'Then why don't you pray in a language we can understand?'.[89] When Ewing's successor, Alexander Chinnery-Haldane, sought in 1894 to establish a house on the island which would be used as a place of prayer, study, contemplation and daily Eucharistic celebration, the parish minister raised a petition of 114 names against this Episcopalian venture. However, the Duke of Argyll was strongly of the opinion that those visiting Iona should be free to worship in their own way and, persuaded that what Chinnery Haldane had in mind was a place of prayer rather than proselytising, he granted permission for the building of what became known as Bishop's House.

The celebrations on Iona to mark the 1,300th anniversary of Columba's death in June 1897 revealed just how far the major denominations were from finding unity in their common Celtic inheritance. On 9 June two Gaelic and two English services were conducted by the Church of Scotland in the Cathedral, which had been given a temporary roof, 'in thanksgiving for the introduction of the Gospel into our land'. Two hymns attributed to Columba, 'Christ is the World's Redeemer' and 'O God, Thou art the Father', were sung in translations provided for the occasion by Duncan MacGregor, who also gave an address describing Columba as 'the wisest of all the rulers of the Church of Scotland', enthusing about his devotion to Scripture, children and dumb animals and identifying his only weakness as being a special love of the Gael. MacGregor quoted the saint as saying 'My nature is frail, and I am yet carnal; for I cannot help loving the Scots more than any other nation'.[90] Chinnery Haldane led clergy from the Episcopal Church in a separate commemoration on the same day in their new retreat house which was formally handed over into the care of the Society of St John the Evangelist, better known as the Cowley Fathers. The Roman Catholics, whose request to come to the island on 9 June had been turned down, had to be content with a service six days later when 615 pilgrims arrived by steamer for a Pontifical High Mass in the Cathedral ruins. As an ecumenical gesture, the Church of Scotland allowed them the use of its covering and seats without charge. Angus MacDonald, Archbishop of St Andrews and Edinburgh, paid tribute to the Church of Scotland service, which had included a celebration of Communion, told his congregation that they should be grateful that 'a learned and earnest company of our brethren in race, though unhappily separated in creed, visited these sacred ruins' and that 'the Saint's influence had inspired such an outburst of devotional feeling of a form so familiar to Roman Catholics'. He went on to pray that 'this devotion would hasten their knowledge of where the strength of the

Columban church lay'.[91] Reporting in the aftermath of this last service, the *Oban Times* commented: 'A chance for the millennium was missed at Iona last week. Instead of three commemorations of St Columba, why not have had one combined celebration in the ancient fane of Iona?'[92]

Away from Iona, Celticists were commemorating the 1,300th anniversary of Columba's death in a more romantic and less partisan spirit. The Scottish seascape artist, William McTaggart, paying his annual visit to his native Kintyre in June 1897 was moved to paint a picture of the saint arriving from Ireland at Gauldrons Bay near Machrihanish, an area which some historians, in fact, see as a more likely initial landing place than Iona. There is some confusion as to the date of this painting. McTaggart's son-in-law and biographer, James Caw, dated it to 1898 and had no doubt that it was inspired by the 1,300th anniversary celebrations. However, the painting itself, which now hangs in the National Gallery of Scotland, appears to bear the date 1895. Lindsey Errington has suggested that McTaggart probably painted the background then and two years later added the figures in the foreground and the two white sailed ships bearing Columba and his companions. I have chosen *The Coming of Saint Columba* for the cover of this book because I feel it beautifully encapsulates the theme of chasing dreams. McTaggart has Columba arriving in the bay where he himself played as a boy. There is a sense of self-identification with the saint, which is carried into a companion painting, *The Preaching of Saint Columba*. There is also a strong sense of expectancy. Errington suggests that McTaggart had been influenced by Blackie and others who portrayed Columba as bringing culture, learning and art as well as Christianity to Scotland. She also points out that *The Coming of Saint Columba* has strong affinities with another picture painted around the same time entitled *Emigrants Leaving the Hebrides*. Like many of his contemporaries, McTaggart was depressed by the steady drain of young and active Highlanders to the New World, leaving only the old and desolate behind. In depicting Columba's arrival on Scottish shores, with its own confused message of exile and longing as well as of hope and beginnings, he was perhaps expressing his own dream of a new dawning of Celtic civilisation.[93]

Meanwhile in Edinburgh another artist was hard at work creating a rather different image of Columba. William Hole had been commissioned by the Scottish National Portrait Gallery to paint a series of murals illustrating the most significant events in Scottish history. A devout Episcopalian and earnest antiquarian, he chose to devote the first tableau to Columba preaching to the Picts (Plate 10). Hole meticulously researched the subject, giving Columba and his followers proper Celtic

Plate 10. Mural by William Hole of Columba preaching to the Picts. (Source: Scottish National Portrait Gallery.)

tonsures, modelling his crosier on St Fillan's crosier in the collection of the National Museum of Scotland and basing the Picts' weapons and jewellery on artefacts dating from the Bronze Age to the eleventh century. While the result was a jumble of anachronisms – virtually none of the clothes or objects depicted in the mural actually dates from the sixth century – the overall impression was unashamedly contemporary. In the words of a recent commentator:

> The gentle saint has become a symbol of the missionary spirit of the nineteenth century. He is a Victorian, preaching to a group of African villagers his own brand of uncompromising faith. Bridei is broody, but behind stands his wife, a Victorian matriarch, un-willing to take any nonsense from either her husband or Columba.[94]

Hole portrayed Columba in similarly muscular Christian pose alongside the equally manly figures of Ninian, Kentigern, Cuthbert and Aidan in the processional frieze of great figures from Scottish history which he painted in 1898 around the walls of the Gallery's entrance hall. In the same year the saints of Scotland were given a further boost when Pope Leo XIII restored the feast days of Adomnan, Colman, Constantine, Donnan, Drostan, Duthac, Fergus, Fillan, Finan, Machar and Maelrubha and extended to the whole of Scotland the feasts of Kentigern and Ninian which had previously only been celebrated in particular areas.

Those involved in the more mystical and esoteric aspects of the Celtic Twilight movement did not let Columba's anniversary pass without producing their own interpretations of the saint's special significance. In *The Light of the West* (1897) Arthur Goodchild, a poet and playwright who was a close friend of William Sharp, presented Columba alongside St John, Pelagius and Simon Magus as a guardian of 'ancient wisdom'. Goodchild made much of a reference in the *Amra Choluimb Chille* (see pp. 17–18) to the fact that Columba had studied both the Christian Scriptures and 'holy wisdom', a term which he took to embrace a corpus of ancient knowledge derived from classical and mythological sources and also including material from the apocryphal gospels and the Jewish Caballa. He argued that Columba's involvement with this secret knowledge had, like the saint's connections with Glastonbury, been deliberately suppressed by Adomnan and subsequent biographers because of their pro-Roman agenda and contempt for Celtic culture. Now was the time to re-discover and re-apply the ancient bardic and Druidic teachings which had survived in the form of the Celtic Church.

A more orthodox but no less effusive tribute to Columba and the enduring spirit of Celtic Christianity came from the pen of an English clergyman who had no Celtic connections. Samuel Stone, best remembered now for his fine hymn 'The Church's One Foundation', was Rector of the City of London church of All Hallows' On the Wall. He had fallen under the spell of Iona after visiting it while on holiday in Scotland in 1872 and begun writing romantic poems about Columba and his legacy. In 1897 Stone gathered these together in a volume entitled *Lays of Iona*. Noting in his preface that 'any real interest in Iona did not generally exist until late in the nineteenth century', he pointed to the 'late birth or revival of interest in the subject of the Celtic ancestry of the Anglican Church'.[95] He referred approvingly to the work of Bishop Lightfoot and robustly expressed his own view of the Church of England's debt to Iona:

As regards the spirit and heart of religion and the noblest and purest principles of missionary work – however great and real is the debt to the Mission by St Augustine, and however much is owing to earlier British sources of evangelisation – the chief debt of Anglo-Saxon Christianity is due to the Celtic Church and its Fathers. In the highest sense, therefore, the cradle of our branch of the Catholic Church is to be identified with the two holy islands of Iona and Lindisfarne, and with the names of St Columba and St Aidan and their spiritual sons.[96]

Stone felt that many 'peculiarities of the Anglican Church in position and in opinion' could be explained by 'the pure Celtic blood in our spiritual ancestry'.[97] They included the Church of England's equidistance from any form of Presbyterianism or Nonconformity and from later medieval and modern Romanism, the persistent Anglican objection to Papal domination and the principles if not the details of the English Reformation. He offered his poems to 'the sons and daughters of the Catholic Church of England' in the hope that they would help them 'to understand what they owe to the pure patient spirit of the Celtic Church, and to look gratefully to the principal Rock from which they have been hewn'.[98] He was determined to show that Celtic Christianity was not dead but remained alive as a spirit, a tradition and an example. Among its contemporary exemplars he cited the East Enders among whom he had ministered for more than twenty years and whom he eulogised for exhibiting those characteristics of endurance, patience, sincerity and high-mindedness that had been displayed by 'the Celtic Christians of the pre-medieval sort'.[99] In a poem entitled 'The Spirit of the Church From Iona, Or the Union of the Celtic, British and Gregorian Churches in the Anglican Church' he took to task those who argued that the Celtic Church had ceased to have any influence following its defeat at the Synod of Whitby:

> Say not the Celtic Church is gone,
>   Like sunset beam from mountain brow;
> The Celtic soul lives on, lives on,
>   The old pure heart is beating now!

> Nor say the British Church is gone,
>   As dies some legendary lay;
> The British Church lives on, lives on,
>   Saint David's Church is here today!

> Say not Iona's Church is gone,
> As memories die and names decay,
> But sing: The British Church lives on
> With Hers and Austin's here today.[100]

Stone's 1897 anthology contained an extraordinary range of poems testifying to the historical significance of Celtic Christianity and its continuing impact on the life of the contemporary church. 'The Church Planets: A Hymn of the Union of the Ancient Churches of Great Britain and the Churches Colonial and American' traced the 'historic line of light' that had started with Patrick, Columba and Aidan and 'is now extended over the Asian, African, American and Australasian world'.[101] A lengthy hymn in praise of the Northumbrian Church proclaimed that 'Our England thrills yet with the Celtic tread' and, after insisting that 'Iona the recluse, not lordly Rome' should be seen as 'England's nursing mother', concluded with a ringing peroration worthy of 'Land of Hope and Glory': 'Forward, Iona's child, Church-Mother of the free'.[102] A sonnet dedicated to Alexander Chinnery-Haldane rejoiced that the establishment of Bishop's House had erected 'once more an altar by Saint Columb's cell'.[103] Other poems eulogised Iona as 'A second Bethlehem, second Nazareth' and repeated the island's name in a way that anticipates some of the songs of the 1990s rock group Iona.[104] Stone's constant refrain, perhaps articulated most clearly in his poem 'Lyric of Iona Past, And to Be' was that Iona would be the centre of a great Christian revival:

> Jesus, Iona waits Thy will!
> Till light upon her smiles;
> Waits, too, in silence dark and chill
> The multitude of Isles:
> Till she may wake their choral throng
> To join her own adoring song.[105]

Two years after the publication of these poems, in the very last year of the nineteenth century, the Duke of Argyll relinquished ownership of all the ecclesiastical buildings on Iona and handed them over to a trust linked to the Church of Scotland. It was charged to re-roof and restore the Abbey Church so that it could be used for public worship and to preserve and where appropriate restore the other buildings. The trustees were also enjoined to allow all branches of the Christian Church to hold services within the restored Cathedral. It was an appropriate curtain-raiser to a century that was to see Iona become the focus both of unprecedented ecumenical activity and also of yet another Celtic Christian revival.

NOTES

1. *Fifeshire Journal*, 11 September 1851.
2. See J. Leerssen, 'Celticism', in Brown, *Celticism*, and P. Sims-Williams, 'The Visionary Celt: the Construction of an Ethnic Preconception', *Cambridge Medieval Celtic Studies*, No. 11, Summer 1996.
3. Rénan, *Poetry*, p. 45.
4. Ibid., p. 41.
5. Ibid., pp. 39, 46.
6. Ibid., p. 9.
7. Arnold, *The Study*, p. 11.
8. Ibid., p. 7.
9. Ibid., p. 71.
10. Ibid., p. 100.
11. Ibid., pp. 177–8.
12. Ibid., p. 178.
13. M. Camille, 'Domesticating the Dragon: The Rediscovery, Reproduction and Re-Invention of Early Irish Metalwork', in Edelstein, *Imagining*, p. 11.
14. Ibid., p. 7.
15. W. Perry, *Alexander Penrose Forbes* (SPCK, London, 1939), p. 158.
16. Skene, *Celtic Scotland*, p. vi.
17. Ibid., p. 418.
18. Forbes, *Kalendars*, p. 1.
19. G. Campbell, *Iona* (Strahan, London, 1870), p. 41.
20. Bieler, *Life and Legend*, p. 17.
21. W. B. Scott, *Collected Poems* (Longmans, Green, London, 1875), p. 158. I owe this reference to Paul Hewison of the English Department, University of Aberdeen.
22. D. McCallum, *The History of the Culdees* (John Menzies, Edinburgh, 1855), p. 76.
23. Ibid., p. 99.
24. Ibid., pp. 105–6.
25. R. W. Morgan, *The British Kymry* (I. Clarke, London, 1857), p. vi.
26. Ibid., p. vii.
27. T. Walsh, *History of the Irish Hierarchy* (New York, 1856), p. vi.
28. W. H. Harding, *Narrative in Proof of the Uninterrupted Consecrational Descent of the Bishops of the Church of Ireland* (Longmans, Green, London, 1869), p. iv.
29. J. Heron, *The Celtic Church in Ireland* (Service & Paton, London, 1898), p. 358.
30. Ibid., p. 358.
31. Ibid., p. 360.
32. D. Moran, *Essays on the Origin, Doctrines and Discipline of the Early Irish Church* (James Duffy, Dublin, 1864), p. vi.
33. Ibid., p. 2.
34. Ibid., p. 2.
35. Ibid., p. 70.
36. Ibid., p. 10.
37. Ibid., pp. 10, 200.

38. Sharpe, *Adomnan*, p. 97.
39. C. de Montalembert, *St Columba, Apostle of Caledonia* (William Blackwood, Edinburgh, 1868), p. 146.
40. Ibid., p. 147.
41. W. Ross, *Aberdour and Inchcolme* (David Douglas, Edinburgh, 1885), p. 58.
42. Stokes, *Ireland and the Celtic Church* (Hodder & Stoughton, London, 1886).
43. Lightfoot, *Leaders*, p. 9.
44. Ibid., p. 5.
45. Ibid., p. 12.
46. G. R. Eden and F. C. MacDonald, *Lightfoot of Durham* (Cambridge University Press, 1932), p. 98.
47. S. Baring Gould, *The Lives of the Saints* (John Hodges, London, 1877), Vol. 1, pp. vii–viii.
48. Payton, *Cornwall*, p. 61.
49. Typescript in possession of family. I am grateful to Tom Davidson Kelly, minister of Govan Old Church, Glasgow, for this reference.
50. D. Masson, *Vestigia Celtica: Celtic Footprints in Philology, Ethics & Religion* (Maclachlan & Stewart, Edinburgh, 1882), pp. 48–9.
51. M. Cragoe, 'A Question of Culture: The Welsh Church and the Bishopric of St Asaph', *Welsh History Review*, Vol. 18, No. 12, December 1996, p. 238.
52. Ibid., p. 243.
53. J. J. O'Riordain, *Irish Catholics* (Veritas, Dublin, 1980) p. 64.
54. A. P. Smyth, *Faith, Famine & Fatherland in the Irish Midlands* (Four Courts Press, Dublin, 1992), p. 117.
55. Hutchison, *The Dynamics*, p. 216. See also J. C. Beckett, *The Anglo-Irish Tradition* (Faber, London, 1976), pp. 102–10.
56. Sheehy, *The Rediscovery*.
57. Errington, *William McTaggart*, p. 111.
58. Ibid., p. 112.
59. See Edelstein, *Imagining*, pp. 44–64 (on Knox) and pp. 106–22 (on Johnson).
60. Foster, *Yeats*, p. 129.
61. Hutchison, *The Dynamics*, p. 61.
62. Foster, *Yeats*, p. 186.
63. Ibid., p. 247.
64. Article in *The Irish Theosophist* quoted in *Circles* (Theosophical Society of Scotland), No. 21, Spring 1995, p. 8.
65. D. Hyde, *The Story of Early Gaelic Literature* (Fisher Unwin, London, 1895), p. 148.
66. J. MacNeill, 'Characteristics of Irish Literature', *Gaelic Journal*, Vol. 5, 1894, p. 76.
67. *The Times*, 1 March 1997.
68. J. W. Bund, *The Celtic Church of Wales* (Nutt, London, 1897), pp. 1–2.
69. Ibid., p. 5.
70. Ibid., p. 25.
71. Ibid., p. 509.
72. Ibid., p. 510.
73. Ibid., p. 515.

156   *Celtic Christianity*

74. N. MacNeill, *The Literature of the Highlands* (John Noble, Inverness, 1892), p. vi.
75. Ibid., p. vii.
76. Ibid., p. 10.
77. Ibid., p. 72.
78. Ibid., p. 72.
79. *The Divine Life of the Church* (Scottish Church Society Conference 2nd Series), Vol. II (Edinburgh, 1895), p. 38.
80. Ibid., p. 42.
81. Ibid., p. 26.
82. Ibid., p. 44.
83. Wotherspoon, *James Cooper*, p. 321.
84. *The Divine Life of the Church*, p. 21.
85. Ibid., p. 15.
86. Wotherspoon, *James Cooper*, p. 321.
87. MacArthur, *Iona*, p. 192.
88. Ibid., p. 192.
89. Ibid., p. 193.
90. D. MacGregor, *St Columba: A Record and a Tribute* (J. Gardner Hitt, Edinburgh, 1897), p. 65.
91. J. McCaffrey, 'The Roman Catholic Church in the 1890s: Retrospect and Prospect', *Scottish Church History Society Records*, Vol. XXV, Part 3 (1995), p. 436.
92. D. P. Thompson, *Iona to Ardnamurchan* (Blackwood, Edinburgh, 1956), p. 3.
93. Errington, *William McTaggart*, pp. 105–12; J. Caw, *William McTaggart: A Biography and Appreciation* (Glasgow, 1917), p. 270.
94. Laing, *Celtic Britain*, pp. 179–80. For the background to Hole's murals, see H. Smailes, *A Portrait Gallery for Scotland* (Trustees of National Galleries of Scotland, Edinburgh, 1985), pp. 49–60.
95. S. J. Stone, *Lays of Iona and Other Poems* (Longmans, Green, London, 1897), pp. i, xvii.
96. Ibid., p. xix.
97. Ibid., p. xix.
98. Ibid., p. xx.
99. Ibid., p. xxii.
100. Ibid., pp. 6, 10.
101. Ibid., p. 72.
102. Ibid., pp. 88–9.
103. Ibid., p. 101.
104. Ibid., pp. 38–9.
105. Ibid., p. 41.

5

The golden evening brightens in the west

Romanticism and the rise of critical scholarship 1900–60

There have been two significant Celtic Christian revivals in the twentieth century. The first two decades saw a continuation of the late Victorian Celtic Twilight movement, its romanticism scarcely tempered by the rise of a new more critical Celtic scholarship. The last two decades have witnessed a new revival which is the subject of the next chapter.

The century opened with the publication of the first volume of a work which has probably done more than anything else to colour modern perceptions of Celtic Christianity and enhance its popular appeal. Alexander Carmichael's *Carmina Gadelica* has certainly been ransacked more than any other single source for paperback anthologies of Celtic prayers and blessings. It strongly reinforced the image of Celtic Christianity as a gentle, 'green', poetic and pagan-friendly inculturation of the Gospel with a particular emphasis on notions of presence, immanence and closeness to the next world. Many of the poems in the *Carmina* invoked the Celtic saints, particularly the familiar trio of Patrick, Brigit and Columba, and portrayed them almost as living figures who could be called and relied on to help solve everyday problems and chores, such as healing a sick cow, curing sickness or blessing the milking.

Unlike many of those who have been attracted by Celtic Christianity, Carmichael came from within the Gaelic world. Born on the island of Lismore, he was a native Gaelic speaker and came from a family that claimed connections with the church established by Moluag, a saint from the golden age said to have been a contemporary of Columba. Carmichael's job as an exciseman checking up on illicit whisky production in the Highlands and islands, while giving him a marvellous opportunity to travel through the remoter reaches of the Gaeltach, might have been expected to put him at a distance from the native inhabitants whose stories and poems he was so keen to note down for posterity. In fact, he seems to have achieved a close rapport with the crofting and fishing communities. A strong supporter of the crofters' cause, he told a friend that his work collecting Gaelic folklore was inspired by a determination to 'show to the world that our dearly beloved people were not the rude, barbarous, creedless, godless, ignorant men and women that prejudiced writers have represented them'.[1]

Carmichael was particularly interested in the religious component of the Gaelic oral folk tradition. Prayers, invocations and blessings dominated the first two volumes of his published collection, the only ones which he himself edited and which appeared in his lifetime. He had an interest in comparative religion and found themes in Hebridean art and verse which he felt were closer to the Indian religious tradition than to that of the West. On close terms with leading members of the Celtic Revival movement, notably J. S. Blackie, he was also sympathetic to the ecumenical endeavours of James Cooper and deplored the fissiparous tendencies in Scottish Protestantism and the bigoted nature of Highland Calvinism. There has been much debate among modern scholars as to how far Carmichael brought these preconceptions and prejudices into his work and fabricated an idealised version of Celtic Christianity that was altogether more syncretistic, eirenic, ecumenical and poetic than the actual raw material he collected. Some have argued that he was guilty of considerable distortion, along the same lines as that practised by his friend, Marjory Kennedy Fraser, who turned the rough working chants of Hebridean fishermen into florid Edwardian art songs. Hamish Robertson believes that there are strong parallels between the *Carmina Gadelica* and James Macpherson's 'Ossian': 'What Macpherson achieved for the fame of the ancient Gaelic bard, Carmichael would achieve for the ancient Gaelic cleric'.[2] Specifically, he accuses Carmichael of deliberately archaizing the language of poems to make them seem older than they actually were, ironing out their roughness to give them a spurious literary polish and allowing his aversion to Calvinism and interest in Eastern religion to distort their indigenous character 'by ascribing Gaelic sacred lore to all but the Scottish Presbyterian tradition, and by making that journey in the imagination to India which is still the pastime of Celtic scholars'.[3]

Other scholars have been kinder to Carmichael. John Lorne Campbell, while agreeing that the *Carmina* should be taken as 'a literary and not as a literal presentation of Gaelic folklore', refused to see them as an exercise in fabrication and deception.[4] In the absence of Carmichael's working notebooks, or any other independent record of his sources, it is difficult to be certain how far he doctored the oral material that he collected to fit in with any of his own feelings or to improve its poetic quality. He may well have tidied up and 'improved' poems to make them more appealing and, perhaps, to emphasise the distinctive rhythms and repetition that give the almost liturgical flavour which has helped to make them so popular for use in churches. It may also be the case that his romantic outlook did sometimes get the better of scholarly detachment, as when he claimed that some of the Gaelic material which he was gathering in the late nineteenth century went back to the golden age of the fifth and sixth centuries. His remark in the preface to the first volume of the *Carmina* that 'some of the hymns may have been composed within the cloistered cells of Derry and Iona' was itself anachronistic.[5] There were no cloisters in the monasteries of Iona or Derry in the time of Columba and his followers. Indeed, there were no stone buildings of any kind. Iona got its first cloisters with the coming of the Benedictines in the twelfth century. The notion of a sacred deposit of religious poetry, originally dating from the golden age of Celtic Christianity and still surviving largely unchanged after nearly one a half millenia of oral transmission from generation to generation, however appealing, is difficult to sustain. The written prayers and poems which survive from the early period are on the whole very much starker and darker in tone, more centred on the themes of sin and judgement and less affirmative of the natural world than the altogether gentler verses found in the *Carmina*.[6]

Carmichael may also have perpetrated, or perpetuated, another mistruth in asserting that the Celtic tradition had all but been knocked out by Protestant Reformers, first at the Reformation and then, more effectively, by the 1843 Disruption, and in seeing the gloomy, world-denying Calvinism of the modern Highlands and islands as fundamentally inimical to the spirit of Columba and his contemporaries. In an interesting and unusual identification of common ground between the Celtic and Roman churches, he wrote that 'the Reformation movement condemned the beliefs and cults tolerated and assimilated by the Celtic Church and the Latin Church'.[7] It is surely significant that although Carmichael was assisted in his labours by Alexander Stewart, parish minister of Onich in Lochaber, and George Henderson, a future Church of Scotland minister, his greatest helper in collecting Gaelic prayers and incantations was Father Allan MacDonald, Roman Catholic priest on Eriskay, a man described by Marjory Kennedy Fraser as 'the gentle enthusiast, the kindly priest, the sympathetic pastor and Celtic dreamer'.[8] Carmichael was scathing about the damage and destruction done to the Celtic tradition by Presbyterian ministers and repeatedly pointed out how much easier it was to find material surviving from it in the Catholic southern Hebrides than the fiercely Protestant islands of Lewis and Harris. There is no doubt that the Catholic islands were repositories of a gentler and more mystical Gaelic culture. Whether this was necessarily closer to the Christianity of Columba's day than the harder evangelicalism of the more northerly isles, however, is a moot point. There are grounds for arguing that the distinctive legacy of Celtic Christianity is to be found just as much in the austerity and simplicity of the religious life of Free Presbyterians on Lewis as in the more lyrical and colourful celebration of the faith by the Catholics of Barra.[9]

Other popular perceptions about Celtic Christianity were reinforced in the pages of the *Carmina Gadelica*. Many of its poems seemed to blend pagan and Christian imagery, a feature which Carmichael himself singled out as being particularly characteristic of Celtic Christian mission: 'The Celtic missionaries allowed the pagan stock to stand, grafting their Christian cult thereon.'[10] This impression was reinforced by the close juxtaposition of pagan charms and Christian prayers. With so much of its contents drawn from the remote Outer Isles on the very edge of Britain, the *Carmina* also contributed to the sense of Celtic Christianity as essentially peripheral. The notion of a faith being lived out on the margins was reinforced by Carmichael's moving descriptions of the Hebridean people going down to the sea-shore to chant their prayers much in the way that Columba, Cuthbert and David had chanted the psalms. The *Carmina* encouraged a view of the Scottish Highlands and islands as a remote region of mystical (and misty) spirituality. The image that it fostered of the spiritual Gael was further enhanced by the publication of Marjory Kennedy Fraser's *Songs of the Hebrides* in 1909.

The format of the *Carmina* as a readily accessible anthology of poems and prayers in English also had a significant impact on the popular appeal and perception of Celtic Christianity. Previous texts from Celtic sources had appeared in more forbidding formats, sometimes only in their original Gaelic, Welsh or Latin and mostly in the rather cramped pages and limited print-runs of academic editions and publications of learned societies. The earliest volumes of the *Carmina* did not achieve large sales but they established the literature of Celtic Christianity as a user-friendly treasure trove of accessible and uplifting poems, prayers and blessings which could be dipped into for pleasure and spiritual profit. This 'pick and mix' quality was to become one of its most appealing features. It also encouraged a view of the Celtic Christian tradition as being as much a cultural as a religious phenomenon. The *Carmina* confirmed what Celticists like Douglas Hyde had already asserted in more critical and analytical works – that Celtic Christianity had given birth to a unique and rich body of prose and verse which had a high literary quality quite apart from its spiritual merit.

Just six years after the first volume of Carmichael's collection appeared, Hyde brought out a very similar anthology of material collected in Ireland. Like the early volumes of the *Carmina*, Hyde's *Religious Songs of Connacht* was part of a general collection of Gaelic folklore and formed a companion to an earlier work, *The Love Songs of Connacht*. Unlike Carmichael, Hyde was not a Gael but he was fired by a similar desire to vindicate the Celts from English criticism and condescension. He too spent many years collecting prayers, charms, blessings and curses that had been transmitted orally for generations and had never before appeared in print. Like Carmichael, he felt that he had only just been in time to rescue the last remnants of a great oral Celtic tradition which, in Ireland's case, had been all but killed off both by Protestantism and by the imposition of the English language. He noted bitterly that the religious poems he had collected and published 'have never lived on in any spot where the English language has been substituted for the Irish ... The English speakers have no welcome for the old religious poems, and they have never "put English on them" as they used often to do with the love songs'.[11] Good Protestant that he was, Hyde acknowledged that 'the old church' had given the Irish 'more to believe than did the new churches' and he approvingly quoted the words of several Catholic priests lamenting Protestant mockery of old people reciting 'the ancient Irish prayers and the old religious poems that had come down to them, perhaps, from the time of St Patrick'.[12] He paid the usual tribute to the natural spirituality of the Celts, introducing his collection with the statement: 'A pious race is the Gaelic race. The Irish Gael is pious by nature. He sees the hand of God in every place, in every time and in every thing. There is not an Irishman in a hundred in whom is the making of an unbeliever'.[13] While identifying a continuous tradition of religious verse running from the seventh to nineteenth century, he also made a point of noting the diversity and variety of the material in his anthology, with prayers, stories and poems 'all mixed together ... just as I myself got them from the mouths of the shanachies and old people'.[14]

An influential study of *The Literature of the Celts* published in 1902 put a similar emphasis on the literary aspects of the Celtic Christian tradition. Its author, Magnus MacLean, a lecturer at Glasgow Technical College, presented the age of the saints as the starting point of a great literary tradition. Chapters on 'St Patrick, the pioneer of Celtic writers' and 'St Columba and the dawn of letters in Scotland' were followed by explorations of Adomnan and the *Book of Deer*, and only after these opening chapters on Christian material were such topics as the mythological and heroic cycles considered. Although MacLean felt that the very best of Celtic literature was to be found in the pre-Christian era, he recognised Patrick and Columba as bards of considerable talent and acknowledged that they had been chiefly responsible for the awakening of literary as well as religious sensibilities in Ireland and Scotland. Since their time there had been a steady decline. Unlike in English literature, where there was a clear developing tradition and progress towards ever better things, 'the Celts produced their best literature first'.[15] Mass emigration and the effects of Anglicisation had left only a tiny remnant of demoralised Celts and effectively put paid to the dreams still entertained by some of laying the foundations of a new Celtic civilisation. Although he blamed Protestantism for destroying aspects of the Celtic tradition, MacLean praised the churches of the Highlands and islands for keeping alive the Gaelic language in their services and noted that virtually all the Gaelic printed literature of the eighteenth and nineteenth centuries had been religious in nature: 'Christianity, through its medium, the Church, besides saving the soul of a departing oral literature, has been the fruitful spring and inspiration of much that is beautiful, pure, and enduring in our Gaelic heritage'.[16]

Three popular anthologies of Celtic verse, all of which began their selections with poems from the golden age of the saints, appeared in the 1910s. The first, *Selections from Ancient Irish Poetry*, was put together in 1911 by Kuno Meyer, who had just completed twenty years in the Department of Teutonic Languages at University College, Liverpool, and was about to take up the Chair of Celtic at Berlin University. The following year Eleanor Hull produced *The Poem Book of the Gael*. Decorated with initials from the Lindisfarne Gospels, it included Irish, Scottish and Welsh poems from the sixth century onwards. The opening section was devoted to extracts from the *Saltair Na Rann*, 150 poems in imitation of the psalms attributed to Oengus the Culdee, and a later section on early Christian poems included the first appearance in verse of 'Be thou my vision'. In 1917 A. P. Graves published *A Celtic Psaltery*, a compilation of 'translations from Irish Scotch Gaelic and Welsh poetry of a serious character' in which 'lays of the Irish saints' and 'lays of monk and hermit' rubbed shoulders with Welsh poems from the *Book of Carmarthen*, eighteenth century evangelical hymns from the Highlands and verses from the *Carmina Gadelica*.[17]

These anthologies reinforced the sense of a continuous tradition of Celtic Christian verse as well as further confirming the image of the

Gaels as an especially spiritual people. Relatively recent compilations stood side by side with ancient texts. The implication was that the actual date of a particular poem did not very much matter. This point was taken up by Eleanor Hull in the introduction to her selection. Discussing a poem the dating of which had been the subject of much dispute, she commented: 'Whether it came to us from the sixth century or from the sixteenth ... it would equally move us'.[18] The effect a poem had was far more important than its provenance. She also defended the apparently unbalanced nature of her anthology which was almost entirely made up of verses on the themes of religion and love. The fact was that this reflected the nature of the Gael, whose character was revealed through a literature which blended 'poetry and fact, dreams and realities, exact detail and wild imagination'.[19]

One particular theme was highlighted in these anthologies and in other critical works that appeared in the early part of the twentieth century. This was the strong affirmation of the natural world found in early Celtic Christian verse. We have already noted the identification of this characteristic of Celtic Christianity by Douglas Hyde and Eoin MacNeill in the 1890s (p. 141). In the following decade it received increasing attention and came to be associated especially with the so-called hermit poems dating from the ninth and tenth centuries but attributed to early Celtic monks (see p. 33). In 1901 Kuno Meyer brought out an edited translation of one of the most striking poems in this cycle, the colloquy between King Guaire of Aidne and his brother Marban, the hermit. Later, in the preface to his 1911 anthology, he enthused:

> In nature poetry the Gaelic muse may vie with that of any other nation. Indeed, these poems occupy a unique position in the literature of the world. To seek out and watch Nature, in its tiniest phenomena as in its grandest, was given to no people so early and so fully as the Celt.[20]

Eleanor Hull was similarly taken with this aspect of early Irish religious verse. In her *Text Book of Irish Literature* (1906) she described the colloquy between Guaire and Marban as 'The Poetry of Nature' and in the preface to *The Poem Book of the Gael* she enthused about the Irish monk's closeness to nature:

> His joy in nature grew with his loving association with her moods. He refused to mingle the idea of evil with what God had made so good ... Amongst his feathered and furred associates, he read his Psalms and Hours in peace; sang his periodic hymn to St Hilary

and St Brigit, and performed his innumerable genuflexions and 'cross vigils'.[21]

That passage contains the germs of several ideas that were to play an important role in the later twentieth century love affair with Celtic Christianity. It suggests that the Celtic Church had a strongly Pelagian strain, believing in the essential goodness rather than the fallenness of creation and being much less hung up on sin than other churches have been. Another passage in the preface to Eleanor Hull's anthology, describing early Celtic Christian poetry as 'wholly joyous', confirms this world-affirming theme.[22] Then there is the specific association with animals and the portrayal of early Irish monks enjoying a particularly close relationship with the non-human part of God's creation.

The uniqueness and significance of what came to be called Irish nature poetry was further explored in three much-quoted studies in the early 1930s. In an article written in 1931 Gerard Murphy argued that it had specifically Celtic Christian origins: 'A mass of evidence seems to point to the monks and hermits of the first Christian ages as the founders of the Irish nature tradition'.[23] He concluded that this distinctive genre was the product of a particular Celtic theology of creation combined with a high degree of education, literary appreciation and the special circumstances of the monastic life. Murphy's thesis was further developed by Robin Flower in a series of lectures delivered in Ireland between 1932 and 1935. Flower linked the emergence of nature poetry to the rise of the anchorite movement in eighth and ninth century Ireland and saw it as an expression of the spirituality of the hermits in their desert places:

> These retreats were on islands, in the depths of woods, or by the borders of rivers; and from their close communion with nature while in the exalted state of contemplation the anchorites developed the exquisite poetry of intense personal religion and close observation of natural things which is the most beautiful product of the European literature of the time.[24]

The third and most comprehensive study of this subject was by Kenneth Jackson, fellow of St John's College, Cambridge, who devoted a whole book to early Celtic nature poetry in 1935. He gave pride of place in it to what, following Flower, he called 'hermit poetry'. The distinguishing marks of this particular genre, he suggested, were 'the solitary hermitage in the wilderness, the life of ascetic purity and humble piety, the spare diet of herbs and water, and the companionship of wild creatures'.[25] Jackson felt that for the Irish hermit:

The very existence of nature was a song of praise in which he himself took part by entering into harmony with nature … It was from
this harmony with nature, this all-perceiving contemplation of it,
that the Irish hermits reached to a more perfect unison with God.[26]

The work of Jackson and his academic colleagues did much to promote
the appeal of early Irish religious verse and to confirm the idealised
picture of solitary hermits living in close communion with nature. Other
scholars, however, took a more sceptical line and sought to debunk some
of the more romantic notions that were growing up about the Celtic
Church. One of the first salvoes in the academic counter-attack against
the excesses of the Celtic Twilight school had been fired in 1896 when
Robert Atkinson, Professor of Comparative Philology at Trinity College,
Dublin, dismissed early Irish literature as 'so much of mere metrical saw-
dust and technical scaffolding, so many pages taken up with genealogical
fact and speculation, such an amount of problematical scriptural history'.[27] When he repeated his comments before the Irish Intermediate
Education Commission in 1898, the Gaelic League rallied a posse of
Celtic scholars, including two leading Continental experts, Heinrich
Zimmer, Professor of Celtic Philology at Berlin, and Ernst Windisch,
Professor of Sanskrit at Leipzig who had worked on Irish texts, to the
defence of the genre. Kuno Meyer published his translation of *The King
and The Hermit* in 1901 partly to rebut Atkinson's accusation and show
the quality of Irish religious verse.

Continental scholars working on early Celtic texts generally adopted
a more rigorous and cautious approach than their British counterparts.
In 1901 an article by Zimmer on the Celtic Church in Ireland provoked
considerable consternation by casting doubt on the historicity of Patrick
and suggesting that *Patricius* was simply the name by which Palladius
came to be known in Ireland. Another German scholar, J. von Pflugh-
Harttung, questioned Patrick's authorship of the *Confessio*. However,
Zimmer was quite happy to join in the general idolisation of the Celtic
Church as a model of proto-Protestant independence:

> The spirit which animated the Celtic clerics at the end of the sixth
> century differed greatly from that of the representatives of the
> Roman Church … On the one side we find a striving for individual
> freedom and personal Christianity, on the other hand a bigoted zeal
> for rigid uniformity and systematizing. The Celt emphasizes a
> Christianity pervading life and deeds, while with the Roman
> Catholic the observance of a formal Christianity is the chief and
> foremost aim.[28]

Perhaps the most prolific Continental scholar working in the field of Celtic Christianity in the early twentieth century was Louis Gougaud, a Benedictine monk who came originally from Brittany. The most influential of his six books and more than 200 articles in scholarly journals was almost certainly *Les Chrétienés Celtiques*, published in Paris in 1911 and translated into English in 1932. It took Rénan to task for idealising the pagan Celts and suggesting they were a naturally religious and sensitive people. On the contrary, Gougaud found them to be 'violent and barabarous ... with beliefs marked by a crude naturalism and utterly devoid of moral character, with minds held captive and enslaved under the tyrannical rule of society. There is nothing in all this to denote a race peculiarly adapted to Christianity'.[29]

Critical scholarship was not just confined to the Continent. In Britain, too, a number of academics were turning their attention to early Celtic Christian history and literature and finding that the reality was not quite as clear-cut or certain as more romantic Celticists made out. They were helped by the publication of critical editions of several major sources, including *Thesaurus Palaeohibernicus*, an important collection of Irish material edited by Whitley Stokes (1901-3), the *Martyrology of Oengus* (1905) and the *Stowe Missal* (1906). In 1905 J. B. Bury, Regius Professor of Modern History at Cambridge, turned his attention from the Roman Empire to write what is generally taken to be the first modern study of Patrick. It acknowledged the considerable problems involved in establishing the saint's historicity. In 1910 another important revisionist work on the Irish saints appeared in the form of Charles Plummer's *Vitae Sanctorum Hiberniae*. The author, who was Chaplain of Corpus Christi College, Oxford, and had previously worked on Bede and the *Anglo-Saxon Chronicles*, was particularly interested in Irish hagiography which he approached with a sceptical eye. He suggested that the Celtic saints might not have been quite as pure and holy as they had been taken to be and noted 'the frequency with which Irish saints distribute curses' which he found to be 'remarkable in persons with a reputation for holiness'.[30] More fundamentally, Plummer argued that the miracle stories which dominated the *Vitae* of the Irish saints had been borrowed almost entirely from pre-Christian and pagan sources. Other supernatural elements in the stories of the saints' lives were explained away in similar terms. References to appearances of heavenly light were taken from pagan solar cults and angelic apparitions were based on visitations by fairies. This exercise in demythologising the saints stripped them of their charismatic qualities and their mystical, supernatural aura and took them back almost where they had been before the first great wave of hagiography and Celtic Christian revival in the late seventh century.

A book which appeared the following year by Charles Plummer's brother Alfred, who was also an Anglican priest and an Oxford don, threw more cold water on the enthusiasms of Celtic revivalists in the Church of England. *The Churches in Britain Before AD 1000* pointed out that the English Church and the British Church were two very different entities, a fact that was often conveniently overlooked in the desire to show that the Church of England 'is, and ought to be, independent of the Church of Rome'.[31] Alfred Plummer believed that the role of missionaries from 'the Scottish Church of Iona' in converting the English to Christianity had been greatly exaggerated. While he conceded that Aidan was a more attractive figure than Augustine, he felt that there was no getting around the fact that 'Augustine was an apostle, and that Aidan was not'.[32] Unlike more romantically inclined contemporaries, Plummer believed in going by results:

> When we are considering the respective claims upon our gratitude which can be urged for Augustine and for Aidan, or (as it perhaps better to say) for the Roman Church and for the Keltic – the important thing to remember is, which system, in the end, swallowed up the other … It was the Roman type of Christianity, and not the Keltic, which became dominant in England.[33]

He also left his readers with the distinct impression that this was a good thing and that the Celts only had themselves to blame for their eclipse. The Roman missionaries had been first in the field, and 'the Keltic bishops in Wales refused to help them'.[34] While accepting that 'it would perhaps be an exaggeration to call it a barbarous form of Christianity', Plummer felt fully justified in describing Celtic Christianity as 'rude and simple in the extreme'.[35] Had 'the insular and stagnant influences of the Keltic Churches' prevailed, English Christianity would have been cut off from the culture and civilisation represented by 'the healthy influences of the Continent, and especially of Rome'.[36]

These strictures did little to stem the enthusiasm felt by a growing number of Anglicans for recovering what they took to be their Celtic roots. Celtic Christian revivalism was especially buoyant in Cornwall where it marched hand in hand with Anglo-Catholicism. The Cornish Celtic Society, formed in 1901, offered a heady mixture of local patriotism, expressed predominantly through renewed interest in the Cornish saints, liturgical revival and an almost pantheistic approach to nature. Its leading light, L. C. Duncombe Jewell, described the Celtic heritage as 'the love of poetry and colour, the pilgrimage of dreams, the pageant of nature'.[37] D. H. Lawrence lauded the Cornish for their special spirituality: 'They have never been Christian in the blue-eyed, or even the truly Roman, Latin sense of the word. But they have been overlaid by our consciousness and our civilisation, smouldering underneath in a slow, eternal fire'.[38] Gilbert Doble, a country vicar and canon of Truro Cathedral, portrayed Cornwall as another land of saints, producing a stream of booklets between 1920 and 1945 on forty-eight Cornish saints whom he described as 'the leaders of a great religious movement' to whom 'we are to look back for inspiration in the difficult times in which we live'.[39] By 1933 the principal Cornish saints had been incorporated within the liturgical observance of the Church of England in the diocese of Truro. A few years later John Betjeman immortalised one of them in verse with his poem 'Oh good St Cadoc pray for me/ Here in your cell beside the sea'.[40]

Glastonbury remained an important focus for less orthodox English Celtic revivalists. An annual festival was launched there and ran through the 1920s, presided over by Rutland Boughton, composer of *The Immortal Hour*, a Celtic opera with a libretto by William Sharp. A study of the Joseph of Arimathea story, published in 1922 by Lionel Smithett Lewis, a former vicar of Glastonbury, was enormously popular, going through ten editions and being still in print in the 1980s. Lewis was convinced of the veracity of the story and proudly proclaimed Glastonbury's position as 'the origin of the national and apostolic church of Britain'. He looked eagerly forward to a recovery of 'the memory of a great and flourishing Celtic Church' which for so long had been 'buried beneath the waves of heathen Saxon and Danish ravages and the Romanizing Norman influence'.[41] Recent developments made him optimistic that revival was imminent: 'Fortunately in recent years a wave of remembrance is surging up, and Glastonbury and Iona, and the whole Celtic Church, are coming into their own'.[42]

Other English writers in the 1920s and 1930s explored the close connections between Celtic Christianity and paganism. *The Circle and the Cross. A Study in Continuity* by A. H. Allcroft (1927) traced a steady evolution from the pagan stone circle to the Christian church. In *Celt, Druid and Culdee* (1938), Isabel Elder invoked the Culdees as the key agents in this transition. Tracing them from Columba, 'a comparatively easy task', she saw the Culdees as Christianised Druids and painted a picture, in which Glastonbury played a prominent role, of Druid priests readily accepting Christianity, becoming ministers and turning their schools into monasteries.[43]

In Ireland the Celtic revival continued, its primary focus remaining on the pre-Christian heroic period but with more than a passing interest being shown by several of its leading figures in themes and symbols from the Christian era. In the early 1900s a group of women, including Susan and Elizabeth Yeats and Evelyn Gleeson, formed an arts and crafts settlement at Dundrum, near Dublin. They named it not after the Christian saint, Brigit, but after Emer, wife of the legendary pagan hero Cú Chulainn. One of the Dun Emer Guild's first major commissions was to make banners for the new Roman Catholic Cathedral dedicated to St Brendan at Loughrea, County Galway. Among the most striking is one designed by W. B. Yeats' painter father, Jack, which depicts Patrick banishing snakes from Ireland with a border of shamrocks. Evelyn Gleeson designed vestments based on Celtic interlacing and scrolls and Sarah Purser designed a stained glass window of Brendan, founder of the nearby Clonfert Abbey and patron saint of the new Cathedral.[44]

The Dun Emer Guild also operated a hand press which printed several of the works of prominent Celtic revivalists in limited editions. They included Lady Augusta Gregory's *A Book of Saints and Wonders* (1906) which attempted to 'disentangle and make clear the Christian miracles and lives that overlaid the primitive legends' and to bring into harmony the beliefs of pagan days, ancient Christian times, and the modern world.[45] Like most of the Irish revivalists, Lady Gregory was more sympathetic to the pagan than the Christian strain in the Celtic tradition. Her *Gods and Fighting Men* (1904) included a chapter on the legendary encounter between Ossian and Patrick which presented the Fianna as altogether more generous and noble than the priests. Stephen Gwynn, journalist and nationalist MP for Galway, took up this episode in a poem, the 'Lay of Ossian and Patrick' (1903), which gave a dramatic description of the encounter of 'the glory of God the Father with the glory of Finn MacCool'. Although it portrayed Ossian in the end becoming a Christian, it ended with an expression of longing for the old pagan ways:

> And still the Gael as he listens
> In a land of mass and bell
> Under the hope of heaven,
> Under the dread of hell,

> Thinks long, like age-spent Ossian,
> For the things that are no more,
> For the clash of meeting weapons,
> And the mad delight of war.[46]

When Ireland itself plunged into the 'mad delight' of the Easter Rising and the subsequent Civil War, it was pagan heroes rather than Celtic saints who tended to be invoked on the nationalist side. Although Patrick Pearse drew on Christian notions of martyrdom and self-sacrifice, he made remarkably little appeal to Irish saints, perhaps because none of them had been martyrs. Similarly, when Yeats described Pearse in a poem at the height of the Easter Rising, it was the pagan hero Cú Chulainn rather than the Christian Patrick whom he imagined at his side. Although Christian and Catholic imagery was taken up in the cause of Irish nationalism, specifically Celtic Christian themes and figures were not, perhaps because they had largely been appropriated by Anglo-Irish Protestants. The bloodshed and bitterness of the Civil War did prompt one moving evocation of the eirenic spirit of the Celtic saints. In her Irish passion play, *The Story Brought by Brigit*, which was performed at the Abbey Theatre, Dublin, in Holy Week 1924, Lady Gregory contrasted the men of violence and error with the sorrowing figure of Brigit and the three women of Jerusalem who were portrayed as instruments of reconciliation and given a keen, or funeral lament, to sing which came from Hyde's *Religious Songs of Connacht*. More scholarly work on Celtic Christianity also flourished in the early years of the Free State, with James Kenney's monumental work on the sources of the early ecclesiastical history of Ireland coming out in 1929 and John Ryan's classic study of Irish monasticism in 1931. Meanwhile, Church of Ireland clergymen continued to use the Celtic Church as a stick with which to bang the anti-Catholic drum. In 1931 W. S. Kerr, Rector of Seapatrick and Archdeacon of Dromore, asked, 'Is the day far off when patriotic Irishmen will unite in a Church self-governing, independent, released from foreign jurisdiction, and reviving the freedom and evangelical traditions of the Church of St Patrick?'.[47]

In Wales the Celtic Christian tradition was more consciously harnessed to a political campaign. Leading Nonconformist advocates of the disestablishment of the Anglican Church in Wales like Howard Evans and William Edwards stressed the independent and tribal nature of the Celtic Church before it had been subjugated by the English.[48] The Celtic card was also played by the establishment. The Edwardian era saw the introduction of St David's Day celebrations in Welsh schools and official encouragement being given to the wearing of leeks and daffodils. This process culminated in the 1911 Investiture, the first of a Prince of Wales on Welsh soil since the thirteenth century, for which elaborate ceremonial was created based around the figure of the Principality's patron saint. It was at the celebrations surounding the Investiture that A. P. Graves conceived the idea of his collection of Celtic religious verse. He mentioned it to David Lloyd George who was highly enthusiastic and when the *Celtic Psaltery* appeared it was dedicated to the Welsh Wizard.[49] Wales experienced its own brand of Celtic twilight romanticism. A Church in Wales clergyman who adopted the name Brother Ignatius styled himself as 'a monk of the British Church' and established a monastery at Llanthony in the Black Mountains. Arthur Machen, the son of another clergyman, joined Yeats' Order of the Golden Dawn and published a number of novels exploring themes in Celtic Christianity, notably *The Secret Glory* (1922) which described a Holy Cup that Teilo had received from the Lord in paradise. Not everyone in the Principality fell under the Celtic Christian spell, however. In a book published in 1934 on *Welsh Christian Origins*, Arthur Wade-Evans tried to persuade his countrymen that there was no historical basis whatsoever for thinking that early British Christians cherished 'a kind of primitive Protestantism, of apostolic purity and simplicity' still less that, as Willis-Bund had suggested, they favoured either a national or a tribal church. Rather he argued, 'Welshman and Irishman alike believed in One Church only, Universal and Catholic, which had begun at Jerusalem, but had its centre at Rome'.[50]

It was perhaps in Scotland that enthusiasm for Celtic Christianity was most marked in the early decades of the twentieth century. Among the Celtic revivalists, Iona continued to weave its magic spell, notably on William Sharp who made it a focus for his fascination with pagan-Christian synthesis, dreams and visions. His *Spiritual Tales* (1903) included three stories set on the sacred isle. The first began with a long conversation on the shore between Columba and a Druid called Ardan about the ancient and the new wisdom. Afterwards, Ardan chanted a rune to the monks telling them to listen to the Birds of Sorrow. Early the following morning Columba had a vision after which a robin in his cell sang a lament for Christ and called on the saint to summon all the birds on the island together and bless them. This he did and a great peace descended. The second story also spoke of Celtic Christianity's closeness to nature and involved Columba blessing flies and fishes. The third described Columba's visions of a Druid, a seal man and a moon child, the message again being the closeness of these beings to God and to the 'deep peace'.[51]

An extended meditation by Sharp, written around the same time under his usual pseudonym of Fiona Macleod but not published until 1910, presented an even more romanticised and mystical picture of Columba's island. Its focus was not on the physical Iona of fisheries and pastures, nor even on the spiritual Iona of sacred memories and prophecies but rather on 'Iona the metropolis of dreams. None can understand it who does not see through its pagan light, its Christian light, its singular blending of paganism and romance and spiritual beauty'.[52] This Iona 'is more than Gaelic, more than a place rainbow-lit with the seven desires of the world, the Iona that, if we will it so, is a mirror of your heart and of mine'.[53] Among the many dreams that Sharp shared in what became a kind of reverie was that Christ would come again upon Iona, possibly in the form of a woman. He then turned his attention to Columba: 'I doubt if any other than a Gael can understand him aright. More than any Celt of whom history tells, he is the epitome of the Celt'.[54] What particularly appealed to Sharp about the saint was his visionary and prophetic power: 'He was the first of our race of whom is recorded the systematic use of the strange gift of spiritual foresight, "second-sight"'.[55] Sharp also made much of Columba's special tenderness towards animals and his closeness to the Druids. He wrote approvingly of the 'half-Pagan, half-Christian basis upon which the Columban Church of Iona stood'.[56] It was, however, to the image of Iona as 'an Isle of Dream' that he kept returning: 'Here for century after century, the Gael has lived, suffered, joyed, dreamed his impossible, beautiful dream'.[57] There was a strong sense of longing for a time long gone and of lament for 'a doomed and passing race'.[58] Yet there was also a note of optimism: 'The Celt fades, but his spirit rises in the heart and mind of the Anglo-Celtic peoples, with whom are the destinies of generations to come'.[59] It is appropriate that Sharp's grave, situated on a wooded slope in Sicily where he died in 1905, should be marked by an Iona cross.

Iona exercised a fascination for another prominent figure in the Scottish Celtic revival movement, the artist John Duncan. The island featured in two of his best-known paintings. *St Bride* (1913) depicts the female saint being transported by angels from Iona to Bethlehem to become hand-maiden to Mary and foster-mother to Christ. *St Columba Bidding Farewell to the White Horse* (1925) draws on an incident recounted in the last chapter of Adomnan's *Vita* and portrays the frail saint in his last hours on earth with the faithful milk horse nuzzling against him. It is a striking representation of Celtic Christianity's closeness to nature (Plate 11).

Columba continued to appeal to people of widely different religious persuasions. The Free Church minister of Dollar in Clackmannanshire wrote a series of articles in 1909 in an attempt to prove that the earliest church in the parish had been dedicated to Columba and 'that there is at least a possibility that that distinguished Irish saint may have himself been the introducer of the Christian faith among the Celtic tribes then resident in this parish, if, indeed he was not the personal founder and

Plate 11. Painting by John Duncan of St Columba bidding farewell to the White Horse. (Source: Carnegie Dunfermline Trust.)

planter of the first church here'.[60] At the other end of the Scottish theological spectrum, Lucy Menzies, a high church Episcopalian, wrote a glowing biography of the saint in 1920 which credited Columba, apparently single-handedly, with subduing the fierce passions of the Picts, securing the independence of the kingdom of the Scots, bringing civilisation to a lawless people and improving their methods of agriculture, their husbandry and their social relations. 'It is impossible for Scotland to exaggerate the debt she owes Columba', she concluded. 'He founded her national unity, he brought about her inter-tribal peace and not only improved her whole mode of living, but set an ideal before her and brought to her the Bread of Life.'[61] It was not only Christians who admired Columba. In a book published in 1908 V. V. Branford, a humanist, used him to illustrate the importance of pilgrimage in personal development and in 1928 Eleanor Merry, a theosophist, made him the central character in a play about spiritual forces older than Christianity. Rudolf Steiner was greatly attracted to Columba and in the 1950s one of his followers who taught at the Waldorf School in Edinburgh wrote a play for young people based on the saint's life. Another more recent play on the same theme, first performed at the Edinburgh Festival Fringe in 1978, was written and performed by members of the Moral Re-Armament movement.

Church architecture as well as art and drama reflected the romantic appeal of the age of the saints. The most remarkable shrine to the Celtic Christian tradition in Scotland is surely St Conan's Kirk on the north side of Loch Awe in Argyllshire which was designed by Walter Campbell, a pious if somewhat eccentric local landowner, and dedicated to one of Columba's supposed disciples. In the grounds of the church, which was built between 1907 and the early 1930s, Campbell erected a high Celtic cross in memory of his mother and laid out a walk dedicated to St Modan. Inside are aisles dedicated to Columba and Fillan and chapels to Conval and Bride. The huge organ screen is decorated with carved Celtic knotwork. This isolated country kirk which serves a tiny local population also has its own cloisters and undercroft and a chapel containing a huge effigy of Robert the Bruce. Other Scottish churches continued to celebrate the Celtic saints more conventionally through the medium of stained glass. A window designed in the 1920s by Karl Parsons for All Saints Episcopal Church in St Andrews features a suitably numerous array of saints grouped around the Madonna and Child. Among those that can be identified from the Celtic tradition are Brigit, Kentigern, Medan, Cainnech, Modan, Columba, Ninian and Patrick, easily outnumbering the Roman trio of Andrew, Wilfrid and Margaret.

Denominational rivalries continued to surface in Scottish writings about the Celtic Church. *A Calendar of Scottish Saints* produced in 1904 by Charles Barrett, a Benedictine monk based at Fort Augustus, chided Presbyterians for their destruction of the Celtic heritage. The entry on Fillan mentioned a well dedicated to the saint in the old parish of Kilfillan in Renfrewshire which had been 'filled up, as a remnant of superstition, by a parish minister in the eighteenth century'. A more recent piece of desecration was deplored in the entry on Modan which noted that a flat stone near Loch Etive traditionally known as St Modan's Seat had been 'broken up for building materials by the Presbyterians not many years ago'.[62]

On the Protestant side, the standard anti-Roman agenda of Celtic enthusiasts was somewhat complicated by a new division between Pictophiles and Gaelophiles. One of the first to champion the hitherto rather neglected Picts was Archibald Scott, minister of Kildonnan near Helmsdale. In *The Pictish Nation* (1918) he paid fulsome tribute to the 'devoted labours of the Pictish *Céli Dé*, who struggled to continue the ancient church'.[63] For the Gaels he had much less time, partly, it has been suggested, because he could not forgive Ireland for its neutrality during the First World War, still raging as he wrote his book which was dedicated to the memory of his brother who had died in the conflict. Scott dismissed the notion that Columba had evangelised the Picts as a Gaelic fabrication. His hero was rather Ninian, the Briton who was the true evangelist of Pictland. Other British saints like Gildas, David and Kentigern were written up at the expense of Irish figures. Scott even managed to find a pupil of Ninian's named Caranoc who had gone as an evangelist to Donegal to win from paganism the very tribe from which Columba himself had sprung.

Several other Scottish ministers and academics shared Scott's belief that Columba's role in the Christianising of Scotland had been over-exaggerated and that more credit should be given to local saints. Frank Knight, a minister in the United Free Church and keen amateur archaeologist, identified eighty men and women who had planted churches in Scotland before Columba set foot on Iona and attempted to raise the profile of indigenous Pictish evangelists like Drostan.[64] Douglas Simpson, librarian of Aberdeen University, championed the cause of Ninian and produced a string of pamphlets in an attempt to prove that the British saint had travelled from his base at Whithorn right through Scotland, getting as far north as Caithness and even to Shetland.[65] There is no doubt that this promotion of Ninian rather than Columba as the true evangelist of Scotland and the more general championship of native British and Pictish saints against Irish ones was partly inspired by anti-Irish sentiment similar to that which had informed the writings of Spottiswoode two centuries earlier (see p. 97). Scott had particularly strong prejudices against the Gaels, claiming that the Gaelic church in Scotland had never had any real independence or integrity but had always been under the control of the secular rulers of Dal Riata. The Pictish church, by contrast, had always been a non-political entity and had not owed allegiance to any monarch:

> The Church of the Picts stands in history as a branch of the
> Church of Christ which, adhering to the simple life and simple
> organization and government of the earliest Apostolic Church,
> fitted itself into the national life of a free people who delighted to
> exercise a control in their own government and education.[66]

Not only did the Picts 'preach their Gospel with the unmatched eloquence of the Celt' but they also did what the Gaels never quite managed, 'they lived the Gospel'.[67] Devoted to the Scriptures, they were models of evangelical puritanism, eschewing infant baptism, celebrating the sacrament infrequently on grounds of unworthiness, loving their native land, having no representation of the Crucifixion on their crosses and no adoration of the mother of Christ.

While Scott felt a special mission to show the spiritual superiority of the neglected Picts over the Gaels, he also fully subscribed to the general Presbyterian view that the Celtic Church as a whole was strongly anti-Episcopal and anti-Roman. He graphically described one of its most distinctive features by drawing on a military allusion, doubtless having in mind the great conflict that was raging as he wrote and which he saw as 'linking in a great array the descendants of Celtic peoples':

> The relations of bishop and abbot were much like those of the chaplain of a modern British regiment to his battalion commander. At divine services the chaplain is the senior officer, but in all other work and service he is subject to his battalion commander; so in the Celtic *muinntirs* at sacramental services the bishop, if invited to act, was for the time being in command of the community; but in all other work and service, he was, with the rest of the community, subject to the Abbot.[68]

Ultimately for Scott the most significant feature of Pictish Christianity was its difference not from the Gaelic branch of the Celtic Church but from Rome:

> On the one hand, there is the Roman Churchman with the imitated pomp and trappings of temporal power, whose aim is the aggrandizement of his Church ... on the other hand there is the Pictish Churchman modelled by S. Ninian, S. Comgall, S. Kentigern or S. Columbanus, clad in hooded cloak of brown coloured wool, helped along by a plain *bachall* or thorn of hazel, carrying a wallet with a few pieces of bread, and a manuscript of the Gospel, rolled in a waterproof casing of hide, demanding a clean, honest, just and merciful life as the first condition of admission into the number of Christ's flock.[69]

Not all enthusiasts for Celtic Christianity shared this anti-Roman agenda. Lucy Menzies, in her 1925 biography of Queen Margaret of Scotland, felt the need to defend her subject against the charge that she had swept a once independent church into the embrace of Rome:

> It is instructive for many of us unhappily-named Protestants, who are sometimes apt to protest more than we reflect, to read how the

clergy of the *Ecclesia Scoticana*, hundreds of years before Margaret was born, made the Sign of the Cross, genuflected reverently and celebrated Mass. Columba himself, the founder under Christ of the Church of Scotland, adapted the beliefs and practices of paganism to the use of his Church, largely by making the Sign of the Cross over them.[70]

Risking the wrath of fellow-Protestants in Scotland, Menzies boldly stated that Columba derived his tradition direct from Rome. She also had a further shock in store for them: 'We Scots are apt to comfort ourselves by Bede's comparison of the laxness of discipline and morals among the Saxon clergy, with the purity of the Celtic missionaries. Taken at their best they were a small body … and left large areas untouched by their ministrations'.[71]

Hers was very much a lone voice, however. Most Scottish writers continued to promote the idea that the Celtic Church was fundamentally anti-Roman. M. V. Hay, a Roman Catholic layman, became so irritated by this that in 1927 he devoted a lengthy book to exposing what he called *A Chain of Error in Scottish History*. Hay sought to show that the letters of the sixth-century Irish monk Columbanus had been selectively and systematically misquoted by Scottish historians to give the impression that the Celtic Church was hostile to Rome. The origins of this chain of error went back to the Reformation but Hay laid particular blame on William Skene's *Celtic Scotland* which had left out crucial words from Columbanus' letters indicating his acknowledgement of Papal superiority. In Hay's view, this had given rise to 'a genealogy of misquotation' as subsequent writers copied Skene without bothering to check the original sources. While most of the culprits were Scottish Presbyterians, distinguished English and Irish scholars had also perpetuated the chain of error. They included Arthur Haddan, a close friend of John Henry Newman, Alexander Forbes, who had sought 'to identify the attitude of St Columbanus with modern Anglicanism and to represent his attitude to Rome as merely one of respect and reverence', and G. T. Stokes, Professor of Church History at Trinity College, Dublin, and author of *Ireland and the Celtic Church* (1887), who had made it appear through plucking a phrase out of context that Columbanus had referred to Pope Gregory the Great as 'a living dog' and suggested that in the Irish monk's homilies 'there is not a word a modern Calvinist might not utter'.[72] Although it was the distortion of Columbanus' words that particularly irked Hay, he was also unhappy with the way in which the Culdees were so often presented as a heroic band of proto-Protestants: 'There is not a scrap of evidence to show that they were hostile to the Roman Church. The credulity of Scotsmen on the subject of the Culdees has been excessive'.[73]

One Protestant writer at least revised his opinions on the nature of the Celtic Church after considering the evidence. In the same year that Hay's *Chain of Error* appeared, John Campbell MacNaught, minister of Kilmuir Easter, produced a book on *The Celtic Church and the See of Peter*. The title suggests yet another piece of Protestant propaganda about the sturdy independence of the Celtic Church. The author admitted in his preface that:

> When he first began to study the history of the Celtic Church he was strongly biassed in favour of this view and fully expected to find it corroborated by the facts; but the more he studied the subject the clearer did it become to him that this oft-repeated assertion requires to be proved.[74]

MacNaught's extensive research obliged him to concede 'in the interests of historical truth that the ancient Celtic Christians recognized the Roman Primacy' although he was at paints to point out that this conclusion should not be taken as an indication 'that he personally acknowledges the validity of the Papal claims'.[75] Even with this proviso, MacNaught's was a bold and rare statement for a Presbyterian minister to make about the relationship of the Celtic Church with Rome. Much more typical was the line taken by John Duke in his influential book *The Columban Church* (1932). For him, independence was:

> The legacy which the Church of St Columba bequeathed to the Church which afterwards was to arise in Scotland; which was to be built at the Reformation upon the ruins of the Church of Rome, and which at last has been completed in the Church of Scotland today – the most independent National Church in Christendom.[76]

Alongside its appropriation by Protestants keen to beat the anti-Roman drum, Celtic Christianity also continued to appeal to Scottish churchmen of a more eirenic and ecumenical disposition. Iona remained an important focus and symbol for those who hoped that the Scottish churches might reunite on the basis of their common Celtic heritage. In 1905 the restored Abbey Church was opened for public worship. The Dowager Duchess of Argyll was present to see Anglicans sharing with Presbyterians in a celebration of Holy Communion, 'surely the beginning of the fulfilment of the prophecy that all denominations would one day worship in the Cathedral of Iona'.[77] However, the Church of Scotland was reluctant to commit money for further rebuilding, much to the frustration of Donald MacLeod, former minister of St Columba's Church in London, who devoted his retirement years to working for the restoration of the Abbey buildings and told members of the General Assembly that it reflected little credit on them 'as Scotsmen, or as Scottish churchmen' that they were so unenthusiastic about the project.[78]

James Cooper was also frustrated that the Church was doing so little to restore Iona's 'spiritual glories'. He canvassed the idea of developing a centre for foreign mission on the island, believing, in the words of his biographer, that it was 'a blunder to leave unutilised the potential appeal of the name and the tradition of the blessed Isle', and had dreams of a training school for missionaries within the Abbey precincts 'from which Columba had carried the Gospel to Pictland and Aidan to Northumbria'.[79] Cooper also dreamed of establishing a boarding school on the island, with Gaelic and sacred music figuring prominently in the curriculum. 'The teaching staff should be a College under a clerical head', he wrote in 1905, 'and to them we should look for work of Celtic learning. Missionary zeal should be encouraged among boys and teachers, and historical lectures on the Columban missions should be delivered. In summer during vacation time clerical and missionary Retreats should be held'.[80] Like Donald MacLeod, he kept putting projects before the Church of Scotland's General Assembly but to no avail. One church committee got as far as suggesting that Iona should be used 'as a place for the bodily recovery of a jaded minister' but even this mild proposal was not acted on.[81] The only significant move towards restoring Iona to its former spiritual glories took place at Bishop's House where the Cowley Fathers were permanently resident between 1906 and 1908, constituting the first monastic presence on the island since the Reformation.

It was, in fact, a layman who put some of Cooper's ideas into practice. In 1920 David Russell, the philanthropically inclined owner of a large paper mill in Fife, paid for a group of twenty-four divinity students to spend a week's retreat on the island. Russell, who had visited Iona regularly since first going there as a nine-year-old boy in 1881, accompanied the students and made sure that each of them was equipped with a copy of Adomnan's *Vita Columbae*. The retreats became an annual event and Russell commissioned Reginald Fairlie, an architect, to draw up plans for the restoration of the cloisters and residential buildings around the Abbey to provide a permanent base for them and for other activities. In 1929 the Iona Fellowship was set up to promote this scheme, its membership drawn from those who had been on the annual retreats and other interested parties, including Marjory Kennedy Fraser who had long expressed the wish that she might be buried on Iona. In 1932 her ashes were interred in the Reilig Oran, the burial ground of Scottish and Norwegian kings. They lie under a granite stone decorated with Celtic interlacing and designed by John Duncan.

Interest in restoring the monastic buildings on Iona was also growing in the United States of America. A speech to the New York Chamber of Commerce in 1929 by the Gaelic scholar Angus Robertson led to the setting up of the American Iona Society. It proposed setting up a Celtic university or college on the mainland (among the preferred sites were Ardchattan Priory, which had been founded by monks from Lismore, and Dunkeld Cathedral with its Columban connections) with an associated retreat centre on Iona. The plan met with a hostile reception from the existing Scottish universities, however, and its promoters, finding it difficult to raise funds in the aftermath of the Wall Street crash and the advent of the Depression, threw in their lot with David Russell who was becoming increasingly enthusiastic about developing Iona as a residential training centre. He was particularly taken with a suggestion mooted in 1936 by Clare Vyner, who owned Fountains Abbey in Yorkshire and had an estate on Mull, that Iona should become a residential centre for training 'missionaries' who would do social work in the Western Isles. Vyner's proposals involved a two year training period in 'health and hygiene, agriculture, fishing and gardening, weaving etc.' with 'a certain amount of theological study'. Russell was adamant that the atmosphere should be non-denominational and described it as 'best visualised by that which is done by such people as the English Society of Friends and the Brotherhood Movement'.[82]

Among those with whom Russell shared this scheme was George MacLeod, Minister of Govan Old parish church in Glasgow and a member of the Iona Fellowship who had acted as a tutor on the student retreats. MacLeod was dismissive of Vyner's proposals, commenting that 'undenominational social service has had its day', but expressed his own enthusiasm for establishing a residential Christian community and ministerial training college in the restored Abbey buildings.[83] Some years earlier, while Minister of St Cuthbert's Church in Edinburgh, he had actively pursued the idea of setting up such a centre on the island of Inchcolm but that project did not come off and he was now convinced that Iona was the right place for it. In 1935 MacLeod put to the Iona Cathedral Trustees a proposal to restore the Abbey buildings as the base for a residential community to equip Church of Scotland ministers for a new type of ministry which would be team based and non-parochial. As in Columba's time, the emphasis would be on developing community life and the creation of a sense of brotherhood. Probationery ministers would come for six months after their theological training and then work in congested urban areas and housing schemes for a period of two to three years during which they would remain in the 'Iona brotherhood' before going into ordinary parish ministry. Directly appealing to the example of Columba, who had 'built his settlement by the labour of his own hands', MacLeod proposed that the building work be done not by 'a contractor and hired labourers at enhanced wages' but voluntarily by skilled masons, carpenters and plumbers, 'loyal members of the Church of Scotland and as proud of her as ever were the monks of their Mother Church ... who would be glad of the opportunity to express their craftsmanship to the glory of God'.[84] He further suggested that these workmen and the first batch of trainee ministers should live together in wooden huts, working together and forming a community.

Yet another project to restore Iona to the spiritual glories it had enjoyed in the golden age of Celtic Christianity surfaced in 1938 when the third Marquess of Bute, a Catholic convert, sought to buy the island from the Duke of Argyll. His dreams of turning the monastic ruins into a Catholic seminary were thwarted, however, both by the Duke of Argyll's reluctance to part with the island and by the terms of the Iona Cathedral Trust. The Trustees decided to allow MacLeod to proceed with his scheme and in the summer of 1938 he took his first party of ministerial candidates and workmen to the island. Work continued throughout the Second World War and an ecumenical community gradually developed with its distinctive emphasis on work and worship. MacLeod dreamed of Iona leading the fragmented church of the twentieth century back to the unity of its Celtic heyday:

> It is our hope that the Abbey will be completed as a Laboratory School of Christian Living where large numbers will come to pray and confer. It is our instinct that the essentials for which we seek, with many others, to stand will soon become the subjects round which the whole Church will be forced to confer. It is our prayer that, increasingly, in such confering we will have gatherings in Iona drawn from many denominations and will together glimpse the day when, as in St Columba's time, Christ's Church shall be one in every land.[85]

Although it was by no means the only model for the Iona Community, George MacLeod was deeply influenced in his great experiment by his understanding of the distinctive character of the Celtic Church and especially by his admiration for Columba. The newsletter that he started in October 1938 to record the progress of the project was named *The Coracle* after the type of leather skinned boat which had brought the saint and his companions to Iona in 563. Some aspects of the life of the new community seem to have been almost deliberately modelled on practices associated with the Celtic monks. Ron Ferguson, MacLeod's biographer, notes that:

> The day, organized with military precision, began with reveille at 6.45 am, and a swim in the freezing sea. George MacLeod would throw off his tattered MacLeod kilt and lead the charge into the water, throwing himself naked into the waves. He insisted that the Celtic monks bathed in the sea every day of the year and resisted the arguments of faint-hearted ordinands who failed to see why they should slavishly follow masochistic Celtic customs.[86]

An incurable romantic, MacLeod shamelessly made up stories about Columba to fit in with his own personal preoccupations and those who heard him talking about the saint were never quite sure whether he was referring to himself or his sixth-century predecessor as leader of the Iona community. The two men were uncannily alike in many ways, sharing an aristocratic background, charismatic personality, visionary quality and somewhat autocratic manner and were even the same age, forty-two, when they began their work on Iona. MacLeod did his bit to perpetuate a romantic view of Celtic Christianity. Laying claim to a remark originally made by an 'old Scotsman' to the English mystic, Evelyn Underhill, he delighted in describing Iona as 'a thin place' where heaven and earth were especially close. His own concern with ecology helped to confirm the 'green' image of the Celtic Church. He also added his powerful voice to those stressing its independence from Rome, although he was also careful to distance it equally from the institutionalism of Calvin's Geneva. He took particular delight in pointing out that Arnold Toynbee in his monumental *Study of History* had entitled one of the decisive crossroads on the path of Christian history 'Iona or Rome?'. MacLeod also emphasised the Celtic Church's particular attachment to the Fourth Gospel, maintaining that 'St John was the patron saint of Scotland for centuries before the Roman dominance placed in his stead St Andrew'.[87]

It was not only on Iona that Columba was exerting his romantic appeal in the 1940s and 1950s. In Ireland, Robert Farren, a Dublin poet, produced an extended poem in 1944 entitled 'The First Exile, the Story of Colmcille'. Seven years later in his classic work, *The Evangelical Movement in the Highlands*, John MacInness hailed him as 'the first of the

Gaelic spiritual bards' and argued that the great Highland evangelical poets of the eighteenth and nineteenth centuries followed in a 'tradition of Gaelic religious verse ... unbroken since his day'.[88] A trio of books by Diana Leatham tackled 'an exciting chapter in the history of Christianity in our islands that has been almost forgotten ... bravely written for us throughout the Dark Ages by our own pioneer saints of the Celtic Church'.[89] *They Built on Rock. The Story of the Men and Women of the Early Celtic Church* (1948) was enhanced by striking art nouveau illustrations by James Harrison Miller showing Columba welcoming the crane and Kentigern striding through Strathclyde in his cowl; *Celtic Sunrise: An Outline of Celtic Christianity* (1951) had an enthusiastic preface by George MacLeod; and *The Church Defies the Dark Ages* (1955) catalogued the substantial achievements of Celtic Christians under chapter headings like 'Welsh Missionaries Convert Brittany', 'Irish Missionaries Convert England' and 'Irish Monks Invade the Continent'.

Leatham remarked that her third book could have been subtitled 'The Story Nobody Knows' and berated historians for largely ignoring the contribution of the Celtic Church. In fact, a number of significant academic studies produced during this period paid considerable attention to it and were highly complimentary about its leading figures. In his seminal work on Anglo-Saxon England, first published in 1943, Frank Stenton followed Bede in giving a glowing picture of Aidan, 'an ascetic evangelist ... influencing men of all ranks by his humility and devotion'. He also lauded Cuthbert for exemplifying 'the Celtic strains in the English Church' and made much of the differences between the Irish and Roman churches in terms of organisation, authority structures and method of calculating Easter.[90] Celtic Christian art was put firmly on the map thanks to the meticulous scholarship and unabashed enthusiasm of Francoise Henry whose *Irish Art in the Early Christian Period* (1940) and *Early Christian Irish Art* (1954) remain classic works on the subject. The positive attitude of Celtic Christianity towards nature was further explored and extolled by several scholars, notably Gerard Murphy in *Early Irish Lyrics* (1956) and J. E. Caerwyn Williams, writing in Welsh in 1958.[91] H. J. Massingham, writer on rural Britain and pioneer of organic farming, developed a particular love for the Celtic places of the British Isles and went so far as to argue in a much-quoted observation that 'if the British Church had survived, it is possible that the fissure between Christianity and nature, widening through the centuries, would not have cracked the unity of western man's attitude towards the universe'.[92]

The churches' growing consciousness and celebration of their Celtic heritage during this period is well demonstrated in the number of hymns and poems written on the subject. Congregations increasingly sang about local and national saints as they gazed on their idealised representation on banners and in stained glass windows. James Archer, Rector of Seagoe in County Down from 1905 to 1935, supplied the Church of Ireland Hymnal with a stirring hymn, 'Lift thy banner, Church of Erin', which stressed the contemporary church's continuity with its Celtic golden age:

> Ages pass, yet with St Patrick
> Firm we hold the faith of God,
> With his 'Breastplate' armed, we follow
> Where the saints and martyrs trod.
> Brave Columba's fearless labours
> Brigid's lifelong work of love,
> Teach us to endure the hardness
> Till we reach the rest above.[93]

In Wales much of the finest writing about local saints was in Welsh and designed for reading rather than congregational singing. A particularly powerful evocation of David by Gwenallt Jones published in 1951 begins:

> I saw Dewi strolling from county to county like God's gipsy, with the Gospel and the Altar in his caravan; and coming to us in the Colleges and schools to show us what is the purpose of learning. He went down to the bottom of the pit with the miners and cast the light of his wise lamp on the coal-face.[94]

Timothy Rees, Bishop of Llandaff from 1931 to 1939, wrote the hymn 'Lord, who in thy perfect wisdom' with a stanza about the coming of the Celtic missionaries:

> To our shores remote, benighted,
> Barrier of the western waves,
> Tidings in thy love thou sentest,
> Tidings of the cross that saves.
> Saints and heroes strove and suffered
> Here thy gospel to proclaim;
> We, the heirs of their endeavour,
> Tell the honour of their name.[95]

A clutch of Cornish saints were remembered in verses written by Miles Brown, who ministered in various parishes in the county for nearly fifty years until his retirement in 1990:

> All these Cornish shores are holy,
> Here the Saints in prayer did dwell,
> Raising font and altar lowly
> Preaching far with staff and bell –
> Piran, Petroc, Paul Aurelian,
> Euny, Samson, Winwaloe.[96]

Hymns devoted to Scotland's saints appeared in *The Hymnal for Scotland*, a kind of tartan wrap around *The English Hymnal* published in 1950 for use in the Scottish Episcopal Church. Columba was commemorated in verses by John Hannah, an Episcopal priest in the Borders, which skilfully explored the complexity of his character by contrasting 'the crafty warrior, Crimthann' and the gentle, dove-like Colmcille.[97] Ninian also received due acknowledgement for his pioneering role in the Christianising of Scotland in a hymn by G. T. S. Farquhar:

> Lord, who sentest Ninian forth,
> First of Bishops to our shore,
> Charged, amid the heathen north,
> To proclaim the Church's lore,
> Now we owe thee thanks and praise
> For the triumph of his days.[98]

Perhaps the most rousing of all the hymns written about the Celtic saints is 'Hail, glorious Saint Patrick, dear saint of our isle' which has long been a favourite among Irish Roman Catholics. I have not been able to trace its exact provenance – it appears in most collections simply as 'traditional' although in one case it is credited to Father Faber (presumably F. W. Faber, the mid-Victorian English Catholic convert and hymnwriter), an attribution that I have been unable to verify and am inclined to distrust. Given a suitably powerful rendition by the tenor Frank Patterson with the Irish Philharmonic Orchestra and Chorus, it is one of the items on a recently issued compact disc 'Faith of Our Fathers – Classic Religious Songs of Ireland' (1997).[99] The phenomenal success of this disc is one of many pointers to the strength of the late twentieth century Celtic Christian revival, the subject of the next chapter.

NOTES

1. J. L. Campbell, 'Notes on Hamish Robertson's Studies in Carmichael's Carmina Gadelica', *Scottish Gaelic Studies*, Vol. XIII, Part 1, Autumn 1978, p. 1.
2. H. Robertson, 'Studies in Carmichael's Carmina Gadelica', *Scottish Gaelic Studies*, Vol. XII, Part 2, 1976, p. 240.

3. Ibid., p. 240.
4. Campbell, 'Notes on Hamish Robertson's Studies', p. 13.
5. Carmichael, *Carmina*, p. 30.
6. Bradley, *Columba*, pp. 78, 101.
7. Carmichael, *Carmina*, p. 24.
8. M. K. Fraser, *A Life of Song* (Oxford University Press, Oxford, 1929), p. 112.
9. Bradley, *Columba*, pp. 98–100.
10. Ibid., p. 29.
11. Hyde, *Religious Songs*, p. xi.
12. Ibid., pp. 5, xv.
13. Ibid., p. 3.
14. Ibid., p. ix.
15. MacLean, *Literature of the Celts*, p. 286.
16. Ibid., p. 303.
17. Graves, *A Celtic Psaltery*, p. vii.
18. Hull, *Poem Book*, p. xxxi.
19. Ibid., p. xxiv.
20. Meyer, *Selections*, p. xii.
21. Hull, *Poem Book*, p. xx.
22. Ibid., p. xxii.
23. G. Murphy, 'The origins of Irish nature poetry', *Studies* (Dublin), 20, 1931, p. 87.
24. R. Flower, 'The Irish high crosses', *J. Warburg, Courtauld Institute* 17 (1954), pp. 90–1.
25. K. Jackson, *Studies in Early Celtic Nature Poetry* (Cambridge University Press, 1935, reprinted Llanerch Publishers, Felinfach, 1995), p. 103.
26. Ibid., pp. 108–9.
27. Kenney, *Sources*, p. 80.
28. H. Zimmer, *The Celtic Church in Britain and Ireland* (David Nutt, London, 1902), pp. 115, 130.
29. L. Gougaud, *Christianity in Celtic Christian Lands* (Four Courts Press, Dublin, 1992), p. 19.
30. C. Plummer, *Baedae Opera Historica*, Vol. 2 (Oxford University Press, Oxford, 1896), p. 260.
31. A. Plummer, *The Churches in Britain Before ad 1000*, Vol. 1 (Robert Scott, London, 1911), p. x.
32. Ibid., p. 103.
33. Ibid., p. 107.
34. Ibid., p. 108.
35. Ibid., p. 108.
36. Ibid., Vol. 2., p. 243.
37. Payton, *Cornwall*, p. 268.
38. D. H. Lawrence, *Kangaroo* (Penguin Books, Harmondsworth, 1975), p. 263.
39. G. H. Doble, *The Saints of Cornwall* (Parret & Neves, Chatham, 1960), p. 9.
40. J. Betjeman, *Collected Poems* (John Murray, London, 1979), p. 98.
41. Lewis, *St Joseph*, p. 17.
42. Ibid., p. 191.
43. I. Elder, *Celt, Druid and Culdee* (Covenant Publishing, London, 1938), p. 87.

44. L. Seidel, 'Celtic Revivals and Women's Work' in Edlestein, *Imagining an Irish Past*, pp. 22–43.
45. Ibid., p. 6.
46. Matthews, *From the Isles of Dream*, p. 172.
47. W. S. Kerr, *The Independence of the Celtic Church in Ireland* (SPCK, London, 1931), p. 160.
48. See, for example, H. Evans, *The Case for Disestablishment in Wales* (The Liberation Society, London, 1907), pp. 32–3, and W. Edwards, *Four Centuries of Nonconformist Disabilities* (National Council of Evangelical Free Churches, 1912), p. 6.
49. Graves, *A Celtic Psaltery*, p. v. On the significance of the 1911 Investiture, see J. Ellis, 'The Prince & the Dragon: Welsh National Identity & the 1911 Investiture', *Welsh History Review*, Vol. 18, No. 2, December 1996.
50. A. W. Wade-Evans, *Welsh Christian Origins* (Alden Press, Oxford, 1934).
51. F. Macleod, 'The Three Marvels of Iona' in *Spiritual Tales* (David Nutt, London, 1903), Vol. 1, pp. 55–84.
52. F. Macleod, 'Iona' in *The Works of Fiona Macleod*, Vol. IV (Heinemann, London, 1910), p. 95.
53. Ibid., p. 95.
54. Ibid., p. 130.
55. Ibid., p. 134.
56. Ibid., p. 241.
57. Ibid., p. 244–5.
58. Ibid., p. 245.
59. Ibid., p. 246.
60. W. B. R.Wilson, 'Peeps into the Past History of Dollar', *Dollar Magazine* Vol. VIII, 1909, p. 112.
61. L. Menzies, *Saint Columba of Iona* (J. M. Dent, London, 1920), p. 194.
62. C. Barrett, *A Calendar of Scottish Saints* (Fort Augustus, 1904), pp. 20, 21.
63. Scott, *The Pictish Nation*, p. xii.
64. G. F. Knight, *Archaeological Light on the Early Christianising of Scotland* (James Clarke, London, 1933).
65. D. Simpson, *The Celtic Church in Scotland* (Aberdeen, 1935), *St Ninian and the Origins of the Christian Church in Scotland* (Edinburgh, 1940).
66. Scott, *The Pictish Nation*, p. 526.
67. Ibid., p. 529.
68. Ibid., p. 334.
69. Ibid., pp. 526–7.
70. Menzies, *St Margaret*, pp. 87–8.
71. Ibid., p. 89.
72. Hay, *Chain of Error*, pp. 102, 169.
73. Ibid., p. 74.
74. J. C. MacNaught, *The Celtic Church and the See of Peter* (Basil Blackwell, Oxford, 1927), p. 1.
75. Ibid., p. 112.
76. J. Duke, *The Columban Church* (Oxford University Press, Oxford, 1932), p. 138.
77. C. MacLeod, *A Short Sketch of the Life of the Rev. Donald MacLeod* (Edinburgh, 1843), p. 13.

78. *Oban Times* report quoted in typescript memoir of Donald MacLeod. I owe these references to Tom Davidson Kelly.
79. Wotherspoon, *James Cooper*, p. 206.
80. Ibid., p. 229.
81. Ibid., p. 229.
82. L. Macintyre, *Sir David Russell* (Canongate, Edinburgh, 1994), pp. 195–6. I owe this reference to Lorn Macintyre.
83. Ibid., p. 196.
84. Ferguson, *George MacLeod*, p. 148.
85. Ibid., p. 197.
86. Ibid., p. 171.
87. D. Leatham, *Celtic Sunrise* (Hodder & Stoughton, London, 1951), p. 9.
88. J. MacInness, *The Evangelical Movement in the Highlands* (Aberdeen University Press, Aberdeen, 1951), p. 265.
89. D. Leatham, *The Church Defies the Dark Ages* (Religious Education Press, London, 1955), p. 5.
90. F. Stenton, *Anglo-Saxon England* (Clarendon Press, Oxford), pp. 119–20; 125–6.
91. J. E. Caerwyn Williams, *Traddodiad Llenwyddol Iwerddon* (University of Wales Press, Cardiff, 1958), p. 72.
92. H. J. Massingham, *The Tree of Life* (Chapman & Hall, London, 1943), p. 40.
93. *Church Hymnal* (APCK, Dublin, 1960), No. 313.
94. Thomas, *Candle*, p. 129.
95. *Church Hymnary*, 3rd edn (Oxford University Press, 1973), No. 473.
96. Payton, *Cornwall*, p. 81.
97. This hymn is quoted in full in Bradley, *Columba*, p. 24.
98. *Hymnal for Scotland* (Oxford University Press, Oxford, 1950).
99. 'Faith of Our Fathers', RTE CD 198 (Squirrel Music, Dublin, 1997). The attribution to Faber is made in the sleeve notes of 'The Contemplative Celt' (Incarnation Music, Glendale, California, 1991).

6

But lo, there breaks a yet more glorious day

The current revival

The current revival of interest in and enthusiasm for Celtic Christianity shares many characteristics with the earlier movements discussed in this book. There is a similar understanding of Celtic Christianity as a distinctive entity and a similar conviction that a return to its central tenets will greatly benefit the contemporary church. It is true that the emphasis has shifted from ecclesiology and denominational considerations to theology and spirituality and that the Celtic golden age has stretched so that in some interpretations it runs right through to the nineteenth century. However, romantic nostalgia and wishful thinking remain key elements in the contemporary revival, with new concerns such as feminism and ecological awareness being projected on to the Celtic Church alongside more long-lasting themes like primitive simplicity, closeness to nature and openness to other religious traditions. While ecclesiastical power politics and denominational point-scoring are much less in evidence than in earlier revivals, the current movement has its less edifying side in the commercialism that has packaged and marketed Celtic Christianity as a commodity to sell books, compact discs and religious trinkets and to promote the burgeoning heritage and tourist industries. Perhaps in reaction to some of these trends, there has been an even sharper divergence between popular and academic treatments of the subject than in previous revivals. Much recent academic work has had an avowedly revisionist and deconstructionist agenda and sought to show that there was no such thing as a Celtic Church and that the whole notion of Celtic Christianity is a myth.

While the current revival only really got into full swing in the late 1980s, its roots can be traced back to a clutch of books that appeared in the early 1960s. The late twentieth-century Celtic Christian revival has been very much a 'bookish' affair and its most characteristic and ubiquitous symbol has been the paperback anthology of Celtic prayers. The first of these appeared in 1960 in the form of two small volumes of 'prayers and blessings from the Gaelic' extracted from Carmichael's *Carmina Gadelica* and published by the Christian Community Press under the titles *The Sun Dances* and *New Moon of the Season*. A more substantial anthology, *Poems of the West Highlanders*, came out the following year with material from the *Carmina* turned into verse by G. R. D. McLean, a priest in the Scottish Episcopal Church. The significance of these collections was not simply that they made widely and cheaply available what had hitherto been confined to expensive volumes of limited circulation. They also presented Celtic prayers not as literary texts or quaint examples of folklore but as aids to personal spiritual devotion:

> They are offered … for the original purpose for which the bulk of them was composed, namely their values of religious expression. They have an especial worth in their nearness in spirit and tradition to the early Christian religion of North Britain, and in their wonderful mirror of the faith of a people who were of necessity individualists, and whose church was nature. Learned by heart and passed on from generation to generation, these are the prayers and hymns of the nomadic Christian missionaries.[1]

McLean's preface to his 1961 anthology touched on several themes that have come to loom large in the current revival. He reiterated Carmichael's conviction that material collected in the late nineteenth century derived from the golden age of Celtic Christianity, arguing that 'it is still possible to discern the spirit of that Columban church in these poems to which even now they are a more durable monument than the stones and crosses of Iona which they inspired'.[2] He noted that the poems contained 'distinctly pre-Christian elements' and revealed 'two great religious conceptions, peculiar to the Celtic Church', namely a sense of the immanence and close presence of God and the ministry of the *anamchara* or soul friend.[3] He stressed the spirituality of the Celtic tradition and the modern relevance of the themes of protection and closeness to nature which figured so prominently in its prayers. His preface ended with a prediction of its 'revivification in these days of a latter Dispersion'.[4]

Another book published in 1961 was perhaps even more influential in sowing the seeds of Celtic Christian revival. In *The Age of the Saints in the Early Celtic Church* Nora Chadwick gave her formidable academic *imprimatur* to the notion of a distinct Celtic Church characterised by spiritual purity and sturdy independence:

The most outstanding feature of this Celtic Church was the wide-spread extent and power of the monastic foundations. By the sixth century these had come to give it an individual character and local tradition to which it clung passionately in the face of attempts from Rome and Canterbury to bring it into full conformity with continental usages.[5]

Her more popular work, *The Celts*, first published in 1971 and never long out of print since, gave an even more positive and romantic spin to the subject of Celtic Christianity, lamenting 'the disappearance of the idiosyncratic Christianity of the Celtic Church' and reflecting that 'a Christianity so pure and serene as that of the age of the saints could hardly be equalled and never repeated ... The Christianity of the Celts has a marked spirituality of its own ... It retained to the end a serene inner life'.[6]

Another scholar was also writing lyrically and enthusiastically in the 1960s about early Irish monasticism. Kathleen Hughes presented a highly attractive picture of the life of the monks, and especially of the hermit poets whom, following Robin Flower, she saw as epitomising the particular Celtic Christian affection for the natural world:

> The hermit retreated to the woods, living under the forest trees, regarding the seasons advance, listening to the birds, watching the wild beasts as they played or came to drink; or he built himself a hut at the lakeside, or within sight of the sea, perhaps on one of the many islands which surround the coast, where he might meditate and pray. A man might come to such a cell after a long period of training in the monastic schools, so that a scholar sophisticated in taste and subtle in expression might enjoy without interruption the beauty of his surroundings at a time when his imagination, stirred by religious emotion, was peculiarly sensitive.[7]

A number of more popular books published in the later 1960s presented Celtic Christianity in a similarly positive and attractive light. Brendan Lehane's *The Quest of Three Abbots* (1968) described Irish Christianity's contribution to civilising Dark Age Europe by focusing on the travels of Brendan, Columba and Columbanus. The travels of the Celtic monks was also the theme of E. G. Bowen's *Saints, Seaways and Settlements* (1969) which suggested close links between native Christian communities on the western edge of Britain and the Coptic churches of Egypt and Syria. Continuing interest in Glastonbury and Arthurian legend showed itself in the popularity of a book published in 1968, and reprinted five times over the next seven years, which argued that Paul, Joseph of Arimathea and the Virgin Mary had all come to Britain and described Ninian as 'a British missionary out of Avalon'.[8] The early 1970s saw the publication of two rather more cautious academic studies, Leslie Hardinge's *The Celtic Church in Britain* (1972) and John McNeill's *The Celtic Churches: A History AD 200 to 1200* (1974), hailed by its publishers as 'the first comprehensive study of Celtic Christianity'. McNeill, a Canadian Presbyterian, was particularly sceptical about 'the ecclesiastically motivated solutions' that had been offered to explain the enigma of the Culdees.[9] Both authors, however, were happy with the notion of a distinct Celtic Church – Hardinge defined it as 'that group of Christians which lived in the British Isles before the coming of the Italian mission of St Augustine and continued for about a century, or a little more, in an independent state'.[10] Even the staunchly orthodox Roman Catholic monk, David Knowles, could write in 1976 that as late as the tenth century there were three distinct regions in north-western Europe in religious terms 'that covered by the organized Church, connected with Rome by bonds of varying strength; that of Celtic Christianity embracing Ireland, Scotland and (though less definitely) Wales; and that of the pagan north'. Knowles also identified a distinctiveness in Celtic monasticism, seeing it as 'more austere and individualistic' than the Benedictine type which he himself professed.[11]

The peculiarly monastic character of Celtic Christianity has been much emphasised in the current revival. So too has the related theme of spirituality – indeed the phrase 'Celtic spirituality' has almost come to eclipse the broader 'Celtic Christianity' in the titles of books, retreats and conferences. One of the first in recent times to identify this particular strain in the Celtic tradition was the American monk and writer, Thomas Merton, who noted shortly before his death in 1968: 'I am reading about Celtic monasticism, the hermits, the lyric poets, the pilgrims, the sea travellers, etc. A whole new world that has waited until now to open up for me'.[12] The earliest modern use of the phrase 'Celtic spirituality' that I have been able to trace is in *Paths in Spirituality*, a book written in 1972 by John Macquarrie, the distinguished Scottish theologian who held chairs in New York and Oxford. In a passage that has been much quoted since, he presents it as a counter-model to the culture of secular materialism that characterises Western society at the end of the twentieth century:

> I choose as an illustration Celtic spirituality. Although it belongs to a culture that has almost vanished, it fulfils in many respects the

conditions to which a contemporary spirituality would have to conform. At the very centre of this type of spirituality was an intense sense of presence. The Celt was very much a God-intoxicated man whose life was embraced on all sides by the divine Being. But this presence was always mediated through some finite this-world reality, so that it would be difficult to imagine a spirituality more down-to-earth than this one. The sense of God's immanence in his creation was so strong in Celtic spirituality as to amount sometimes almost to a pantheism. Of course Celtic Christianity was continuous with the earlier Celtic paganism ... It must also be made clear that their spirituality was in fact christianized. It is strongly trinitarian, and transcendence is combined with immanence.[13]

The spirituality of Celtic Christianity was also emphasised in *God in Our Midst*, an anthology of 'prayers and devotions from the Celtic tradition' that appeared in 1974. Its compiler, Martin Reith, a priest in the Scottish Episcopal Church, included several of McLean's verse versions of prayers from the *Carmina Gadelica* together with translations of hymns attributed to Columba and prayers and poems written in the 1930s by Alistair Maclean, Minister of Daviot near Inverness and father of the famous novelist. This diverse material was presented as coming from a distinctive spiritual tradition which Reith investigated further in a later book, *Beyond the Mountains* (1979). Like Maclean, he emphasised the devotional nature of his anthology, writing that 'many readers should find in these poems a powerful incentive to lead them into deeper ways of silent prayer'.[14] He also stressed the contemporary relevance of the Celtic spiritual tradition: 'The prayers reveal a grasp of the wholeness of creation in marked contrast to that disintegrated and unsacramental view of life which is bedevilling much of Christian witness today'.[15] Drawing on Nora Chadwick's work, and enthusiastically quoting Macquarrie, Reith presented Celtic Christianity as monastic, holistic, imbued with a sense of God's presence in creation, preferring the small- to the large-scale and above all deeply spiritual:

> The Celt may never have excelled at developing institutions, but in an age when structures in government, industry, and even the Church are increasingly criticized for crushing the spirit that ought to exist in them, the Celt has something very vital to contribute. The current development of the 'house church' and Christian cell movements are entirely in keeping with Celtic tradition.[16]

Unlike many of those involved in the modern revival, Martin Reith was not content just to write about Celtic Christianity but also sought to live out what he took to be its cardinal principles. He felt called to the eremetical life and gave up parish ministry to live simply in a small cottage at Scotlandwell, an ancient Celtic site near Loch Leven and the island retreat of Serf. He conducted occasional retreats there but spent much of his time in solitary study and prayer. The growing fashion for a rather easy and self-indulgent 'Celtic' spirituality through the later 1980s deeply disturbed him. Shortly before his sudden death in 1992, he spoke of the need to get back to the 'missing ingredient' of asceticism: 'The image of Celtic spirituality that is put across so often today is twee, drawing room religion. It's comfortable – part of the affluent society. The emotional side is toned down. In fact it's whisky served up with an awful lot of water'. For Reith the distinctive hallmark of the early Celtic Christians was that 'they took the Gospel whole and didn't leave out the bits that they didn't like. For example, they realised that prayer goes with fasting. They didn't compromise the Cross out of the Gospel'.[17]

On the whole, enthusiasm for Celtic Christianity in the 1960s and 1970s was confined to certain individuals. There was not much interest at an institutional level in the churches although major anniversaries connected with the saints were celebrated. The Roman Catholic Archdiocese of Dublin put on a pageant in 1961 to mark the 1,500th anniversary of Patrick's death and two years later the 1,400th anniversary of Columba's arrival on Iona was celebrated with a service of Holy Communion in the Abbey at which 'the Moderator of the General Assembly of the Church of Scotland received communion at the same table as an Anglican bishop'.[18] The ecumenical associations of Celtic Christianity in Scotland were further displayed when a new church in Bridge of Don, Aberdeen, shared by Roman Catholic and Presbyterian worshippers was dedicated to Columba. Some Scots however, were uneasy about the new portrayal of Columba and his contemporaries as patron saints of ecology and inter-faith dialogue. A poem written by Edwin Morgan in the early 1970s had the saint protest at his arrival on Iona 'there's too much nature here', and remind his twentieth-century admirers that 'it wasn't for a fox or an eagle I set sail'.[19]

It was perhaps in Ireland that the rediscovery of the Celtic Christian tradition was first taken up by more than a few isolated individuals. A growing mood of national self confidence reinforced the message of the Second Vatican Council that the Catholic church should look more to its native traditions and be less in thrall to Rome. An important series of lectures on Irish spirituality delivered at the Mater Dei Institute of

Religious Education in Dublin in 1978–9 signalled a new appreciation of the Celtic heritage. All but one of the contributors were Catholics, the sole Protestant being George Simms, former Primate of the Church of Ireland and a keen enthusiast for Celtic Christianity who was particularly devoted to the *Book of Kells*. The lectures arose out of a feeling among staff at the Catholic teacher training college that the courses offered in religious education 'lacked a specifically Irish dimension ... and gave scant attention to the Celtic religious tradition'.[20] Later published in paperback form, they indicated a growing acknowledgement and affirmation of the Celtic heritage of Irish Catholicism and identified several highly relevant contemporary themes within it – the lecture on the place of the Bible in Irish spirituality, for example, concluded by observing that 'the early Irish Church has the same message for us regarding scripture in the Church as has the Second Vatican Council'.[21] Tomás O'Fiaich, Archbishop of Armagh and Primate of Ireland from 1977 to 1990, was a vigorous proponent of the Celtic strain in Irish Christianity, which he sometimes expounded in terms that were construed to be nationalistic and anti-English, and published studies of the travels of early Irish monks on the Continent.

Although Celtic Christianity has had much less appeal in Northern Ireland, those seeking a way out of the terrible sectarian violence that has gripped the province since the 1960s have sometimes pointed to its potential to bring Catholics and Protestants closer on the basis of their common religious heritage. The Corrymeela Community, founded in 1965 on Presbyterian initiative as a force for reconciliation and consciously modelled on the Iona Community, has never strongly emphasised the Celtic tradition, doubtless because it still grates with many Protestants. It does, however, affirm that 'all of us have a common heritage in Christ received through St Patrick, the Apostle of Ireland, and the Celtic Church, whose spirituality predates our modern divisions and has had an influence on both Protestant and Catholic traditions'.[22] Other would-be peace-makers have sought to remind Irish Catholics and Protestants of their shared spiritual ancestry as 'Patrick's People' and resisted the narrow identification of Celtic Christianity, and Patrick in particular, with the nationalist cause.[23]

A number of events and publications in the late 1970s indicated a growing fascination with Celtic Christianity on the other side of the Atlantic. Perhaps the best publicised was the project dreamed up by Tim Severin, a Harvard professor, to reconstruct Brendan's voyage across the Atlantic. Sailing from Ireland in a boat constructed according to principles laid down in an eighth-century Hiberno-Latin text, Severin and his crew travelled via the Faroes, Iceland and Greenland to Newfoundland. The book chronicling their year-long journey, *The Brendan Voyage*, became a bestseller on both sides of the Atlantic and revived speculation that Celtic monks had reached the shores of America and planted monasteries there. In 1946 William Goodwin had argued in *The Remains of Greater Ireland in New England* that an ancient site in North Salem, New Hampshire, had once been a *Céli Dé* monastery. In 1976, Barry Fell, a Harvard professor, claimed that there were several pre-Christian Celtic sites in America. Two years later a large-scale conference on 'Celtic Consciousness' was held in Toronto. William Thompson, an American with Welsh, Scottish and Irish blood, told delegates that reading *The Quest of Three Abbots* had inspired him to quit 'the institutional routines' of academic life and described the Celtic Church as 'the mystical Church of John ... decentralized, shamanistic, and simple' in contrast to the 'centralized, hierarchical, complex and worldly' Church of Rome.[24]

In Britain, a steady stream of attractively packaged new anthologies of Celtic prayers and poems appeared throughout the 1980s. One of the first to range beyond the usual selections from the *Carmina Gadelica* and include extracts from saints' *Vitae* and early Irish poems was *Celtic Christianity: Ecology and Holiness*, first published in 1982 by the Lindisfarne Association and reprinted in 1986 by Floris Books, a publishing house connected with the Rudolf Steiner movement. An introductory essay by Christopher Bamford emphasised Celtic Christianity's embrace of the natural world and assimilation of druidic and bardic traditions and lauded the Celtic Church, 'or as it is also called, the British Church', as:

> An ideal for those who have known of it, not simply as a Golden Age of innocence and purity ... but as an alternative seed, 'a light from the west', perhaps obscure and even alien, but nevertheless powerful and true with the kind of reality we need in Britain today.[25]

In *God Under My Roof*, a collection of poems and blessings from the *Carmina* published by a small press run by an Anglican community of nuns in 1984, Esther de Waal offered a more orthodox and less 'alternative' view of Celtic Christianity but was equally enthusiastic about its relevance to an age hungry for a new spirituality and for a greater sense of identity and roots:

> Recent years have seen the enormous growth in exploration of other religious traditions, particularly those of the East; yet have we not failed to recognize the wealth of a tradition much nearer to us, a tradition 'at home' in our own native islands?[26]

The publication in 1985 of a volume of 'prayers in the Celtic tradition' written by David Adam, Vicar of Lindisfarne, marked a significant new departure and heralded one of the most successful and influential manifestations of the modern Celtic Christian revival. *The Edge of Glory* contained short rhythmic prayers decorated and encircled by the characteristic interlacing designs found on illuminated manuscripts and high crosses. It was an almost instant bestseller and has been followed by a succession of similar collections. Most, like *Tides and Seasons*, *Power Lines*, *The Open Gate* and *The Rhythm of Life*, are collections of modern prayers in the Celtic idiom, but others involve sustained meditations on early Irish prayers – *The Cry of the Deer* (1987) focuses on 'St Patrick's Breastplate' and *The Eye of the Eagle* (1990) on 'Be thou my vision'. Adam's books have appealed to Christians of a wide variety of denominational and theological persuasions and have done much to raise the profile and increase the popularity of Celtic Christianity as well as boosting Lindisfarne as a place of pilgrimage and retreat.

David Adam stands very much in the tradition of those Anglicans from the north of England who have felt a special affinity for the Celtic tradition. Born and brought up in Northumberland, he visited Lindisfarne as a young boy and was much taken with the stories of Cuthbert and Aidan. Later, working as a priest in the North Yorkshire Moors near Whitby and Lastingham, he came to appreciate the legacy of Hilda, Cedd and Chadd. Talking to Adam and reading his prayers one very much has the sense that these figures are a living reality for him, just as they were for Bede and Lightfoot in earlier centuries. His appreciation of Celtic Christianity is rooted in his fondness for these saints and, indeed, in a more general conviction about the importance of saints in contemporary Protestant Christianity. He is fond of saying that 'a church without saints is a church without heaven'.[27] He eschews a romantic approach, stressing the down-to-earth nature of the Celtic tradition which he feels has the effect of pulling modern society back towards reality rather than away from it. While he deplores the wild flights of fancy engaged in by some modern enthusiasts for Celtic Christianity – it is, indeed, to a remark of his that I owe the title for this book – his own approach is unashamedly enthusiastic rather than academic. For him Celtic Christianity is first and foremost a resource of insights and approaches to be taken up and adapted by contemporary Christians. His concern is with what it can say to us today rather than what we can say about it in terms of dates and historical details. Discussing 'St Patrick's Breastplate', for example, he comments that it does not matter when it was written. The important thing is that 'It expresses so well much of the early Celtic Christian Faith.

It vibrates still with the God who surrounds us, the Christ who is with us, and the Spirit within us'.[28]

Adam's books of 'prayers in the Celtic tradition' originated in the work of a small group in his North Yorkshire parish in the early 1980s. Having found material from Celtic anthologies particularly enriching and relevant, the group took to crafting their own prayers in a similar style and producing accompanying artwork. How 'Celtic' they actually are is a moot point. *Power Lines*, subtitled 'Celtic Prayers about Work' includes contributions from Aquinas, Alcuin, Augustine, Clement of Rome, Ignatius Loyola and Robert Runcie. On the whole, Adam's prayers reflect the reconstructed Celticism of Carmichael's *Carmina Gadelica* and McLean's *Poems of the West Highlanders* rather than the tone of much earlier works like Columba's *Altus Prosator*. It is true that they do stand firmly in the tradition of the ninth- and tenth-century Irish breastplate and hermit prayers with their strong emphasis on protection, the enfolding and encircling nature of God's love and the reality of the Divine presence in the physical world but there is little of the darker, more sin-centred approach found in much of the early Celtic Christian material.

The same could be said of all the anthologies of Celtic prayers that appeared in the later 1980s. As with Adam's books, most of these were presented primarily as devotional rather than literary works. *Threshold of Light*, a small volume of 'Prayers and Praises from the Celtic Tradition' compiled by Esther de Waal and Donald Allchin in 1986, included Irish poems from the eighth to tenth centuries and medieval Welsh verse as well as the inevitable *Carmina* selection. Its appearance as one in a series of 'selections from the spiritual classics in a form suitable for daily reading and meditation' might perhaps be taken to mark the coming of age for Celtic spirituality which could now stand alongside devotional 'greats' like Dame Julian of Norwich and St John of the Cross.[29] Two years later, in *The Celtic Vision*, de Waal made a more substantial selection of material from the *Carmina* which she insisted should not simply be approached in a mood of nostalgia: 'To read the *Carmina Gadelica* is not merely to be transported back into a vanished world. It is to be given a vision of a world which still lies to hand, a gift waiting for us if we should choose to take it'.[30] Also in 1988 *The Sun Dances* and *New Moon of the Seasons* were reprinted by Floris Books and a selection of McLean's *Poems of the Western Highlanders* was included in a paperback entitled *Praying with Highland Christians* with a foreword by the broadcaster Sally Magnusson, who gushed 'It is a privilege to pray with these Celtic Christians'.[31] While material from the Scottish Highlands and islands dominated these anthologies, other Celtic regions of the British Isles were also gaining recognition. In 1986 *The Deer's Cry* brought together 'a treasury of Irish religious verse' and three years later *The Welsh Pilgrim's Manual* provided a generous selection of prayers and poems in both Welsh and English from the ninth to the twentieth centuries.

Several of these books were more likely to be found shelved both in bookshops and homes alongside works on Zen Buddhism and reading tarot cards than next to Bibles and Christianity. There was a widespread suspicion among evangelicals and other conservative Christians that what was being presented as 'Celtic Christianity' owed more to New Age influences and modern ultra-liberalism than to early expressions of the eternal truths of the Gospel. These suspicions were not allayed by the appearance in 1990 of *Celtic Fire*, an anthology of Celtic Christian literature culled from a wide variety of (unidentified) sources. Its compiler, Robert Van de Weyer, a somewhat unorthodox Anglican priest, made much of the esoteric and syncretistic nature of Celtic Christianity which he saw as drawing on the apocryphal as well as the canonical Gospels and having some resemblances to Eastern religions. He described Welsh gnomic poems as having 'something of the quality of the "koan" in Zen Buddhism'.[32] For Van de Weyer, the Celtic fire, 'burning anew in the late twentieth century', had three main sources: ancient Druid religion, the desert fathers of Egypt and 'the doctrines of the great British heretic Pelagius'.[33] This last element he regarded as particularly important. Introducing a theme that has been taken up in several other popular recent books about Celtic Christianity, he suggested that the early British Church had been strongly Pelagian in outlook, taking a much more affirmative view of both human and physical nature than either Roman Catholicsm or later Protestant Churches. He also argued that elements of this distinctive Celtic tradition still lingered, noting that 'the rugged individualism of the Celtic monk, his conviction that each person is free to choose between good and evil, and his insistence that faith must be practical as well as spiritual, remain hallmarks of Christians in Britain' and quoting Karl Barth's description of British Christianity as 'incurably Pelagian'.[34] He even portrayed the British tradition of pastoral poetry and landscape painting and the national obsession with gardening and pets as distinctively Celtic legacies. Like Esther de Waal, Van de Weyer portrayed the Celtic Christian revival of the 1980s as the exciting rediscovery of a long lost treasure: 'For over a millennium the treasures of Celtic poetry, and the wisdom of the great Celtic saints, lay largely hidden'.[35] He also shared her enthusiasm for the home-grown nature of a movement that could help people rediscover their own roots: 'All of us born and bred in the British Isles, whatever blood runs in our veins, have the Celtic fire in our hearts.'[36]

These and other anthologies published in the 1980s put 'Celtic spirituality' firmly on the map and provided a wealth of easily accessible material for both public worship and private devotion. It has so far been in the area of liturgy that the current revival has had most impact on the churches. The prayers of David Adam and the *Carmina Gadelica* in particular have been widely used in services and several churches have adopted Celtic-style liturgies. The Church of Scotland's 1994 *Book of Common Order* has orders for morning and evening worship based on a Celtic pattern and a Celtic Communion service, using rhythmic prayers in the style of the *Carmina*. There has also been a boom in retreats, quiet days and conferences on Celtic spirituality, most of which are based around use of the prayers and poems, both ancient and modern, found in the anthologies.

Along with the promotion of Celtic spirituality as an important resource for (more or less orthodox) Christian devotion, the 1980s also saw a heightened general interest in the subject as part of a wider fascination with all things Celtic. One of the first books to provide a broad popular survey of Celtic Christianity, Peter Berresford Ellis' *Celtic Inheritance* (1985) significantly appeared under the imprint of a general rather than a religious publisher. The author, a novelist and historian, avoided the excesses of romanticism and pointed out that the term 'Celtic Church' is not strictly accurate, although he went on to use it 'because any other term would be too cumbersome' and because he felt that it was possible to discern 'a singular cultural entity within the greater Christian movement, delineated by its practices, philosophies, social concepts and art forms'.[37] He also made much of the Celtic input into the formulation of the Christian doctrine of the Trinity, singling out the contribution of Hilary, the fourth-century 'Celtic' Bishop of Poitiers. The notion that the Trinity is a peculiarly Celtic concept, deriving from an emphasis in pre-Christian times on triads of deities, is taken up in several other recent books.

Another book first published in 1985, Shirley Toulson's *Celtic Journeys*, reflects a theme that has loomed particularly large in the current revival. Essentially a travel guide, it offers detailed directions for those wishing to follow in the footsteps of the Celtic saints. Celtic Christian sites have become a mecca for pilgrimages, retreats, day-trips and holidays. Several books have been written to facilitate this spiritual tourism. Van de Weyer's *Celtic Fire* provides a 'pilgrims' guide to the main Christian sites' with suggestions of 'comfortable hotels and campsites' nearby.[38] In *The Celtic Year* (1993), which gives details of a different pilgrimage to a holy site for each month of the year, Toulson writes:

> All places are holy, if we will only keep ourselves aware of where we are, but the hermitages, caves, holy wells and ruined oratories associated with the Celtic saints are both numinous in themselves and instrumental in awakening us to the general sanctity of earth and water.[39]

The pantheistic 'New Age' overtones of that remark are not accidental. Shirley Toulson has been prominent among those who have emphasised the 'alternative' nature of Celtic Christianity and its closeness to other religions. In *The Celtic Year* she links Celtic saints' days to pre-Christian festivals and argues that the Celtic Church took on many of the rites and traditions of the Druids. Her earlier work, *The Celtic Alternative: A reminder of the Christianity we lost* (1987), argues that Celtic Christianity 'had more in common with Buddhism than with the institutional Christianity of the West' and also notes close parallels with the Jewish faith in which she herself grew up.[40] This book is a lament for a lost Christianity with much to teach us today in terms of 'tolerance, persistence and a tough but gentle kindness'.[41] In particular, it is a lament over the outcome of the Synod of Whitby, Bede's account of which is printed in full as an appendix:

> When matters came to a head at Whitby and the Celtic Church ceased to exist, we lost a form of individual Christianity which, through its druidic roots, was truly linked to the perennial philosophy of humanity. It is possible that the battle of words waged in 644 was even more of a turning point in the history of these islands than the battle fought out by contending armies at Hastings in 1066.[42]

For Toulson, the essence of Celtic Christianity is that it was 'primarily concerned with the relations between people, a religion of an isolated rural landscape, in which to meet a fellow human being is to hail him'. At Whitby that had been given up for 'a city based religion' in which 'people are amassed in crowds, to be manipulated'.[43]

> Now that we are realizing the deadly dangers of our mass technological society, it is time, I think, to turn back and consider the humanity of the men and women of the Celtic Church. Their Church could have been our inheritance – as it is, we can still visit the places associated with it, look at some of the things that were

202   *Celtic Christianity*

made by its adherents and catch something of the spirit of its leaders in the descendants of the people who were their friends.⁴⁴

Here was a new way of recovering the faith that had been lost. It could be recaptured not just by visiting its sacred sites and contemplating the beauty of its surviving artefacts but also by encountering contemporary Celts. At a time when the English are facing an identity crisis and suffering from guilt about their imperial past, this romanticisation of the inhabitants of the Celtic fringes and recovery of such mythical stereotypes as the Spiritual Gael and the Visionary Celt has proved very appealing.

The Celts as a whole were much in vogue in the mid-1980s, as evidenced by the large audiences for Frank Delaney's BBC 2 television series in 1986. Much interest was focused on pre-Christian Celtic religion and books like P. MacCana's *Celtic Mythology* (1983) and Miranda Green's *The Gods of the Celts* (1986) sold well. Glastonbury became a mecca for Celtic revivalism and the unofficial capital of 'New Age' Britain with many of the shops in its high street given over to selling healing crystals, holistic remedies and books on goddess worship and the Arthurian legends. To some extent Celtic Christianity was incorporated into this 'alternative' agenda, with its syncretistic and panentheistic elements being stressed at the expense of its more orthodox Christian aspects. To its conservative and evangelical critics, the Celtic Christian revival seemed to have been hi-jacked by the New Age movement and neo-paganism.

Suspicions about the orthodoxy of Celtic Christianity were, if anything, confirmed by the presentation of Pelagius, the fifth-century British heretic, and John Scotus Eriugena, a ninth-century Irish monk whose writings were later condemned by the Pope, as 'Celtic' theologians whose affirmative view of human nature and the physical world was in total contrast to the teachings of Augustine of Hippo which had come to be accepted by both the Roman Catholic and Protestant churches. Pelagius' rediscovery and rehabilitation owed much to the work of Brian Rees whose *Pelagius: A Reluctant Heretic* was published in 1988. Eriugena was strongly championed by John Macquarrie who described him in a 1983 article on Celtic Spirituality as 'the greatest thinker of the Celtic Church' and the author of its distinctive immanentist spirituality in which God was seen as being present in all things.⁴⁵ He was also the subject of a major study by J. J. O'Meara in 1988. Augustine of Hippo became the bogeyman for a new breed of pro-Celtic theologians who blamed him for giving Western Christianity its obsession with sin and guilt. In the words of one of them: 'The pessimism and anti-humanism of the later Augustine has cast a chilling gloom across Western Christendom. Only Celtic Christianity has entirely escaped this shadow. In this tradition men and women have opened to God and have trusted human nature in each other'.[46]

Celtic Christianity has been strongly championed by Matthew Fox, the controversial proponent of creation-centred spirituality. Eriugena appears eighth in line after Jesus Christ and gains a three-star award in the bizarre 'family tree' at the end of his seminal work *Original Blessing* (1983) and is taken to represent 'the Celtic love of God in nature and nature in God'.[47] Other works by Fox, who fell foul of the Roman Catholic Church for his apparent denial of the doctrine of original sin, laud the Celtic contribution to creation-centred spirituality and put Eriugena and Cuthbert alongside Hildegaard of Bingen, Francis of Assisi, Meister Eckhart and Teilhard de Chardin as 'the finest wisdom figures of the West'.[48] Shirley Toulson has written that 'if we want to understand the depths of Celtic spirituality we shall find the nearest parallels in the Buddhist teaching of today as well as in the creation spirituality of such Christian teachers as Matthew Fox'.[49] Catalogues of books on Creation Spirituality regularly list works on Celtic Christianity alongside the writings of Fox and gurus of the green movement like Chief Seathl and E. F. Schumacher.[50]

The identification in Celtic Christianity of elements more usually found in pagan religion continues to be a marked feature of books appearing under the imprint of 'New Age' publishers like Element Books. Michael Howard's *Angels and Goddesses* (1994) emphasises the syncretistic nature of Celtic Christianity and its many Druidical elements. In similar vein, Caitlin Matthews' *The Celtic Tradition* (1995) notes that 'the transition between Celtic paganism and Celtic Christianity was surprisingly easy. So easy that ... druidism and Christianity mutually upheld common concepts'.[51] Commenting on the story of Patrick's encounter with King Leagaire at Tara, she notes that 'Patrick shares both the druidic ability to create invisibility and also to shapeshift'.[52] C. James' *An Age of Saints: Its Relevance for Us Today* (1996), which ends with a hymn to Gaia, strongly emphasises the 'Original Blessing' theme: 'Not for the Celtic saints of the heroic age chilling and childish depictions of hell and eternal damnation, and little for them of mortal sin and original sin. It seems that they spoke rather of the sweetness and beauty of this life on Earth'.[53]

A clutch of books that came out in the early 1990s under the imprint of well-established Christian publishers portrayed Celtic Christianity in a more orthodox if equally positive light. Although this objective is nowhere explicitly stated by their authors, they represent an attempt to reclaim this particular tradition for Christianity and counter its appropriation by New Agers and neo-pagans. More specifically, they were aimed at those who had bought and used anthologies of Celtic prayers and wanted to know more about the theology and culture that lay behind them. Common to these books is the presentation of Celtic Christianity as a set of distinctive themes, all of which have contemporary relevance. First in the field was Esther de Waal with *A World Made Whole – The Rediscovery of the Celtic Tradition* (1991). Her preface announced: 'I have written this book with one purpose and one hope, and that is that it will encourage others to discover for themselves some of the riches that I have myself found in the Celtic tradition'.[54] While stressing that 'the Celtic way of seeing the world ... cannot be understood only in cerebral terms' and that 'like poetry, it must remain ultimately elusive', she encapsulated its central themes under three main headings: 'The Dedicated Life', 'The Celebration of Creation' and 'The Light and the Dark'.[55]

Very similar both in intention and structure was my own *The Celtic Way* which appeared in 1993 and grew out of a series broadcast in the late-night devotional slot on BBC Radio 4, 'Seeds of Faith' in March 1992. Like de Waal's, my book was written to inspire and encourage others to take up and follow the Celtic way that I myself had begun to explore and found enriching. I, too, identified certain themes such as 'Presence and Protection', 'The Goodness of Nature' and 'The Power of Imagination' which I felt struck a contemporary chord:

> Celtic Christianity does seem to speak with almost uncanny relevance to many of the concerns of our present age. It was environment-friendly, embracing positive attitudes to nature and constantly celebrating the goodness of God's creation. It was non-hierarchical and non-sexist, eschewing the rule of diocesan bishops and a rigid parish structure in favour of a loose federation of monastic communities which included married as well as celibate clergy and were often presided over by women. Like the religions of the Australian Aborigines and the native American Indians which are also being rediscovered today, it takes us back to our roots and seems to speak with a primitive innocence and directness which has much appeal in our tired and cynical age.[56]

Philip Sheldrake's *Living Between Worlds* (1995) has a more specific focus, exploring the theme of 'Place and Journey in Celtic Spirituality' and relating the 'present fascination with Celtic Christianity' to the fact that 'the last thirty years have seen a strong reassertion of regional identity in the British Isles'.[57] It ends with a note of caution about the current revival not found in most books of this kind:

In one sense, the Celtic spirituality that I have described is not simply a rediscovery but a *reinvention*. There is a danger that either we force the history and tradition of particular spiritualities into the shape of other, modern experiences or we seek to shape our own contemporary spiritual quest naively in terms of some presumed golden age.[58]

The authors of two other books published in 1995 are much less troubled by this danger. Michael Mitton and Ray Simpson both come from the charismatic wing of the Church of England. Their studies, *Restoring the Woven Cord: Strands for Celtic Christianity for the Church Today* and *Exploring Celtic Spirituality: Historic Roots for Our Future*, signal a significant broadening in the appeal of Celtic Christianity that took place in the middle 1990s. In the early stages of the current revival, the 'Celtic fan club' was largely confined to Christians of a liberal disposition. Charismatics were the first from outside this circle to break clear of evangelical suspicions about the New Age and pantheistic aspects of Celtic Christianity and to recognise its orthodoxy and Biblical basis. Not surprisingly, they were particularly attracted to the stories of signs and wonders, miracle working, healing and prophesying that fill the *Vitae* of the Celtic saints. Mitton, formerly director of Anglican Renewal Ministries and now associated with the Acorn Healing Trust, is an especially enthusiastic exponent of the charismatic nature of Celtic Christianity, even going so far as to tell a New Wine gathering in 1993 that its adherents spoke in tongues. His book, while sensibly dropping that particular claim for which there is no definitive evidence, argues that 'the Celtic Church was quite at ease with God intervening miraculously in the affairs of his people ... and would have been quite at home with John Wimber's phrase "power evangelism" '.[59] Ray Simpson, in his book, similarly emphasises the themes of healing, prophesying and spiritual warfare.

The enthusiasm for Celtic Christianity among contemporary charismatics has been one of the most striking aspects of the current revival. 'Celtic style' worship, involving short, rhythmic prayers and songs based on those found in the *Carmina Gadelica*, has been a prominent feature in 'alternative' services such as those in the ill-fated Sheffield Nine o'Clock experiment and has been widely taken up by the new 'house' churches. It is through the charismatic movement that many evangelicals have come to a much more positive view of Celtic Christianity. Sessions on Celtic spirituality are now a regular fixture on the programmes of the great evangelical jamborees like Greenbelt and Spring Harvest. There is particular interest among the so-called 'post-evangelicals' who are seeking to deepen their spirituality and go on growing in faith.

A number of evangelicals have become attracted to the missionary approach which they discern in the Celtic Church and the model that it is seen as providing of a style of evangelism rooted in indigenous culture. Anglicans in particular have suggested that this Celtic approach may offer an appropriate strategy for evangelism in contemporary post-Christian Britain. In *Recovering the Past: Celtic and Roman Mission* (1996), John Finney, Bishop of Pontefract and former Anglican Officer for the Decade of Evangelism, argues that the Celtic model of mission, which he identifies as emphasising spirituality rather than doctrine, and belonging to a community rather than hard-selling the Gospel, is more effective for reaching a society predominantly non-Christian in its make-up and ethos, while the more settled institutional Roman model, as practised by Augustine, is more appropriate in a situation where conversion has already been achieved. A more measured and academic study of this theme by Douglas Dales, Chaplain of Marlborough College, *Light to the Isles* (1997), which gives rare praise to the Anglo-Saxons as well as to the more glamorous Celts, shares the sense that there are lessons for the modern church to learn from these early missionary efforts.

It is not just in its approach to evangelism that the Celtic Church is increasingly being seen as a model for the contemporary church to follow. Robert Van de Weyer's *A Celtic Resurrection* (1996) argues that it also offers lessons on church organisation and structure that Anglicans in particular would do well to heed. This book portrays the rebellion of a number of parish churches in Norfolk and Suffolk against episcopal authority as a replay of the Synod of Whitby, this time with the Celtic side winning. It pleads for more local autonomy and power for the laity in the Church of England and strongly attacks modern bishops whom Van de Weyer sees as chief executives wholly out of keeping with the Celtic model of episcopacy epitomised by Aidan and Cuthbert who 'had no executive power at all' but were 'apostles who travelled from place to place, talking to people about the gospel and inspiring them to change their lives in accordance with Christ's teaching'.[60]

There is one especially striking feature about the books that have played so important a role in the current Celtic Christian revival. Their authors are virtually all English, albeit in some cases with Celtic connections. It is reminiscent of the contribution made by the Anglo-Saxon Bede and the Anglo-Norman chroniclers, Giraldus Cambrensis, Geoffrey of Monmouth and William of Malmesbury, to the first two revivals. There is a similar agenda of romantic idealisation, compounded by a certain guilt-induced acknowledegment of the validity of a marginalised tradition and a fascination with the 'outsider' and the 'other'. Several of the key manifestos of the current revival begin with personal testimonies describing a conversion experience. In the preface to *A World Made Whole*, Esther de Waal notes that 'it was in fact one September evening, several years ago, when I was staying in Ireland and taken to see the high crosses at Monasterboice that I now look back on as the moment of true conversion'.[61] Donald Allchin is equally precise about the event which first made him aware of the whole Celtic Christian tradition. A visit to a remote Celtic site in Wales was 'like opening a door into a hitherto unexpected part of the house in which you live' and led him to realise that 'the island of Britain is larger than England'.[62] Ray Simpson writes in the preface to *Exploring Celtic Spirituality* of the importance in his spiritual journey of a visit to Lindisfarne in 1985. Michael Mitton tells the most dramatic conversion story:

> In March 1992 I set off on a journey that has changed the direction of my life. I travelled to the holy island of Lindisfarne … Here, during the course of two blustery wet and cold days I became acquainted with this historic place, researching the lives of Aidan and Cuthbert who had lived here during the Christian dawn of these isles of Britain and Ireland. For me it was like a homecoming. Something about the island and its history connected with a deep longing within me, and brought together many different strands of my own faith. As I explored the Celtic faith of this ancient mission centre I discovered something that I had been searching for during the past twenty years.[63]

The zeal of the convert is noticeable in the writings of many of those who have been in the forefront of the current revival. So too is the importance of sacred places, journeys and pilgrimage. For several of us 'conversion' to Celtic Christianity has been bound up with a physical as well as a spiritual change of direction. In Esther de Waal's case this has been a move from Canterbury to the Welsh borders, in mine from Surrey to Scotland, in Donald Allchin's from Oxford to North Wales and in Ray Simpson's from Norwich to Lindisfarne. Then there is the sense of coming home and discovering roots that were long hidden. At a time of cultural fragmentation and growing nationalism, rediscovery of the Celtic dimension in the British make-up perhaps has a special resonance, particularly for the English who have more difficulty defining their identity than the Irish, Scots and Welsh. To find that the Christianity of Cuthbert and Aidan is as much part of the Church of England's heritage as that of Augustine and Lanfranc has been a liberating experience for many Anglicans. The Celts are, after all, so much more romantic and exotic than the dull, prosaic Anglo-Saxons.

It is noticeable that the great majority of those both speaking at and attending conferences and retreats on Celtic Christianity have English accents (and mostly southern English accents). In my experience, this is as true of events taking place in Scotland and Wales as in England, although not in Ireland. In its early stages at least the current Celtic Christian revival has been a predominantly English and Anglican phenomenon. Some of its fiercest critics have come from the ranks of the indigenous Celtic population of the British Isles, most notably the Gaelic-speaking Scots.

This strongly English bias has had another interesting consequence. If Iona was the place at the symbolic heart of the late nineteenth- and early twentieth-century Celtic Christian revival, then Lindisfarne has come to occupy much the same role in the current one. In part this is because of the enormous success of David Adam's prayers but it also reflects a desire to find and affirm an authentic English expression of Celtic Christianity. There are times when it has looked as though the agenda is nothing less than an English (and Anglican) take-over bid for the entire Celtic Christian heritage. In John Finney's *Recovering the Past*, Ireland and Scotland go largely unmentioned, Wales scarcely more so, while England takes centre stage. Iona is totally eclipsed, if not ousted by Lindisfarne which is even claimed (on the book's cover as well as in the text) as the place where Columba died. Such blatantly Anglo-centric rewritings of history are mercifully rare but there is no doubt that the general tendency of several recent books has been to play up the significance of Lindisfarne and the English Celtic tradition represented by Cuthbert and Aidan.[64] It is also striking that the two most significant new religious movements to emerge from the current Celtic Christian revival, the Northumbria Community and the Community of Aidan and Hilda, both draw their inspiration from that tradition and are centred on Lindisfarne.

The Northumbria Community was established in 1992 when a small group of charismatic Christians from different denominations moved into a large house in north Northumberland which stands near a cave where Cuthbert's body is said to have been carried by monks from Holy Island fleeing from Viking invaders. They included a Baptist minister, an Anglican priest, and a Roman Catholic layman who had drawn inspiration from the rhythm of daily prayer on Lindisfarne while living there in the late 1970s. What brought them together was a conviction of the 'importance of the Celtic brand of Christianity, its emphasis on monastery and mission, the fire of continual devotion, and obedience to initiatives of the Spirit'.[65] The Community is not just restricted to those living in Northumbria but has members throughout the country who follow a 'way of living' which emphasises availability and vulnerability. There is a strong emphasis on mission, developing techniques of spiritual warfare associated with the Celtic saints, music and liturgy. The Community has its own daily office, combining 'traditional Celtic services' with contemporary songs and readings and has published two books of daily readings, *Celtic Daily Prayer* and *Celtic Night Prayer*.

The Community of Aidan and Hilda is also rooted in the charismatic renewal movement. It was launched in 1994 at an Anglican Renewal Conference in Swanwick by a group which included Michael Mitton and Ray Simpson. It draws direct inspiration from the lives of the Northumbrian saints and seeks a revival of their particular brand of Christian practice and witness today:

> The Community of Aidan and Hilda is a scattered community, a body of Christians who share the belief that God is once again calling us to the quality of life and commitment that was revealed in the lives of the Celtic saints, who once so effectively evangelised the isles of Britain, Ireland and beyond. Its aim is the healing of the land through men, women and children who draw inspiration from the Celtic saints.[66]

Those involved in the Community make much of the significance of the twentieth century's rediscovery of the long lost treasures of Celtic Christianity. A chronology at the front of Ray Simpson's book jumps from 793 ('A century of Viking invasions destroys monastic communities') to 1938 ('The Iona Community is founded by George MacLeod') and the 1990s ('As the Age of Enlightenment ends, waves of re-kindled Celtic spirituality bring hope') and ends in 1994 ('The Community of Aidan and Hilda is founded'), making an even more dramatic leap than the church history course until recently pursued in a certain Scottish divinity faculty which stopped in 664 and did not resume again until 1560.[67] The Community is specifically committed:

> To restore the memory, landmarks, witness and experience of the Celtic Church in ways that relate to God's purposes today, and to research the history, beliefs, lifestyle, evangelism and relationships to cultural patterns of the Celtic Church and how they apply to the renewal of today's church and society.[68]

Those seeking to join are first allocated a soul friend who guides them in

210   Celtic Christianity

the 'first voyage of the coracle' which leads to becoming a member and subscribing to a rule of life which involves a commitment to prayer, study, care for creation, mission and wholeness. In 1996 Ray Simpson left parish ministry in Norwich and moved to a small cottage in Lindisfarne where he conducts retreats and acts as the Community's main resource person. His *Celtic Worship Through the Year* (1997) provides a collection of daily liturgies and special services for Celtic saints' days and seasons of the Christian year. Simpson is also developing links with churches of different denominations throughout the British Isles with an interest in exploring Celtic models of ecclesiology and mission. His presence on the island has made Lindisfarne even more of a mecca for those seeking to refresh their own faith and 'learn from the Celts a way of mission that gets under the skin of people in non-church culture'.[69]

Iona has also inevitably been a major focus for the renewed interest in Celtic Christianity in the last two decades of the twentieth century. The island now attracts over 250,000 visitors a year. The majority are day-trippers but an increasing number stay in the restored Abbey or the recently built MacLeod Centre nearby. Bishop's House is booked solidly for retreats and holidays for much of the year and a new Roman Catholic residential house of prayer has recently been built on the island. Weeks on Celtic spirituality are a regular feature of the Iona Community's island programme and the Abbey shop has a huge turnover in Celtic Christian material. Overall, Celtic Christianity does not have quite the same prominence in the thinking of the Iona Community as it does for the more recently established Lindisfarne-leaning movements. Contemporary issues of peace and justice occupy a higher place on the Community's agenda and its two most recent leaders, who are based along with most of the Community's full-time staff not on Iona but in Glasgow, have tended to distance themselves from several aspects of the contemporary Celtic Christian revival.[70]

It is perhaps in its liturgy that the modern Iona Community most consciously draws on the Celtic tradition. The preface to the worship book used for daily morning and evening services in the Abbey and by members and associates around the world proclaims:

> We are the inheritors of the Celtic tradition, with its deep sense of Jesus as the head of all, and of God's glory in all of creation. So we use prayers from the Celtic Church for welcome, for work, and in expressing the need of the world.[71]

Most of the material in it is more obviously inspired by the gentle, world-affirming spirituality of the *Carmina Gadelica* than the darker, sin-centred prayers of Columba and his followers. The *Carmina* is also acknowledged as the major influence behind 'a weekly cycle of prayers from Iona in the Celtic Tradition' written by Philip Newell, joint warden of Iona Abbey in the early 1990s, and published in 1994 under the title *Each Day and Each Night*. Long regarded with considerable suspicion in conservative evangelical quarters for its over-incarnational bias and flirtation with 'New Ageism', the worship at Iona now seems to attract opprobium in equal measure for being either too Christian or not Christian enough, as well as winning much praise from those who find its Celtic cadences a welcome change from the prosy diet they are used to getting in church.

The songs of the Iona Community's Wild Goose worship group have played a considerable role in the current revival and are a virtually indispensable feature of services and retreats built around the theme of Celtic spirituality. The group's title is supposedly derived from an ancient Celtic symbol for the Holy Spirit but no historical evidence can be adduced to support this and there is a strong suspicion that the connection was first made in the fertile imagination of George MacLeod. Similar questions about authentic Celticity could be asked about many of the group's songs which are often very modern in approach and set to folk tunes. They certainly have little in common with the chants sung by Columba and his monks. Yet there are undeniably Celtic echoes both in their subject matter and their imagery and rhythmic style. Some derive from ancient Irish poems, like 'Today I arise' which is based on a poem attributed to Patrick. John Bell, the group's leading member and most prolific song writer, discerns three themes in Celtic Christianity which have strongly influenced his own work – 'mention of nature and the world as something affirmed by God rather than denied, seeing Jesus as a person and the marriage of the life of the world to the worship of God's people'.[72]

Several other contemporary Christian musicians have been influenced by the current Celtic Christian revival. Iona, a band founded in 1991, has recorded an album of instrumental and vocal music directly inspired by the *Book of Kells*, and two others, 'Heaven's Bright Sun' and 'Journey Into the Moon', inspired by David Adam's meditations on 'Be thou my vision' and, more generally, by the spiritual atmosphere of both Iona and Lindisfarne. Liam Lawton, a Roman Catholic priest who is Director of Music at Carlow Cathedral and came close to being chosen to represent Ireland in the 1998 Eurovision Song Contest, writes and performs songs in a contemporary Celtic idiom which draw on the language and themes of ancient Irish prayers. In Ireland an explosion of 'spiritual Celtic music' has blurred the already fuzzy edges between pagan and Christian Celtic religion with songs about Druid stone circles and Christian monasteries featuring equally prominently in the repertoires of the Anuna choir, Clannad and Enya. In Scotland, there is less overlap. Sammy Horner, lead singer in the Christian band, the Electrics, has produced a series of albums entitled 'Celtic Praise', setting modern worship songs to characteristically Scottish melodies. Part of his agenda has been to 'redeem' Celtic music from its New Age and pagan associations. Some of the songs written and recorded by the popular Gaelic band, Runrig, have reflected the more hard-edged Celtic spirituality of the Western Isles with its attachment to the Psalms.

In Wales, poetry continues to be a major vehicle for both celebrating and keeping alive the indigenous Christian tradition. Several modern Welsh poets have followed Gwennallt's lead and written about Celtic saints (see p. 184). Saunders Davies, Vicar of the Welsh-speaking Anglican church in Cardiff, sees a number of contemporary Welsh poems as belonging to a long and distinctive Celtic Christian tradition that expresses the voice of a marginalised and oppressed people with a strong sense of the power of sacrifice and suffering.[73] Donald Allchin, discovering the Welsh spiritual tradition as an outsider after a lifetime's fascination with Orthodox Christianity, has identified its distinctive characteristic as the expression of praise and blessing through poetry. In his books, *Praise Above All: Discovering the Welsh Tradition* (1991) and *God's Presence Makes the World: The Celtic Vision through the Centuries in Wales* (1997), he has traced this tradition from the earliest extant piece of verse in Welsh, a ninth-century hymn in praise of the Trinity, via the work of the eighteenth-century Methodist poet, Ann Griffiths, to modern poets like Euros Bowen, Saunders Lewis and R. S. Thomas.

The unbroken nature of the Celtic Christian tradition in Wales has been an especially strong theme in the writings of Patrick Thomas, the vicar of a group of remote hill parishes in the Carmarthenshire hills. Brought up on the Anglo-Welsh border, he spent most of his childhood and teenage years in England, but then returned to Wales and learned the language. His two books, *The Opened Door – A Celtic Spirituality* (1990) and *Candle in the Darkness: Celtic Spirituality from Wales* (1993), were to some extent written to counter the impression given by many of the anthologies that appeared in the 1980s of a lost culture that had only just been rediscovered. Thomas was particularly incensed by the statement on the cover of Van de Weyer's *Celtic Fire* that 'composed in languages long extinct, Celtic literature has been inaccessible for many centuries'. For him, 'such a remark shows a startling ignorance of (and possibly a hidden contempt for) the hundreds of thousands of people who continue to live and think and pray through the medium of the Celtic languages'.[74] His second book begins with a diatribe against the BBC commentator at George Carey's enthronement as Archbishop of Canterbury for describing Augustine 'as the man who brought Christianity to Britain in 597'. Such a statement 'is calculated to make Welsh, Irish and Scottish hackles rise, for there were Christians in Britain long before Augustine's mission'.[75] In another swipe at English imperialism, Thomas launched a campaign in 1994 to bring the Lichfield Gospel back to Wales. He claimed that the Gospel, traditionally associated in England with Chad, in fact had associations with Teilo and had been stolen from Llandeilo in the tenth century. This was hotly disputed by the Chancellor of Lichfield Cathedral who said that it had in fact been stolen from Lichfield during a raid by the Welsh in the eighth century.

It is in Ireland where there is perhaps most sense of Celtic Christianity as a continuing living presence. This is partly because of the persistence of long-established practices involving popular devotion to the saints, such as pilgrimages to Lough Derg and the annual climb up Croagh Patrick. There have been some notable Protestant contributions to the general upsurge of interest in aspects of the country's early Christianity, such as Hilary Richardson's work on high crosses and metalwork and Lesley Whiteside's books on *The Spirituality of St Patrick* (1996) and *In Search of Columba* (1997). Most of the work in this area, however, has been done by Roman Catholic priests. Peter O'Dwyer, a Carmelite, has written about the *Céli Dé* and traced a distinctive tradition of Irish spirituality from Patrick to modern times. Diarmuid O'Laoghaire, a Jesuit, has collected and translated early Irish prayers. Hugh Connolly, a priest in the Diocese of Dromore, has written on the Irish penitentials and argued that they offer a model of spiritual growth and pastoral care based on the theme of pilgrimage and the understanding of the minister as fellow-sufferer and soul friend which is very helpful today. His book, *The Irish Penitentials and their Significance for the Sacrament of Penance Today*, is one of a number of important recent academic studies on aspects of Celtic Christianity published by the Four Courts Press in Dublin. This press has also responded to the booming interest in the subject by republishing such classics as Ryan's *Irish Monasticism* and Gougaud's *Christianity in Celtic Lands*. At a more popular level, there has also been a distinctive Irish contribution to the more romantic and nostalgic side of the current revival. It is epitomised in Herbert O'Driscoll's *The Leap of the Deer: Memories of a Celtic Childhood* (1994) in which an Anglican priest who has spent most of his life in Canada fondly reminisces about his childhood in Kerry in the 1930s. J. J. O'Riordain, a Redemptorist priest based at Dundalk, has written a number of books interweaving anecdotes about religious life in modern Ireland with stories from the age of the saints. The 'blurb' for one of them notes that 'Celtic spirituality is often spoken of as something ancient, remote and in need of re-discovery. John J. O'Riordain, however, speaks of it as a lived experience even in modern Ireland'.[76]

The worlds of academic scholarship and Celtic twilight romanticism are to some extent brought together in the work of Noel O'Donoghue, a Carmelite priest who grew up and trained in Ireland but has spent much of his life as a lecturer in the faculty of Divinity at Edinburgh University. Schooled in classic Thomist theology, O'Donoghue has come to be gripped by the power of the Celtic imagination. For him the distinctive feature of Celtic Christianity is its intuitive, mystical nature. He locates Patrick firmly in the tradition of Christian mystics like St John of the Cross and Teresa of Avila. He is fascinated by the notion of presence and by the interweaving of pagan and Christian themes that pervade both St Patrick's Breastplate and the *Carmina Gadelica*. O'Donoghue's translation of the Breastplate provides an altogether starker and more faithful rendition of the original than Mrs Alexander's Victorian versification. For him Celtic Christianity 'is a Catholic tradition that does not define itself negatively in opposition to the Reformation or positively in terms of a strongly centralised ultramontane Catholicism'.[77] It 'reaches back and reaches out behind and beyond Christianity, not only to tribal and aboriginal religions, but also to the Muslim and Hindu worlds'.[78] Above all, it is 'an enchanted country' populated by angels and presences which can be visited by those who have the imagination to see 'the mountain behind the mountain' and find 'that Celtic vision of another world within the everyday world of common perception and things that pass away'.[79]

Ireland has been at the forefront of developments to cater for the growing number of 'spiritual tourists' produced by the Celtic Christian revival. Michael Rodgers, Roman Catholic priest at Glendalough, has set up a retreat centre and opened a pilgrimage trail through the valley that once housed one of the largest early medieval monastic 'cities' so that modern-day pilgrims can 'pray following in the footsteps of St Kevin and the Celtic Saints'.[80] Meanwhile, the *Céli Dé* programme run by Glendalough's Church of Ireland minister, Marcus Losack, offers study-pilgrimage programmes which 'have a contemplative and spiritual intent, drawing on the wealth of the Celtic Tradition for our own spiritual formation and deepening'.[81] Tours offered in 1997 included pilgrimages to Jerusalem and Sinai as well as to Irish sites, Iona, Lindisfarne and

Durham and quiet days at Glendalough to tie in with saints' days and pre-Christian festivals. An imaginative cross-border 'Columba trail', opened in 1997 as part of the celebrations to mark the 1,400th anniversary of the saint's death, links sites in Ulster with his supposed birthplace in Donegal. An application has recently been made for European Union funding to help establish a multi-media presentation on Columba's life in the Church of Ireland parish church at Drumcliffe, near Sligo, a place best known for its associations with W. B. Yeats but also supposedly the location of a Columban monastery and near the site of the battle of Cúl Drebene which may have occasioned the saint's enforced departure to Iona. A recent brochure advertising a tour of 'Enchanted Ireland', with a reproduction of Petrie's 'Pilgrims at Clonmacnoise' on its cover, offers 'a magical journey to Sacred Sites of the Emerald Isle' taking in Clonmacnoise, Glendalough, Skellig Michael, and holy wells associated with the saints as well as pre-Christian sites like Tara. For the visit to Brigit's well, 'a place of the Earth mother that is still in use to this day', tourists are invited to 'bring a piece of cloth to tie on the tree as a prayer'.[82]

The increasing attraction of visiting Celtic Christian sites has also been reflected in developments in other parts of the British Isles. A number of guide books have been published over the last few years for the new breed of pilgrim-tourist who want to follow in the footsteps of the Celtic saints. They include John Marsden's *Sea-Road of the Saints: Celtic Holy Men in the Hebrides* (1995), Roger Race's *Celtic Tide in Cornwall* (1996), Donald Smith's *Celtic Travellers: Scotland in the Age of the Saints* (1997) and special 'Pilgrim Guides' to Iona, Lindisfarne, St David's and Durham. A pilgrim way has been established along the shores of the Solway Firth, its route indicated by markers bearing the distinctive logo of the Celtic Cross. It ends at Whithorn, which has been enthusiastically promoted as the 'Cradle of Christianity' and 'an all-weather attraction', offering 'live archaeology' as the team excavating Ninian's monastery dig up their finds in front of visitors.[83] A new visitors' centre on Mull allows tourists to bone up on Columba before they take the ferry across to the overcrowded island of Iona. A modern museum adjacent to the ruins of Lindisfarne Priory portrays the lives of Aidan and Cuthbert in heroic terms and offers an interpretation of Celtic Christianity worthy of the post-Reformation revival: 'The Celtic Church had developed largely independently of the mainstream Roman tradition. The monks were withdrawn and ascetic, contrasting with the worldly, sophisticated missionaries of Rome'.[84] Similarly romanticised and stereotyped images are purveyed at Celtica, an exhibition at Machynlleth near Aberystwyth which enables visitors 'to experience the mysterious and magical world of the Celts ... using the latest audio-visual technology' and the nearby 'King Arthur's Labyrinth' where tourists are regaled with Arthurian legends as they take a boat ride through subterranean caves.[85]

Other less tourist-oriented projects have sought to find a new spiritual and pastoral role for ancient Celtic Christian sites. The remote church in mid-Wales which houses the shrine of Melangell (see p. 50), rebuilt and reopened in 1992 after decades of disuse, is now used as a healing centre and has a small respite care unit for cancer sufferers attached to it. A secluded well at Glamis in Scotland traditionally associated with St Fergus was restored under a youth employment scheme in the early 1990s. Visitors following a trail from the parish church to the well are encouraged to reflect on the Celtic tradition of seeing God through the beauty of creation, and on the value of hospitality, tolerance and learning through journeying. One aspect of the way that this last theme has been put into practice is the popularity of travels in the wake of Celtic saints by clergy taking sabbaticals. In addition to periods in the retreat centres on Iona and Lindisfarne this can also involve staying in less frequented places like Bardsey Island, much used by hermits in the sixth century and still without electricity or indoor sanitation and with only one boat a week to the mainland.

Interest in the ascetic and eremetical character of Celtic monasticism is not just confined to the British Isles. At St Dolay in Brittany a small group of monks live according to what they take to be principles of Celtic monasticism and undertake social service in the local community. Established in 1977, the Monastery hosts an annual colloquy on Celtic Christianity which attracts several hundred participants and publishes a journal which makes much of the distinctive Breton legacy of Gildas and Dol. The monks belong to the Celtic Orthodox Church, which has links with Coptic Christian communities and has recently been joined by a section of the British Orthodox Church. In both the United States and Australia there is increasing interest in Celtic Christianity in the context of the churches' engagement with native peoples and their faiths. Studies are pointing to the similarity of Celtic and native spirituality, while concern about the marginalisation and exploitation of indigenous people by the churches is prompting suggestions that there may be lessons to be learned from the missionary approach adopted by the Celtic Church, with its emphasis on inculturation and respect for native customs and beliefs.

America has also had its fair share of modern hagiography idealising the Celtic saints. In a book designed to do for them what Thomas Merton's *The Wisdom of the Desert* did for the desert fathers, Edward

Sellner, assistant Professor of Pastoral Theology at the College of St Catherine in St Paul, Minnesota, presents the Irish and Welsh saints of the golden age as spiritual gurus for today:

> Listen with your hearts to the stories and sayings of these Celtic saints. Allow them to become spiritual mentors again, teaching contemporary Christians about soul friendship and about an ancient spiritual heritage ... The wisdom of these saints is still very much alive. Like the tiny coracle boats of the Celtic missionaries skimming swiftly over the ocean depths, they travel in our dreams and our imagination. They give us a rich vision of a more inclusive church, and perhaps new directions in our own spirituality.[86]

North Americans have also been responsible for putting Celtic Christianity on the internet. There is now a profusion of web sites, ranging from the general ('Celtic Christian links', 'Apostolate of Celtic Christian Communities', 'The Fellowship of Celtic Christian Ministries', 'The Franciscan Order of Céli Dé', 'New Hinba Cyber Monastery' and 'Real Celtic Christianity is Orthodox') to the specific ('St Bede's Episcopal Church' and 'St Columbanus' Community: A Franciscan and Celtic Christian Community in Memphis, Tennessee'). Tony Nolan has researched these sites and discovered that the groups responsible for them hold two principles in common:

> Firstly, all profess a belief that at some point a distinct Celtic Church had existed, whose members had fought a gallant but doomed battle against a legalistic and continental Roman Church. Secondly, all stress the equality of women within this system and its singularly non-hierarchical nature.[87]

Many of the sites appear to be run by splinter groups from the Orthodox Communion and have a strongly anti-Roman agenda.

One of the most detailed web sites is that of 'The Celtic Christian Communion, formerly the Synod of Celtic Christian Churches'. It uses the symbol of the burning bush, long the emblem of the Church of Scotland, and proclaims: 'We are happy to work with Ordained Catholic, Anglican and Orthodox Clergy and dedicated lay people who desire to form Celtic Christian Communities'.[88] The presiding Archbishop of the Communion, Ivan MacKillop, based in Springfield, Oregon, is also the presiding Abbot in the Church of the Culdees and can be conveniently be e-mailed at *culdee@continent.com*. The home pages for this church repeat the old myth about the Culdees:

It is most likely that the term was in use in the Celtic Church from its earliest days. Later the term came to be applied to those Celtic and Anglo-Saxon Christians who refused to submit to the Roman Church's heretical claims to authority, but preferred to continue in the Christian traditions of the great Celtic Saints.[89]

After lengthy descriptions of the arrival of the 'haughty and ambitious' Augustine in Britain and the tragedy of Whitby, the Church of the Culdees is identified as the spiritual descendant of the original Culdee Church which survived on Iona after most of the rest of the British Isles had given in to Rome:

> We are ready to enjoy ecumenical relations or intercommunion with other churches but we are not and will not be governed by other than our own bishops and sacred traditions ... The Church of the Culdees is Celtic in its spiritual style. We do not claim to be identical with the Orthodox and Catholic Celtic Church of the first centuries, rather we respond to the call of the Holy Spirit to bring the unique vision of the Celtic Church into the reality of our present place and time.[90]

The Church of the Culdees identifies eight special emphases in 'the primitive Celtic Church' which it seeks to maintain: a profound respect and care for the environment; a passion for scholarship and learning; a great desire to explore the unknown and carry the Good News beyond the horizon; a love of solitude and silence; a particular concept of time, emphasising the interpenetration of time and eternity; living a life of simplicity; the importance of personal rather than institutional relationships; and the fact that 'much more than any of the other churches, the Celtic Church upheld the equality and dignity of women'.[91] Anyone over eighteen, able to pass an entrance exam and prepared to take vows of moral purity, apostolic poverty, obedience and stability, can be admitted into the Order of the Celtic Cross.

The arrival of Celtic Christianity on the internet confirms its position as one of the 'brand leaders' in the new pick-and-mix, post-modern spiritual supermarket. Those surfing the net can experience the virtual reality of a Celtic cyber-monastery without leaving their homes and having to endure the discomfort of days of fasting in some damp cave. Some other recent developments suggest a similar process of dumbing down and trivialisation as the current revival becomes ever more commercially exploited. With the appearance of Melvyn Bragg's best seller *Credo*, set in seventh-century Northumbria, Celtic Christianity is now the stuff of airport novels. Those daunted by the proliferation of paper-backs on Celtic models for the contemporary church can take refuge in another novel, Robert Van de Weyer's *Celtic Gifts* which follows the fortunes of a new bishop trying to recreate the ancient Celtic orders of ministry. The children's market has been catered for by Maeve Friel's *The Deerstone* (1992), set in Glendalough, Eileen Dunlop's *Tales of St Columba* (1992) and Mary Rhind's *Iona Boy* (1997). Celtic Christian titles have moved from the spirituality and New Age shelves to the gift sections of bookshops where they rub shoulders with replica high standing crosses, cassettes and compact discs of 'easy listening' Celtic music and cards with David Adam's prayers decorated with interlacing designs. *The Little Book of Celtic Prayers* and *The Little Book of Celtic Blessings* are among the best-selling titles in a series of attractively packaged series pocket companions which also includes volumes on 'Arthurian Wisdom', 'Iron John', 'Native American Wisdom' and 'Zen Wisdom'.

Are these products so much religious tat, like the plastic saints and madonnas of commercialised Catholicism, or genuine icons which can lead people into a deeper faith and spirituality? There is no doubt that putting the word Celtic on anything nowadays enormously enhances its sellability. The marketing potential of Celtic Christianity has not been lost on commercial companies. Aer Lingus' fleet of passenger jets are named after Irish saints. A German pharmaceutical firm which manu-factures an anti-depressant drug developed from the herb St John's wort, also known as Columba's wort, has toyed with the idea of a television commercial on Iona to stress its links with Celtic monasticism. At the same time, contemporary religious artists are being inspired by Celtic symbols. Ben Coode-Adams' recent work for Chadkirk Chapel in Stock-port includes a crucifix based on an eighth-century Irish plaque, candle-sticks modelled on figures from the Durham Gospels, and a frieze of local saints, the 'good' ones who supported the old ways at Whitby looking inwards, the 'bad' ones looking outward.

The most instantly recognisable symbol of Celtic Christianity is almost certainly the Celtic cross. Is it a commercial logo or a religious icon? On the one hand, it appears on tourist signs and travel posters and is worn on neck chains as a fashion accessory. On the other, in Scotland especially, it has become a statement of ecumenism and intent on the part of the churches. In 1991 Norma Henderson of the Church of Scotland's Board of National Mission conceived the idea of using it on publicity material throughout the church in the run-up to the millennium. An artwork pack providing versions for church magazine covers, posters, orders of service, letterheads, badges and teeshirts was produced to present 'the corporate

Plate 12. Celtic cross logo used by Scottish churches in the pre-millennium campaign, 1997–2000.

symbol of the Celtic Cross as a common theme recognisable inside and outside the church' and churches were urged to use 'this strong and central image until it begins to soak into the consciousness of people'.[92] In fact, the Celtic cross 'logo' has been adopted by churches of many denominations and proved one of the most successful devices to raise the corporate image and awareness of Christianity in contemporary Britain (Plate 12).

Although its general thrust has been enthusiastically ecumenical, the current revival has provided an opportunity for some denominational point-scoring. The old anti-Roman agenda still surfaces in some Protestant treatments of the Celtic Church:

> Back in the seventh century, when our Christian forefathers on the Scottish island of Iona sought to maintain Biblical Christianity, not entertaining the iniquitous ambitions nor embracing the erroneous doctrines of Popery, the charge of being a sectarian element was levelled against them.[93]

On the Roman Catholic side a more gentle bias can be detected in Basil Hume's *Footprints of the Northern Saints*, a book published in 1996 to coincide with a Channel 4 television series which explored the monastic culture of seventh- and eighth-century Northumbria and included Anglo-Saxon saints like Wilfrid and Benedict Biscop as well as Aidan, Cuthbert and Hilda. Hume's pro-Roman approach is particularly evident in his treatment of the Synod of Whitby. Portrayed in most recent books as a tragic crushing of the free, gentle anarchic Celtic spirit by the might of Roman bureaucracy, he sees it rather as a victory for the principle of Catholicity against the notion of a multitude of sects each doing their own thing:

> This is very important for us today. The Church must have authority, for whatever people may say we cannot live without it. We need to be in communion with Saint Peter and the local churches need to be in communion with each other. It is only through Peter, the guardian of the gates of heaven, that we can have a guarantee and protection of the faith we have ... The Synod of Whitby united all of Christian England in one tradition and practice of the faith, and also united England with the greater universal tradition of the Roman Church.[94]

Overall, denominational rivalry has played a much less significant role in this than in previous Celtic Christian revivals. Academic input and debate, by contrast, has been much more marked. While some scholars have been largely supportive of the revival and happy to accept the notion of a distinctive Celtic Christianity, others have been highly sceptical and questioned the validity of the whole concept. To some extent, the division has been drawn according to subject areas. Broadly speaking, those in departments of divinity and religious studies have tended towards the former view and those in Celtic studies and social anthropology to the latter. There has also been a geographical dimension to the debate, with Scots academics being noticeably more hostile to the revival than many of their Welsh and Irish colleagues.

A huge amount of academic work has been done over the last three decades of the twentieth century in the field of early church history and literature and in the more general area of Celtic studies. The 1990s alone have seen the publication of major interdisciplinary studies such as the volume edited by S. Moscati to accompany the Venice Celtic exhibition in 1991 and Miranda Green's compilation, *The Celtic World* (1995) as well as more specific studies such as Lloyd and Jennifer's Long's *Celtic Britain and Ireland* (1995). Archaeology has considerably illuminated our knowledge of early Christian communities in the British Isles, with the pioneering studies by Charles Thomas being supplemented by detailed reports on recent work like Peter Hill's account of the Whithorn excavations.[95]

Art historians have also been active in this area, with Hilary Richardson continuing to bring out important articles on the high standing crosses.[96] Both the accessibility and intelligibility of early texts have been greatly increased by the work of Máire Herbert, David Dumville, Thomas O'Loughlin, Alan Macquarrie and Richard Sharpe, whose Penguin edition of Adomnan's *Life of Columba* (1995) is a model of its kind. Important work on the *Vitae* and cults of the Celtic saints is also being pursued by younger scholars like Tom Clancy, Jonathan Wooding and Elva Johnston. New scholarly editions of many important sources have appeared and the Archive of Celtic-Latin Literature, a joint initiative by the Royal Irish Academy and an electronic publishing firm based in Belgium, is providing a permanent electronic database containing the entire corpus of Celtic-Latin literature from the period 400–1200. Altogether, 1,300 texts covering saints' *Vitae*, liturgical, legislative and penitential works, annals, verses and letters will be available on CD Rom.

Much of this academic activity has undoubtedly been stimulated by the general revival of interest in Celtic Christianity. This has been particularly true of work undertaken in university departments of theology and religious studies. The first major department to take a lead in this area was the Faculty of Divinity at Edinburgh where the initiative came from Noel Dermot O'Donoghue, and James Mackey, Professor of Theology since 1979. It was as much as anything a personal quest which sent both these two Irish-born Catholics back to their ancient roots. Mackey has commented that he started exploring Celtic Christianity 'when years of feeding upon largely teutonic philosophy and theology began at last to fail to refresh my spirit and was beginning to fail my Christian faith'.[97]

The first fruit of this initiative was the publication in 1989 of *An Introduction to Celtic Christianity*. Conceived by O'Donoghue and edited by Mackey, this rather eclectic collection of essays aimed to provide 'an introductory map for beginners'.[98] Although published in Edinburgh, its focus was almost entirely Irish. Of its fifteen contributors, thirteen were Irish and two Welsh. The only saint dealt with is Patrick, the one essay on Scotland (which deals entirely with post-Protestant Highland culture) is by an Irishman and the modern figures taken to represent the continuing Celtic Christian tradition are James Joyce and Seán Ó Rioradin.

In an introductory essay Mackey poses the question: 'Is There a Celtic Christianity?' The fact that he chooses to use the present rather than the past tense is significant. Subsequent essays focus as much on the continuing Celtic spiritual tradition shown in the evangelical revival in Wales and Joyce's *Ulysees* as on the golden age of the sixth and seventh centuries. In his introduction Mackey goes on to endorse many prevalent myths. He notes that 'the Celts seem to have taken quite quickly and early to Christianity' and detects 'the presence of unreconciled Celtic pagan culture within the Christian literature of the Celtic territories'.[99] Emphasising the extent to which Celtic Christianity embodied itself in local culture, he identifies certain distinctive themes, notably 'a pervasive sense of spiritual presence', 'the full and uninhibited acceptance of the natural world', 'the Celtic penchant for wandering around' and 'the Celtic way of adapting the natural religious (or so-called pagan) heritage'.[100] He writes warmly of Pelagius and raises the 'very real possibility that there is a characteristically Celtic theology of nature, sin and redemption which ... avoid the clear excesses and failures of its Augustinian counterpart'.[101] Overall, Mackey's introduction gives the clear impression that there is a distinct Celtic Christianity and that it offers some important pointers for contemporary Christians. He ends by expressing the hope that 'further explorations' will lead eventually 'to discernment of a distinctively Celtic mentality still living perhaps in the depths of consciousness, a Celtic culture still flowering in hidden places, still waiting to be fully christianized and to shape again a distinctive Christianity to all that is best in itself'.[102]

Despite these echoes of Twilight romanticism, some of the contributors to this collection were out to puncture the myths that had grown up around the subject of Celtic Christianity. Writing about St Patrick, R. P. C. Hanson felt compelled to point out:

> He did not banish snakes from Ireland. He did not illustrate the doctrine of the Trinity by the example of the shamrock; he did not climb Croagh Patrick nor institute his Purgatory in Lough Derg in Donegal. He did not meet any High-King, whether called Laoghaire or not, on the hill of Tara in Co. Meath. We cannot even with confidence associate him with the foundation of the see of Armagh.[103]

Hanson also rebuked those who claimed Patrick as the prototype of a particular kind of Christian minister:

> He was not like a modern Roman Catholic bishop, very much conditioned by an elaborate ecclesiastical law and constantly keeping in mind the existence of the autocrat of his centralised church. He was not like a modern Anglican bishop, existing in a much looser framework of ecclesiastical law, much concerned to reconcile different traditions within his diocese, conscious of exercising leader-

ship within a national church. He was not like a Methodist or Presbyterian minister; far less did he resemble a lone evangelist on the model of the Plymouth Brethren.[104]

Yet for all these negatives, Hanson's portrayal of Patrick was ultimately highly positive, if not even idealised:

> He deserves the title 'Apostle of the Irish People'. We can perhaps credit him also with that missionary impulse which was so strong a trait in early Irish Christianity ... we can perhaps see in the peculiar self-abandonment of the Irish monks of the sixth and seventh centuries something of Patrick's spirit ... There is no remote, stormswept island off the west coast of Ireland, Brittany and Scotland which has not the remains of a Celtic monastery on it. Here Patrick's example and spirit were bearing their finest fruit.[105]

A similarly committed and enthusiastic approach characterised the work of doctoral students supervised by Mackey and O'Donoghue in Edinburgh in the 1990s. It can be seen in Mary Low's study, *Celtic Christianity and Nature* (1996) which is essentially descriptive rather than analytical and literary rather than theological. Interweaving Biblical, pre-Christian and Christian sources and references, it provides a rich stock of stories and poems from the seventh to the sixteenth century without ever quite engaging with the question of how 'green' Celtic Christianity actually was or distinguishing the earlier from the later material. A similar syncretistic approach mixing pre- and post-Christian sources characterises Karen O'Keefe's fascinating study of references to music in early Irish literature, *From Ireland to Iona: Music and the Celtic Otherworld* (1999).

Since the mid-1990s the lead in the academic study of Celtic Christianity has passed from Edinburgh to Lampeter. Thanks largely to the enthusiasm of Oliver Davies, an MA course in Celtic Christianity, the only one of its kind in the country, began there in 1995. The course brochure nails its colours firmly to the mast by stating that its purpose 'is to introduce students to the concept of a distinctive type of Christianity in the Celtic countries during the middle ages which results from the fusion of pre-Christian Celtic religion with Christianity'.[106] Even more than at Edinburgh, the ethos of the Lampeter course, which is being undertaken predominantly by part-time students, including a good number of clergy, is very much in sympathy with the spirit of the current revival.

Oliver Davies has argued the case for the distinctiveness of Celtic

Christianity in two recent books. In *Celtic Christianity in Early Medieval Wales* (1995) he defines it in terms of 'the interaction between Christianity and native forms of Celtic primal religion'.[107] The introduction to *Celtic Christian Spirituality: An Anthology of Medieval and Modern Sources* (1995), a collaboration with his wife, Fiona Bowie, which brings together a huge corpus of material, ranging from a ninth-century Welsh poem to a prayer for New Year by a Breton poet who died in 1981, initially adopts a more cautious approach. It concedes that the term 'Celtic' would have had no meaning in the Middle Ages and is 'all too often used in a way which suggests that nineteenth-century Scotland and pre-Christian Gaul, eighth-century Ireland and modern Brittany all somehow form a unified cultural unit'.[108] It further acknowledges that the idea of a distinctive 'Celtic Church' is erroneous and was largely the invention of post-Reformation Protestant apologists. Nonetheless, Davies and Bowie feel justified in using the term 'Celtic Christianity' for two reasons:

> First, because there undoubtedly are some distinctive and important Christian emphases which thread their way through the religious imagination of Celtic speaking peoples, and second, though just as important, many Christians living in Celtic countries today choose to regard themselves as Celts.[109]

Davies and Bowie enumerate three distinct ways in which Celtic religion differed from Roman. It was oral rather than written in character, drawing especially strongly on poetry, mythology and imagery; it had a tribal dimension; and it was a markedly local phenomenon. The distinctiveness of Celtic Christianity lies in the fusion of this old Celtic religion with the new faith of Christianity. For them, as for Mackey and O'Donoghue, it is a living rather than a dead tradition with much to teach us today. Specifically, they point to a further trio of themes which Celtic Christianity offers to the contemporary church: 'a persistent emphasis upon the place of nature within the Christian revelation', 'a valuing of the creative imagination of the individual' and 'the spirit of community'.[110] Displaying their own share of the romantic nostalgia that has suffused every movement of Celtic Christian revivalism, they look back longingly 'to an earlier age, to the remote margins of north west Europe', and find there 'precious *possibilities* of Christian consciousness and existence which yet retain their power and which the churches of Christ have neglected for far too long'.[111]

Ranged against these enthusiastic revivalists are a number of scholars who take a diametrically opposed line on the subject of Celtic Christianity. For them it is a bogus and misleading concept, the notion of a Celtic

Church even more so, with no historical reality and existing only as the invention and in the imagination of outsiders. Unease about use of the term 'Celtic Church' has a longer pedigree and is considerably more widespread than dislike of the broader phrase 'Celtic Christianity'. An article by Kathleen Hughes, published posthumously in 1981, pointed to the considerable organisational differences between Welsh and Irish Churches during the early medieval period and concluded that 'The "Celtic Church" is a rather misleading phrase'.[112] Another early medieval historian, Wendy Davies, noted in her study of the Welsh Church, published in 1982, that 'romantic views of a Celtic church, spanning Celtic areas, with its own institutional structure and special brand of spirituality, have often been expressed, but have little to support them'.[113] Ten years later in an article on 'The Myth of the Celtic Church' she made the point even more emphatically: 'There was no such thing as a Celtic Church: the concept is unhelpful, if not positively harmful'.[114] More recently, Sally Foster, writing about Scotland, has described it as 'an unhelpful concept, since it implies uniformity throughout Celtic parts of Europe, which was certainly not the case'.[115] I myself have now stopped using the term 'Celtic Church' and prefer to think in terms of smaller, more localised entities such as 'the Columban Church'.[116]

But if we cannot talk accurately about a Celtic Church, can we still hold to the concept of a distinctive Celtic Christianity? It is this latter concept which has come under particular assault from Celticists in the last few years. This is partly the result of a wider unease about the whole notion of Celticity. As early as 1963 J. R. R. Tolkien, who knew a bit about myth-making himself, noted that the term 'Celtic' was 'a magic bag, into which anything may be put, and out of which almost anything may come … Anything is possible in the fabulous Celtic twilight, which is not so much a twilight of the gods as of the reason'.[117] During the 1980s a number of anthropologists questioned whether the Celts were any more than a construct. This view reached its zenith in Malcolm Chapman's *The Celts* (1992) which argued that 'romanticism created the fringe Celtic minorities as figures of wish-fulfilment, of opposition to the prevailing philosophy and actuality of industrialising England'.[118] From the time that the Greeks first coined the term *Keltoi*, Celts were essentially outsiders, defined in terms of their 'otherness'. So for the Anglo-Saxons, who essentially created the British version, the Celt was all that they were not: 'A magical figure, bard, warrior, and enchanter, beyond the reach of this world, and an object of love and yearning for those doomed to wander among material things in the cold light of reason'.[119] Chapman was particularly uneasy about the catch-all nature of the concept of Celtic

Christianity which was used to describe everything from imported Egyptian monasticism to the Calvinism of the Western Isles:

> The fringe religiosity of the 'Celts', their peculiarity and fervour, can be reconstituted with every new change of fashion. Pan-European pre-Christian religion, crystallised around anachronistic collocations of druids and stone circles, is widely considered to be a kind of Celtic prerogative. The Christianity of the Roman Empire becomes, after the fall of Rome, 'Celtic Christianity'. Early Christian Mediterranean styles in monumental religious stonework come to Ireland, and are called 'Celtic crosses'. Roman Catholicism, in turn, finds an appropriate home in the Celtic fringe. And Swiss theological fashions of four centuries ago have assumed a 'timeless' Celtic guise.[120]

The most sustained academic criticism of the whole notion of Celtic Christianity, and of the current revival in particular, has come from Donald Meek, Professor of Celtic at Aberdeen University. As a considerable Celtic scholar and native Gaelic speaker, he deplores the fact that most of those who write about Celtic Christianity are ignorant of the Celtic languages and have not engaged with the primary sources; as an evangelical Christian he is uneasy about the New Age, syncretistic and ecumenical overtones of the revival; and as someone who grew up on the Hebridean island of Tiree, he does not recognise what passes for Celtic spirituality as authentic to the religious tradition of the Scottish Highlands and islands. In a number of articles and papers he has identified the salient characteristics of what he calls 'the Celtic new religious movement'.[121] These include its largely bookish and undemanding nature – he points out that 'few of the movement's advocates have yet taken to living on Rockall or the Old Man of Hoy, although such eremitic sites offer stacks of potential, in keeping with the aspirations of several Celtic saints'[122] – and its unscholarly and distorting emphasis on such themes as closeness to nature, gentleness and primitive simplicity at the expense of the more brutal and severe elements that were undoubtedly present in early Christianity in the British Isles. Overall, Meek views the present revival as an exercise in invention and myth-making largely carried out by non-Celts, and especially by English Anglicans. For him 'Celtic Christianity' is not the same entity as 'Christianity in the British Isles in the period *c*.400–1100 AD ... It is a re-creation'.[123]

Several other Celtic scholars have sought to puncture particular myths about Celtic Christianity. Patrick Sims Williams has shown the extent to which the notion of the Celts' peculiarly visionary and spiritual qualities has been built up through centuries of myth-making by both Celts and non-Celts. Among those whom he cites as having contributed to the construction of the 'ethnic preconception' of 'the Visionary Celt' are Geoffrey of Monmouth, Gerald of Wales, James Macpherson, Ernest Rénan, Matthew Arnold and Alexander Carmichael.[124] Donnchadh Ó Corráin has cast grave doubt on the authenticity of the so-called hermit poems, which have been so important in establishing the 'green' credentials of Celtic Christianity, and suggested that they represent the wishful thinking of 'urban' monks (see pp. 33–5). In a further assault on the notion that there was anything especially 'green' about Celtic Christianity, Thomas Clancy and Gilbert Markus, have published early poems associated with the Iona monastery which reveal a strong sense of the fallenness of creation and a fear of many aspects of the natural world. They conclude that 'delight in nature ... is no more Celtic than Hebrew or Roman-African'.[125] As a result of engaging with these and other recently translated and published sources, I have myself been forced to revise my own views about the attitude to nature among early Celtic Christians.[126]

Gilbert Markus, a Dominican currently based in Glasgow, has been especially active and enthusiastic in demolishing long-cherished shibboleths about Celtic Christianity. His suggestion that Columba's dealings with animals and birds as recorded in Adomnan's *Vita* are entirely a matter of political symbolism (see p. 20) raises serious questions about whether the Celtic saints did, in fact, have a particularly close relationship with non-human creatures. Markus has described Columba as a 'hijack victim' and demonstrated how hagiographers and spin-doctors from Adomnan onwards have created a wholly distorted and unhistorical picture of him as 'missionary, eco-patron and pastoral agent'.[127] In a more recent salvo against those who characterise Celtic Christianity as being egalitarian, anti-Roman, pro-feminist and Pelagian, he adduces evidence to show that it was in fact hierarchical, subordinate to and in close conformity with Rome, markedly chauvinistic and distinguished for an exceptionally strong attachment to the doctrines of the Fall and the reality of hell. Markus reckons that the excessive romanticism of the current revival will puncture the myth of Celtic Christianity for good: 'it doesn't actually preserve anything or introduce us to our Christian fathers and mothers, but is simply the last nail in the coffin of the Celtic Christian past'.[128]

Equally dismissive comments have come from the evangelical Presbyterian theologian, Donald MacLeod:

Everyone from Free Presbyterian to Roman Catholic to Baptist to Robbie the Pict is suddenly discovering that he is a direct descendant of Colum Cille; and also that his own particular way of spending weekends (whether in church, temple, chapel or mountainside) is the only religion in harmony with the Highland habitat. I am more and more inclined to think that the whole business is a lot of nonsense ... Celtic spirituality? Or New Age under another name?[129]

It is significant that these strong attacks on the current revival should have come from Scotland and from a Roman Catholic and two evangelical Protestant academics. The English, and those in the liberal Protestant middle ground, have on the whole been much more favourably disposed towards the notion of Celtic Christianity. Even south of the border, however, it has its critics. Clifford Longley, the *Daily Telegraph*'s unfailingly perceptive and stimulating religious commentator, chose the beginning of 1997, the year dedicated to celebrating Columba and Britain's Celtic Christian heritage, to launch a fierce attack:

Is it time for a backlash against 'Celtic Christianity'? It is the latest fad in British religion. Its enthusiasts regard it as the answer to the spiritual needs of the age. Courses in it are oversubscribed, 'Celtic Christian' events are standing room only.

It is ecological, feminist, spontaneous, non-cerebral, poetic, mystical, almost pantheistic. It easily shades off into New Age paganism. It is exciting to young people because it seems unconventional and newly discovered. And it helps the Scots to vindicate themselves against the English, just as it helps English Anglicans and Protestants to vindicate themselves against Roman Catholics.

It is truly the myth whose time has come. But its very convenience, its extraordinary ability to meet so many current needs, should make us suspicious. For it is also, to use an old Celtic expression, phony baloney – a legend still in the process of being invented ... It will be all things to all men and score high in the ballyhoo department. A touch of scepticism would be timely.[130]

Longley's article did nothing to check the progress of the revival. In the same week that it appeared, an evangelical gathering on worship in Eastbourne offered a seminar on 'Celtic Passion – rediscovering our radical roots'. Subsequent months saw groups of pilgrims visiting Celtic Christian sites across the British Isles as part of the churches' official celebrations to mark the 1,400th anniversary of Columba's death on Iona

and Augustine's arrival at Canterbury. It was undoubtedly the former
rather than the latter event which caught both the popular imagination
and the media's attention. While Augustine was given a relatively low-key
commemorative service at Canterbury Cathedral, Columba was celebrated in books, conferences, television documentaries, an oratorio
written by the leading Scottish poet, Iain Crichton Smith, and trans-
missions of the main BBC radio and television worship programmes
from Iona Abbey.

Several aspects of the 1997 celebrations recall themes that we have
encountered in earlier periods of Celtic Christian revival. They had a
political dimension, with Columba's anniversary providing the occasion
for a visit to Scotland by Mary Robinson, President of Ireland, and a
number of events to strengthen Scottish-Irish links and provide an
alternative Celtic axis at a time when Scotland's ties with England were
weakening with the vote for a separate Edinburgh parliament. Denomi-
nationalism as well as nationalism reared its head. On Iona, the opening
of a Roman Catholic house of prayer provoked similar anxieties in certain
quarters to those expressed when Bishop's House had opened nearly a
century earlier. A claim by the novelist Allan Massie that Columba's
church 'had no link with Rome' was attacked by Thomas Clancy as 'a
musty bit of sectarian spin doctoring'.[131] In Ireland, the Orange Order
published a pamphlet accusing nationalists and Catholics of hi-jacking
Patrick and claiming that, as someone who had fact seldom if ever left
Ulster, he should be regarded as the apostle of Northern Ireland and
not of the south.[132] In Scotland, there was an echo of the rivalry between
different monasteries which had played so important a part in promoting
the cults of Celtic saints in the early Middle Ages. Determined that
Columba, and Iona, should not have all the glory, Whithorn sought to
present itself as the real cradle of Scottish Christianity and claimed that
1997 marked the 1,600th anniversary of its foundation by Ninian.
Blithely ignoring recent scholarship which suggested a much later date
and more limited role for Ninian, his latest local hagiographers hailed
him as the man 'who established the Christian church in Scotland which
is recognizable to this day' and credited him with 'the transformation of
the Picts from an aggresive, raiding warlike people to creative scholars
skilled in metalwork, sculpture and book illumination'.[133]

Meanwhile the books and merchandise keep coming. My last visit to
a religious bookshop yielded two new titles, *Prophetic Lifestyle and the
Celtic Way*, the work of two English charismatics now resident in the
United States who discovered Celtic Christianity on a retreat to Lindisfarne in 1989 and relate it to their own awareness of God speaking to

them through his Spirit, and *Listening for the Heartbeat of God – A Celtic Spirituality*, in which Philip Newell traces a line from Pelagius to George MacLeod via Alexander Carmichael and finds both a feminist agenda and a particular emphasis on the Fourth Gospel in the Celtic tradition.[134] I resisted the temptation to buy a double album of 'Celtic Expressions of Worship' (one of the best-selling Christian compact discs of 1997, I was told), which gives favourite hymns like 'Let all mortal flesh keep silent', 'The day thou gavest', 'The King of Love' and 'I will sing the wondrous story' a 'Celtic' treatment with harp and pipe arrangements. I did, however, pick up a copy of a glossy brochure entitled 'Celtic Times' which carried details of twenty-eight recent paperbacks, eight compact discs and eleven Celtic-cross design necklaces and enthused:

> We are seeing such a renewed interest in and commitment to Celtic spirituality and its principles that it is little wonder church leaders today are looking, with breathless anticipation, for an outpouring of God's Holy Spirit on our land. Such revival brings freedom – freedom from rigid tradition and from frozen formality in worship. In fact, all the evidences and expressions found in the Celtic Church when it was in full bloom between the 5th and 12th centuries.[135]

Huge expectations are riding on the current Celtic Christian revival. The cover story of a recent issue of *The Plain Truth*, the magazine of the Worldwide Church of God, entitled 'Celtic Christianity – back in fashion?', suggests that Francis of Assisi acquired his love of animals and Luther his unease about Roman Catholic theology from exposure to the Celtic tradition in Irish monasteries on the Continent. It goes on to speculate:

> If the Celts had won at Whitby, our world might be less materialistic and less steeped in consumerism. Our waters might be less polluted, our rain forests and ozone layer might still be intact, and our fellow creatures might be less endangered. Life might be simpler, less frantic and happier.[136]

Of course these claims are wildly exaggerated and profoundly unhistorical. So too were the statements made by seventh- and eighth-century hagiographers about the lives and activities of the early saints, the legends dreamed up in the twelfth century about the Holy Grail and the origins of Patrick's Purgatory, the post-Reformation myth of an independent British Church and the romantic nostalgia of the late nineteenth- and early twentieth-century Celtic Twilight movement. As they have done so often in the past, Christians are once again projecting their own hopes and desires on to that misty and distant period that has carried so many dreams and expectations over the centuries. At least the current agenda is a great deal more idealistic and edifying than that in many previous revivals. If we are to chase Celtic dreams, and history suggests that we always will, better surely that they be about unpolluted waters and intact ozone layers than about having bigger and better relics than the church down the road.

NOTES

1. McLean, *Praying with Highland Christians*, p. xv.
2. Ibid., p. xv.
3. Ibid., pp. xiii, xvi.
4. Ibid., p. xx.
5. Chadwick, *Age of Saints*, p. 70.
6. Chadwick, *The Celts*, pp. 218–19.
7. Hughes, *The Church in Early Irish Society*, pp. 185–6.
8. G. Jowett, *The Drama of the Lost Disciples* (Covenant Publishing Company, London, 1968), p. 238.
9. J. T. McNeill, *The Celtic Churches – A History AD 200 to 1200* (University of Chicago Press, Chicago, 1974), p. 208.
10. L. Hardinge, *The Celtic Church in Britain* (SPCK, London, 1972), p. xi.
11. I. Cowan and D. Easson, *Medieval Religious Houses: Scotland* (2nd edn, Longman, London, 1976), p. ix.
12. Sellner, *Wisdom*, p. 9.
13. Macquarrie, *Paths in Spirituality*, pp. 122–3.
14. Reith, *God in Our Midst*, p. 6.
15. Ibid., p. 5.
16. Ibid., p. 23.
17. Interview with author, December 1991.
18. *Oban Times*, 6 June 1963.
19. E. Morgan, 'Columba's Song' in *Poems of Thirty Years* (Carcanet Press, Manchester, 1982), p. 221.
20. Maher, *Irish Spirituality*, foreword.
21. Ibid., p. 46.
22. *Celebrating Together* (Corrymeela Community, 1998), p. 5
23. See, for example, Mary Kenny's article 'St Patrick's People' in *The Tablet*, 11 March 1995, p. 316.
24. O'Driscoll, *Celtic Consciousness*, pp. 598–9.
25. C. Bamford and W. P. Marsh, *Celtic Christianity* (Floris Books, Edinburgh, 1986), pp. 9–10.
26. E. De Waal, *God Under My Roof* (SLG Press, Oxford, 1984), p. 1.
27. Interview with author, December 1991.
28. D. Adam, *The Cry of the Deer* (SPCK, London, 1987), p. xiv.
29. Allchin and de Waal, *Threshold*, back cover.
30. E. De Waal, *The Celtic Vision* (Darton, Longman & Todd, London, 1988), p. 14.
31. McLean, *Praying with Highland Christians*, p. ix.

32. Van de Weyer, *Celtic Fire*, p. 113.
33. Ibid., pp. 1–3.
34. Ibid., p. 11.
35. Ibid., p. 12.
36. Ibid., p. 13.
37. P. Berresford Ellis, *Celtic Inheritance* (Constable, London, 1985), p. 1.
38. Van de Weyer, *Celtic Fire*, pp. 123–35.
39. Toulson, *Celtic Year*, p. ix.
40. Toulson, *Celtic Alternative*, p. 1.
41. Ibid., p. 154.
42. Ibid., p. 9.
43. Ibid., p. 11.
44. Ibid., p. 11.
45. G. Wakefield (ed.), *A Dictionary of Christian Spirituality* (SCM Press, London, 1983), p. 83.
46. O'Donoghue, *Patrick*, p. 93.
47. M. Fox, *Original Blessing* (Bear & Co., Santa Fé, 1983), p. 308.
48. E. Conn and J. Stewart (eds), *Visions of Creation* (Godsfield Press, Alresford, 1995, foreword.
49. Toulson, *Celtic Year*, p. 15.
50. See, for example, the catalogues issued by Alan Shephard, Warminster.
51. C. Matthews, *The Celtic Tradition* (Element Books, Shaftesbury, 1995), p. 91.
52. Ibid., p. 97.
53. C. James, *An Age of Saints. Its Relevance for Us Today* (Llanerch, Lampeter, 1996), pp. 95–6.
54. De Waal, *A World*, p. 7.
55. Ibid., p. 7.
56. Bradley, *Celtic Way*, pp. vii–viii.
57. Sheldrake, *Living*, p. 2.
58. Ibid., pp. 93–4.
59. Mitton, *Restoring*, pp. 93, 101.
60. Van de Weyer, *Celtic Resurrection*, p. 13.
61. De Waal, *A World*, p. 9.
62. Allchin, *Threshold*, p. ix.
63. Mitton, *Restoring*, p. 1.
64. I have written about this at more length in reviews of *Restoring the Woven Cord* (*Church Times*, 25 August 1995) and *Recovering the Past* (*A Better Country*, No. 42, March 1997).
65. A. Raine and J. T. Skinner, *Daily Prayer: A Northumbrian Office* (Marshall Pickering, London, 1994), p. 443.
66. Simpson, *Exploring*, p. 11.
67. Ibid., p. xii.
68. Ibid., p. 11.
69. *Lindisfarne Mustard Seed Project Prayer Letter*, Vol. 1, No. 4, Spring 1997, p. 1.
70. See the comments of John Harvey in Bradley, *Celtic Way*, pp. 75–6.
71. *Iona Community Worship Book* (Wild Goose Publications, Glasgow, 1991), p. 8.

72. Interview with author, 12 December 1991.
73. S. Davies, 'Light in Darkness. The Relevance of Celtic Spirituality Today' (unpublished paper).
74. Thomas, *Candle*, p. 11.
75. Ibid., p. 11.
76. O'Riordain, *The Music*, back cover.
77. N. O'Donoghue, 'Celtic Spirituality', *Priests and People*, March 1995, p. 117.
78. O'Donoghue, *The Mountain*, p. 21.
79. Ibid., p. 137.
80. 'Come to Glendalough' (brochure issued by Fr Michael Rodgers, 1997).
81. *Céli Dé Ireland. Programmes in Celtic Spirituality* (Annamoe, Co. Wicklow), leaflet, 1997.
82. 'Enchanted Ireland' (Gothic Image Tours, Glastonbury, 1992).
83. 'Visit Whithorn' (brochure issued by Whithorn Trust, 1997).
84. Display panel at Lindisfarne Priory Museum (English Heritage, 1997).
85. 'Celtica' (brochure issued by Celtica Cyf., Machynlleth, 1997); 'King Arthur's Labyrinth' (Corris Craft Centre, Mid-Wales, 1997).
86. Sellner, *Wisdom*, p. 205.
87. A. Nolan, 'Celtic Christianity on the Internet' (essay submitted for MA in Celtic Christian Studies, Lampeter, 1997). Quoted with the permission of the author.
88. http://www.continet.com/culdee/synod.html.
89. http://www.continet.com/culdee/intro.html.
90. Ibid.
91. Ibid.
92. N. Henderson, 'Artwork Pack: Celtic Cross Theme' (Church of Scotland Department of National Mission, Edinburgh, 1997).
93. *The Reformer*, November–December 1994, p. 3.
94. B. Hume, *Footprints of the Northern Saints* (Darton, Longman & Todd, London, 1996), pp. 41–2.
95. C. Thomas, *The Early Christian Archaeology of North Britain* (Cambridge University Press, Cambridge, 1971); *And Shall These Mute Stones Speak?* (University of Wales Press, Cardiff, 1993); P. Hill, *Whithorn & St Ninian: the excavation of a monastic town* (Sutton Publishing, Stroud, 1997).
96. See, for example, H. Richardson, 'Celtic Art' in Mackey, *Introduction*, pp. 359–85.
97. Mackey, *Introduction*, p. 10.
98. Ibid., p. 1.
99. Ibid., pp. 8, 5.
100. Ibid., pp. 12, 13, 18, 21.
101. Ibid., pp. 17–18.
102. Ibid., p. 6.
103. Ibid., p. 24.
104. Ibid., p. 38.
105. Ibid., pp. 43–4.
106. MA in Celtic Christianity (course brochure, University of Wales, Lampeter, 1997).
107. Davies, *Celtic Christianity*, p. 143.

108. Davies and Bowie, *Celtic Christian Spirituality*, p. 3.
109. Ibid., p. 4.
110. Ibid., p. 20.
111. Ibid., p. 21.
112. K. Hughes, 'The Celtic Church: Is this a valid concept? *Cambridge Medieval Celtic Studies* No. 1, Summer 1981, p. 15.
113. Davies, *Wales*, p. 141.
114. Davies, 'The Myth of the Celtic Church' in N. Edwards and A. Lane, *The Early Church in Wales and the West* (Oxbow Books, Oxford, 1992).
115. Foster, *Picts, Gaels and Scots*, p. 82.
116. Bradley, *Columba*, pp. 65–7.
117. J. R. R. Tolkien, *Angles and Britons* (University of Wales Press, Cardiff, 1963), pp. 29–30.
118. Chapman, *The Celts*, p. 214.
119. Ibid., p. 253.
120. Ibid., p. 116.
121. D. Meek, 'Modern Celtic Christianity: The Contemporary "Revival" and Its Roots' in *Scottish Bulletin of Evangelical Theology*, Vol. 10, No. 1, Spring 1992, p. 9.
122. Ibid., p. 9.
123. D. Meek, 'Modern Celtic Christianity' in Brown, *Celticism*, pp. 143–4; see also Meek's article 'Surveying the Saints: Reflections on Recent Writings on "Celtic Christianity"' in *Scottish Bulletin of Evangelical Theology*, Vol. 15, No. 1, Spring 1997, pp. 50–6.
124. P. Sims-Williams, 'The Visionary Celt: the Construction of an Ethnic Pre-conception', *Cambridge Medieval Celtic Studies*, No. 11, Summer 1996.
125. Clancy and Markus, *Iona*, p. 93.
126. I. Bradley, 'How green was Celtic Christianity?', *Ecotheology*, No. 4, January 1998, pp. 58–69.
127. G. Markus, 'Columba: Monk, Missionary and Hi-jack Victim', *Spirituality* No. 12, May–June 1997, pp. 131–5.
128. G. Markus, 'The End of Celtic Christianity', *Epworth Review*, Vol. 24, No. 3, July 1997, p. 54.
129. *West Highland Free Press*, 7 March 1997.
130. *Daily Telegraph*, 31 January 1997.
131. *Scotsman*, 7 June 1997.
132. *The Times*, 13 March 1997.
133. *St Ninian and the Christian Heritage of Wigtonshire* (Whithorn, 1997), p. 1.
134. A and J. Fitzgibbon, *Prophetic Lifestyle and the Celtic Way* (Monarch, London, 1977); P. Newell, *Listening for the Heartbeat of God* (SPCK, London, 1997).
135. *Celtic Times* (brochure produced in 1997).
136. *The Plain Truth*, December 1997–January 1998, p. 8.

Bibliography

Listed below are all major sources cited more than once in the notes following individual chapters. Full bibliographical details of minor sources cited only once are given in the chapter notes.

Abou-El-Haj, B., *The Medieval Cult of Saints* (Cambridge University Press, Cambridge, 1990).

Aitchison, N. B., *Armagh and the Royal Centres of Early Medieval Ireland* (Cruithne Press, Boydell and Brewer, Woodbridge, Suffolk, 1994).

Allchin, A. M., *Praise Above All: Discovering the Welsh Tradition* (University of Wales Press, Cardiff, 1991).

Allchin, A. M., *God's Presence makes the World: The Celtic Vision through the Centuries in Wales* (Darton, Longman & Todd, London, 1997).

Allchin, A. M. and E. De Waal, *Threshold of Light* (Darton, Longman & Todd, London, 1986).

Anderson, A. O., *Early Sources of Scottish History AD 500 to 1286*, Vol. 2 (Paul Watkins, Stamford, 1990).

Arnold, M., *The Study of Celtic Literature* (Smith, Elder & Co., London, 1891).

Ashe, G., *St Brendan's Voyage to America* (Collins, London, 1962).

Ashe, G., *King Arthur's Avalon: The Story of Glastonbury* (Fontana, London, 1990).

Barrow, G. W. S., *Kingship and Unity: Scotland 1000–1306* (Edward Arnold, London, 1981).

Bede, *Ecclesiastical History of the English People* (various editions).

Bede and His World: The Jarrow Lectures, Vols 1 (1958–78) and 2 (1979–93) (Variorum, Aldershot, 1994).

Bieler, L., *The Life and Legend of St Patrick* (Clonmore and Reynolds, Dublin, 1949).

Bieler, L., *St Patrick* (Davis Lectures, 1958).

Bieler, L., *Studies on the Life and Legend of St Patrick* (Variorum Reprints, London, 1986).

Bourke, C. (ed.), *Studies in the Cult of St Columba* (Four Courts Press, Dublin, 1997).

Bradley, I. C., *The Celtic Way* (Darton, Longman and Todd, London, 1993).

Bradley, I. C., *Columba, Pilgrim and Penitent* (Wild Goose Publications, Glasgow, 1996).

Brooke, D., *Wild Men and Holy Places. St Ninian, Whithorn and the Medieval Realm of Galloway* (Canongate Press, Edinburgh, 1994).

Brown, P., *The Cult of the Saints* (University of Chicago Press, Chicago, 1981).

Brown, T. (ed.), *Celticism* (Studia Imagologica 8, Rodopi, Amsterdam, 1996).

Buchanan, G., *History of Scotland* (2nd edn, J. Bettenham, London, 1722).

Burgess, T., *Tracts on the Origin and Independence of the Ancient British Church* (F. C. & J. Rivington, London, 1815).

Calderwood, D., *History of the Kirk of Scotland* (Woodrow Society, Edinburgh, 1842).

Carmichael, A., *Carmina Gadelica* (Floris Books, Edinburgh, 1992).

Chadwick, N., *The Age of the Saints in the Celtic Church* (Oxford University Press, Oxford, 1961).

Chadwick, N., *The Celts* (Penguin Books, Harmondsworth, 1971).

Chapman, M., *The Gaelic Vision in Scottish Culture* (Croom Helm, London, 1978).

Chapman, M., *The Celts. The Construction of a Myth* (Macmillan, London, 1992).

Clancy, T. O. and Markus, G., *Iona: The Earliest Poetry of a Celtic Monastery* (Edinburgh University Press, Edinburgh, 1995).

Coe, J. B. and S. Young, *The Celtic Sources for the Arthurian Legend* (Llanerch Publishers, Felinfach, 1995).

Connolly, H., *The Irish Penitentials* (Four Courts Press, Dublin, 1995).

Dales, D., *Light to the Isles: Missionary Theology in Celtic and Anglo Saxon Britain* (Lutterworth Press, Cambridge, 1997).

Davies, O., *Celtic Christianity in Early Medieval Wales* (University of Wales Press, Cardiff, 1996).

Davies, O. and F. Bowie, *Celtic Christian Spirituality. An Anthology of Medieval and Modern Sources* (SPCK, London, 1995).

Davies, W., *Wales in the Early Middle Ages* (Leicester University Press, Leicester, 1982).

De Paor, L., *St Patrick's World* (Four Courts Press, Dublin, 1993).

De Paor, M. and L. De Paor, *Early Christian Ireland* (Thames and Hudson, London, 1958).

De Pontfarcy, M. H. and Y. De Pontfarcy, *The Medieval Pilgrimage to St Patrick's Purgatory* (Clogher Historical Society, Enniskillen, 1988).

De Waal, E., *A World Made Whole* (Harper Collins, London, 1991).

Doble, G. H., *Lives of the Welsh Saints* (University of Wales Press, Cardiff, 1971).

Doherty, C., 'The Problem of Patrick' in *History Ireland*, Spring 1955.

Dumville, D. N. (ed.), *St Patrick AD 493–1993* (Boydell Press, Woodbridge, 1993).

Duncan, A. A. M., *Scotland: The making of the Kingdom* (Mercat Press, Edinburgh, 1975).

Edelstein, T. J., *Imagining an Irish Past. The Celtic Revival 1840–1940* (The David and Alfred Smart Museum of Art, University of Chicago, 1992).

238 *Bibliography*

Errington, L., *William McTaggart 1835–1910* (National Gallery of Scotland, 1989).

Ferguson, R., *George MacLeod* (Collins, London, 1990).

Finney, J., *Recovering the Past: Celtic and Roman Mission* (Darton, Longman & Todd, London, 1996).

Fitzgibbon, A. and J. Fitzgibbon, *Prophetic Lifestyle and the Celtic Way* (Monarch Publications, London, 1997).

Forbes, A. P., *Kalendars of Scottish Saints* (Edmonston & Douglas, Edinburgh, 1872).

Foster, R. B., *W. B. Yeats: A Life*, Vol. 1 (Oxford University Press, Oxford, 1997).

Foster, S., *Picts, Gaels and Scots* (Historic Scotland and B. T. Batsford, London, 1996).

Godwin, M., *The Holy Grail* (Bloomsbury Publishing, London, 1994).

Graves, A. P., *A Celtic Psaltery* (SPCK, London, 1917).

Greene, D. and F. O'Connor, *A Golden Treasury of Irish Poetry* (Macmillan, London, 1967).

Hale, R., *The Magnificent Gael* (MOM Printing, Ottawa, 1976).

Haren. M. and Y. de Pontfarcy, *The Medieval Pilgrimage to St Patrick's Purgatory* (Clogher Historical Society, Enniskillen, 1988).

Hay, M. V., *A Chain of Error in Scottish History* (Longmans Green, London, 1927).

Head, T., *Hagiography and the Cult of Saints: The Diocese of Orléans, 800–1200* (Cambridge University Press, Cambridge, 1990).

Henderson, G., *From Durrow to Kells.The Insular Gospel-books 650–800* (Thames and Hudson, London, 1987).

Henken, E., *Traditions of the Welsh Saints* (D. S. Brewer, Cambridge, 1987).

Henken, E., *The Welsh Saints. A Study in Patterned Lives* (D. S. Brewer, Cambridge, 1991).

Hughes, K., *The Church in Early Irish Society* (Methuen, London, 1966).

Hull, E. (ed.), *The Poem Book of the Gael* (Chatto and Windus, London, 1912).

Hunter-Blair, P., *Northumbria in the Days of Bede* (Gollancz, London, 1976).

Hunter-Blair, P., *The World of Bede* (Cambridge University Press, Cambridge, 1990).

Hutchison, J., *The Dynamics of Cultural Nationalism: The Gaelic Revival and the Creation of the Irish Nation State* (Allen and Unwin, London, 1987).

Hyde, D., *The Story of Early Gaelic Literature* (T. Fisher Unwin, London, 1895).

Hyde, D., *A Literary History of Ireland* (T. Fisher Unwin, London, 1899).

Hyde, D., *The Religious Songs of Connacht*, Vol. 1 (T. Fisher Unwin, London, 1906).

Jackson, K., *The Gaelic Notes in the Book of Deer* (Cambridge University Press, Cambridge, 1972).

Johnson, S., *A Journey to the Western Islands of Scotland* (Clarendon Press, Oxford, 1985).

Kenney, J. F., *The Sources for the Early History of Ireland; Ecclesiastical* (Columbia University Press, 1929; reprinted by Irish University Press, Shannon, 1968).

Kirby, D. P., *Saint Wilfred at Hexham* (Newcastle, 1974).

Knott, E. and G. Murphy, *Early Irish Literature* (Routledge, Kegan and Paul, London, 1966).

Lacey, B., *Colum Cille and the Columban Tradition* (Four Courts Press, Dublin, 1997).

Laing, L., *The Archaeology of Late Celtic Britain and Ireland c.400–1200* (Methuen, London, 1975).

Laing, L., *Celtic Britain* (Routledge and Kegan Paul, London, 1979).

Laing, L. and J. Laing, *Celtic Britain and Ireland AD 200–800* (Irish Academic Press, Dublin, 1990).

Leerssen, J. T., *Mere Irish and Fíor-Ghael. Studies in the idea of Irish nationality, its development and literary expression prior to the nineteenth century* (John Benjamins, Amsterdam, 1986).

Lewis, L. S., *St Joseph of Artimathea at Glastonbury* (James Clarke, Cambridge, 1988).

Lightfoot, J., *Leaders in the Northern Church* (Macmillan, London, 1870).

Low, M., *Celtic Christianity and Nature* (Edinburgh University Press, Edinburgh, 1996).

MacArthur, E. M., *Iona* (Edinburgh University Press, Edinburgh, 1990).

Macfarlane, L., *William Elphinstone and the Kingdom of Scotland* (Aberdeen University Press, Aberdeen, 1995).

Mackey, J. (ed.), *An Introduction to Celtic Christianity* (T. & T. Clark, Edinburgh, 1989).

Mackinley, J. M., *Ancient Church Dedications in Scotland: Non-Scriptural Dedications* (David Douglas, Edinburgh, 1914).

McKitterick, R. (ed.), *The Uses of Literacy in Early Medieval Europe* (Cambridge University Press, Cambridge, 1990).

McLean, G. R. D., *Praying with Highland Christians* (new edn, SPCK, London, 1988).

MacLean, M., *The Literature of the Celts* (first published 1902; reprinted by Kennikat Press, New York, 1970).

Macquarrie, A., *The Saints of Scotland. Essays in Scottish Church History AD 450–1093* (John Donald, Edinburgh, 1997).

Macquarrie, J., *Paths in Spirituality* (SCM, London, 1989).

MacQueen, J., *St Nynia* (Polygon Books, Edinburgh, 1990).

Maher, M. (ed.), *Irish Spirituality* (Veritas Publications, Dublin, 1981).

Matthews, J. (ed.), *From the Isles of Dream. Visionary Stories and Poems of the Celtic Renaissance* (Floris Books, Edinburgh, 1993).

Menzies, L., *St Margaret Queen of Scotland* (first published 1925; reprinted 1992 by J. M. F. Books, Llanerch).

Meyer, K. (ed.), *Selections from Early Irish Poetry* (Constable, London, 1911).

Mitton, M., *Restoring the Woven Cord: Strands of Celtic Christianity for the Church Today* (Darton, Longman & Todd, London, 1995).

Murphy, G. (ed.), *Early Irish Lyrics* (Clarendon Press, Oxford, 1956).

Newell, J. P., *Each Day and Each Night* (Wild Goose Publications, Glasgow, 1994).

Newell, J. P., *Listening for the Heartbeat of God* (SPCK, London, 1997).

Ó Corráin, D. (ed.), *Sages, Saints and Storytellers: Celtic Studies in Honour of Professor James Carney* (An Sagart, Maynooth, 1989).

Ó Cróinín, D., *Early Medieval Ireland 400–1200* (Longman, London, 1995).

O'Donoghue, N. D., *Patrick of Ireland* (Michael Glazier, Wilmington, Delaware, 1987).

O'Donoghue, N. D., *The Mountain Behind the Mountain* (T. & T. Clark, Edinburgh, 1993).

O'Driscoll, H., *The Leap of the Deer* (Cowley Publications, Boston, Massachusetts, 1994).

O'Driscoll, R., *The Celtic Consciousness* (Canongate, Edinburgh, 1992).

O'Dwyer, P., *Towards a History of Irish Spirituality* (Columba Press, Dublin, 1995).

O'Riordain, J. J. *The Music of What Happens: Celtic Spirituality – A View from the Inside* (Columba Press, Dublin, 1996).

O'Sullivan, P., *The Creative Migrant* (Leicester University Press, Leicester, 1994).

Payton, P., *Cornwall* (Alexander Associates, Fowey, 1996).

Picard, J. M. (ed.), *Ireland and Northern France AD 600–850* (Four Courts Press, Dublin, 1991).

Piggott, S., *The Druids* (Thames & Hudson, London, 1968).

Piggott, S., *Ancient Britons and the Antiquarian Imagination* (Thames & Hudson, London, 1989).

Reeves, W., *The Culdees of the British Islands, As They Appear in History* (M. H. Gill, Dublin, 1864).

Reith, M., *God in Our Midst* (SPCK, London, 1975).

Reith, M., *Beyond the Mountains* (SPCK, London, 1979).

Rénan, E., *Poetry of the Celtic Races and Other Essays* (Walter Scott, London, 1896).

Scott, A., *The Pictish Nation, Its People and Its Church* (T. N. Foulis, Edinburgh, 1917).

Selmer, C. *Navigatio Sancti Brendani Abbatis* (University of Notre Dame Press, Indiana, 1959).

Sellner, E. C., *Wisdom of the Celtic Saints* (Ave Maria Press, Notre Dame, Indiana, 1993).

Sharpe, R., *Medieval Irish Saints' Lives* (Clarendon Press, Oxford, 1991).

Sharpe, R. (ed.), *Adomnan of Iona's Life of St Columba* (Penguin Books, Harmondsworth, 1995).

Sheehy, J., *The Rediscovery of Ireland's Past. The Celtic Revival 1830–1930* (Thames & Hudson, London, 1980).

Sheldrake, P., *Living Between Worlds: Place and Journey in Celtic Spirituality* (Darton, Longman & Todd, London, 1995).

Simpson, R., *Exploring Celtic Spirituality: Historic Roots for Our Future* (Hodder & Stoughton, London, 1995).

Simpson, R., *Celtic Worship Through the Year* (Hodder & Stoughton, London, 1997).

Skene, F .H. (ed.), *The Book of Pluscarden* (William Paterson, Edinburgh, 1880).

Skene, W. F., *Celtic Scotland: A History of Ancient Alba*, Vol. II (David Douglas, Edinburgh, 1877).

Southern, R., *The Making of the Middle Ages* (Hutchinson, London, 1967).

Spottiswoode, J., *The History of the Church of Scotland* (R. Norton, London, 1666).

Thomas, P., *Candle in the Darkness. Celtic Spirituality from Wales* (Gomer Press, Llandysul, 1993).

Toulson, S., *Celtic Journeys* (Hutchinson, London, 1985).

Toulson, S., *The Celtic Alternative* (Century Hutchinson, London, 1987).

Toulson, S., *The Celtic Year* (Element Books, Shaftesbury, 1993).

Van de Weyer, R., *Celtic Fire* (Darton, Longman & Todd, London, 1990).

Van de Weyer, R., *A Celtic Resurrection* (Harper Collins, London, 1996).

Von Maltzahn, N., *Milton's History of Britain. Republican Historiography in the English Revolution* (Clarendon Press, Oxford, 1991).

Watt, D. (ed.), *Scotichronicon* (Mercat Press, Edinburgh, 1989–95), Vols. 1–6.

Welsh History Review (University of Wales Press, Cardiff), 1968–.

Whitelock, D., R. McKitterick and D. Dumville (eds), *Ireland in Early Medieval Europe* (Cambridge University Press, Cambridge, 1982).

Williams, G., *Welsh Reformation Essays* (University of Wales Press, Cardiff, 1967).

Williams, G., *Reformation Views of Church History* (Lutterworth Press, London, 1970).

Williams, G., *Religion, Language and Nationality in Wales* (University of Wales Press, Cardiff, 1979).

Williams, G., *The Welsh and their Religion* (University of Wales Press, Cardiff, 1991).

Wotherspoon, H. J., *James Cooper: A Memoir* (Longmans, London, 1926).

Index of names and places

Goodwin, William, 196
Gougaud, Louis, 166, 213
Grant, Peter, 144
Graves, A. P., 162, 170–1
Green, Miranda, 202, 221
Greene, David, 59
Gregory, Lady Augusta, 169–70
Gregory the Great, 30, 93, 177
Gwenallt, 184, 212
Gwynn, Stephen, 169

Haddon, Arthur, 177
Hallstat, 122
Hannah, John, 185
Hanson, R. P. C., 223–4
Hardinge, Leslie, 192
Hardinge, W. H., 129
Hawker, R. S., 133
Hay, M. V., 177–8
Henderson, George, 21
Henderson, Norma, 219
Henken, Elissa, 45, 46, 47
Henry, Francoise, 183
Henry II (king of England), 72
Henry VII (king of England), 89
Herbert (bishop of Glasgow), 54
Herbert, Algernon, 111
Herbert, Máire, 59, 222
Herdman, Robert, 136
Heron, James, 129–30
Hilda, 132, 197, 208–9, 221
Hill, Peter, 221
Hole, William, 149–50
Horner, Sammy, 212
Howard, Michael, 203
Hughes, Kathleen, 191, 226
Hull, Eleanor, 162, 163–4
Hume, Basil, 220–1
Hunt, Robert, 133
Hutchison, John, 135, 139
Hyde, Douglas, 140–1, 160–1, 163, 170

Illtud, 44, 49, 120
Inchcolm, 50–1, 55, 56, 83, 85, 85–6
Innes, Thomas, 105
Innocent III (Pope), 43
Iona, 1, 17–22, 24, 26, 55, 58, 83, 108, 111, 127, 133, 147–9, 151–3, 159, 167, 168, 171–2, 178–82, 194, 208, 210–11, 214, 215, 216, 220, 230

Jackson, Anthony, 23
Jackson, Kenneth, 164–5
James IV (king of Scotland), 85, 87, 89
Jamieson, John, 111
Jarrow, 26, 29, 41, 42
Jewel, John, 92, 93
Jewell, L. C. D., 167
Jocelin (bishop of Glasgow), 54
Jocelin of Furness, 54, 61, 62, 63, 89
John of Fordun, 84, 88, 97
John of Tynemouth, 86
Johnson, Edmond, 137–9
Johnson, Samuel, 74, 109
Johnston, Elva, 11, 222

Jonas, 3
Jones, Owen, 123
Joseph of Arimathea, 71, 72, 80, 91, 92, 103, 108, 168, 192
Joyce, James, 222

Kells, 22, 24, 55, 58, 70
Kenney, James, 3, 8, 12, 59, 65, 68, 170
Kentigern, 46, 51, 54, 61, 70, 84, 85, 87, 98, 125, 145, 151, 174, 175, 176
Kenwyn, 80
Kermode, P. M. C., 138
Kerr, W. S., 170
Kessog, 66
Kevin, 74, 85
Kildare, 9–11, 15, 58, 76, 80
Kilkenny, 80
Kilpatrick, 39
Kilwinning, 89
Kirby, D. P., 35, 48
Knight, Frank, 175
Knowles, David, 192
Knox, Archibald, 137–8

La Tène, 122
Lach-Szyrma, W. S., 133
Lapidge, Michael, 72
Lastingham, 29, 197
Laurence (bishop of Dublin), 64, 99
Laurencekirk, 51
Lawrence, D. H., 168
Lawton, Liam, 211
Leagaire (high king of Ireland), 13, 16, 20, 203
Leatham, Diana, 183
Ledwick, Edward, 112
Leerssen, Joseph, 102, 107
Lehane, Brendan, 191
Leland, Thomas, 112
Lewis, L. S., 168
Lhuyd, Edward, 106
Lightfoot, Joseph, 132, 151, 197
Lindisfarne, 1, 21, 26, 29, 30, 31, 43, 131, 152, 162, 196, 197, 207–10, 214, 215, 216, 230
Lismore, 63, 157, 180
Llandaff, 46, 48
Llantwit Major, 1, 9, 49
Lloyd, William, 104
Lloyd George, David, 171
Lombard, Peter, 102
Long, Lloyd and Jennifer, 221
Longley, Clifford, 229
Losack, Marcus, 214
Low, Mary, 224
Lucius, 92
Ludgvan, 80

Mac Ailpín, Kenneth, 22–3
Macaulay, Lord, 122
MacCaghwell, Hugh, 101
McCallum, Duncan, 128
MacCana, P., 202
MacDonald, Allan, 159
MacDonald, Angus, 148
Macfarlane, Leslie, 87, 88
MacGregor, Duncan, 144–6, 148